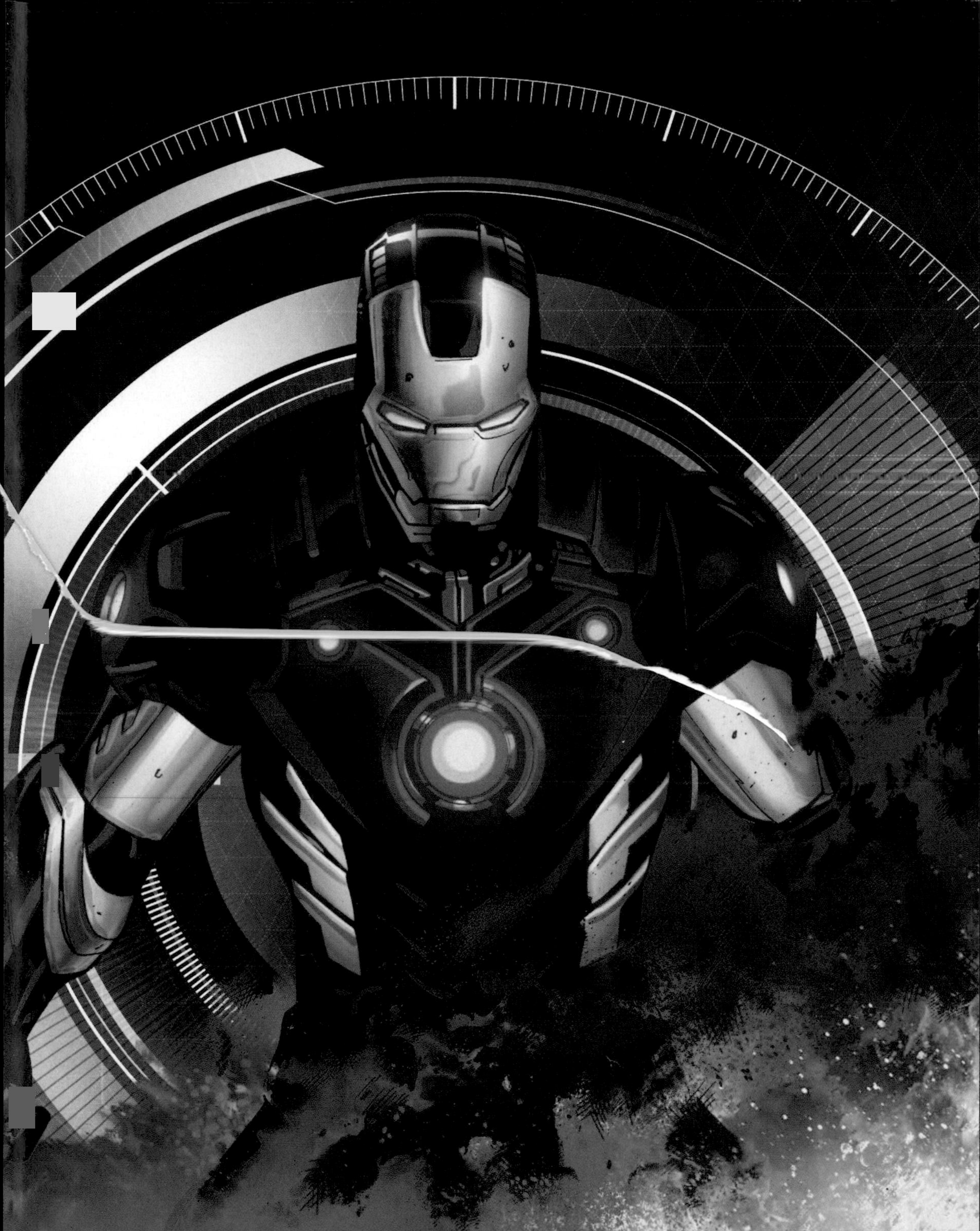

IRON MAN

BELIEVE

IRON MAN VOL. 1: BELIEVE. Contains material originally published in magazine form as IRON MAN #1-5. First printing 2013. Hardcover ISBN# 978-0-7851-6833-1. Softcover ISBN# 978-0-7851-6665-8. Published by MARVEL WORLDWIDE, INC., a subsidiary of MARVEL ENTERTAINMENT, LLC. OFFICE OF PUBLICATION: 135 West 50th Street, New York, NY 10020. Copyright © 2012 and 2013 Marvel Characters, Inc. All rights reserved. All characters featured in this issue and the distinctive names and likenesses thereof, and all related indicia are trademarks of Marvel Characters, Inc. No similarity between any of the names, characters, persons, and/or institutions in this magazine with those of any living or dead person or institution is intended, and any such similarity which may exist is purely coincidental. **Printed in the U.S.A.** ALAN FINE, EVP - Office of the President, Marvel Worldwide, Inc. and EVP & CMO Marvel Characters B.V.; DAN BUCKLEY, Publisher & President - Print, Animation & Digital Divisions; JOE QUESADA, Chief Creative Officer; TOM BREVOORT, SVP of Publishing; DAVID BOGART, SVP of Operations & Procurement, Publishing; RUWAN JAYATILLEKE, SVP & Associate Publisher, Publishing; C.B. CEBULSKI, SVP of Creator & Content Development; DAVID GABRIEL, SVP of Print & Digital Publishing Sales; JIM O'KEEFE, VP of Operations & Logistics; DAN CARR, Executive Director of Publishing Technology; SUSAN CRESPI, Editorial Operations Manager; ALEX MORALES, Publishing Operations Manager; STAN LEE, Chairman Emeritus. For information regarding advertising in Marvel Comics or on Marvel.com, please contact Niza Disla, Director of Marvel Partnerships, at ndisla@marvel.com. For Marvel subscription inquiries, please call 800-217-9158. **Manufactured between 2/4/2013 and 3/8/2013 (hardcover), and 2/4/2013 and 11/8/2013 (softcover), by R.R. DONNELLEY, INC., SALEM, VA, USA.**

10 9 8 7 6 5 4 3 2 1

3 1969 02178 2429

Tony Stark is a technological visionary... a famous, wealthy and unparalleled inventor. With the world's most advanced and powerful suit of armor, Stark valiantly protects the innocent as an invincible bright knight known as...

IRON MAN

KIERON GILLEN
WRITER

GREG LAND
PENCILER

JAY LEISTEN
INKER

GURU-eFX
COLORIST

VC'S JOE CARAMAGNA
LETTERER

GREG LAND & **GURU-eFX**
COVER ART

JON MOISAN
ASSISTANT EDITOR

MARK PANICCIA
EDITOR

COLLECTION EDITOR: **JENNIFER GRÜNWALD**
ASSISTANT EDITORS: **ALEX STARBUCK** & **NELSON RIBEIRO**
EDITOR, SPECIAL PROJECTS: **MARK D. BEAZLEY**
SENIOR EDITOR, SPECIAL PROJECTS: **JEFF YOUNGQUIST**
SVP OF PRINT & DIGITAL PUBLISHING SALES: **DAVID GABRIEL**
BOOK DESIGNER: **RODOLFO MURAGUCHI**

EDITOR IN CHIEF: **AXEL ALONSO**
CHIEF CREATIVE OFFICER: **JOE QUESADA**
PUBLISHER: **DAN BUCKLEY**
EXECUTIVE PRODUCER: **ALAN FINE**

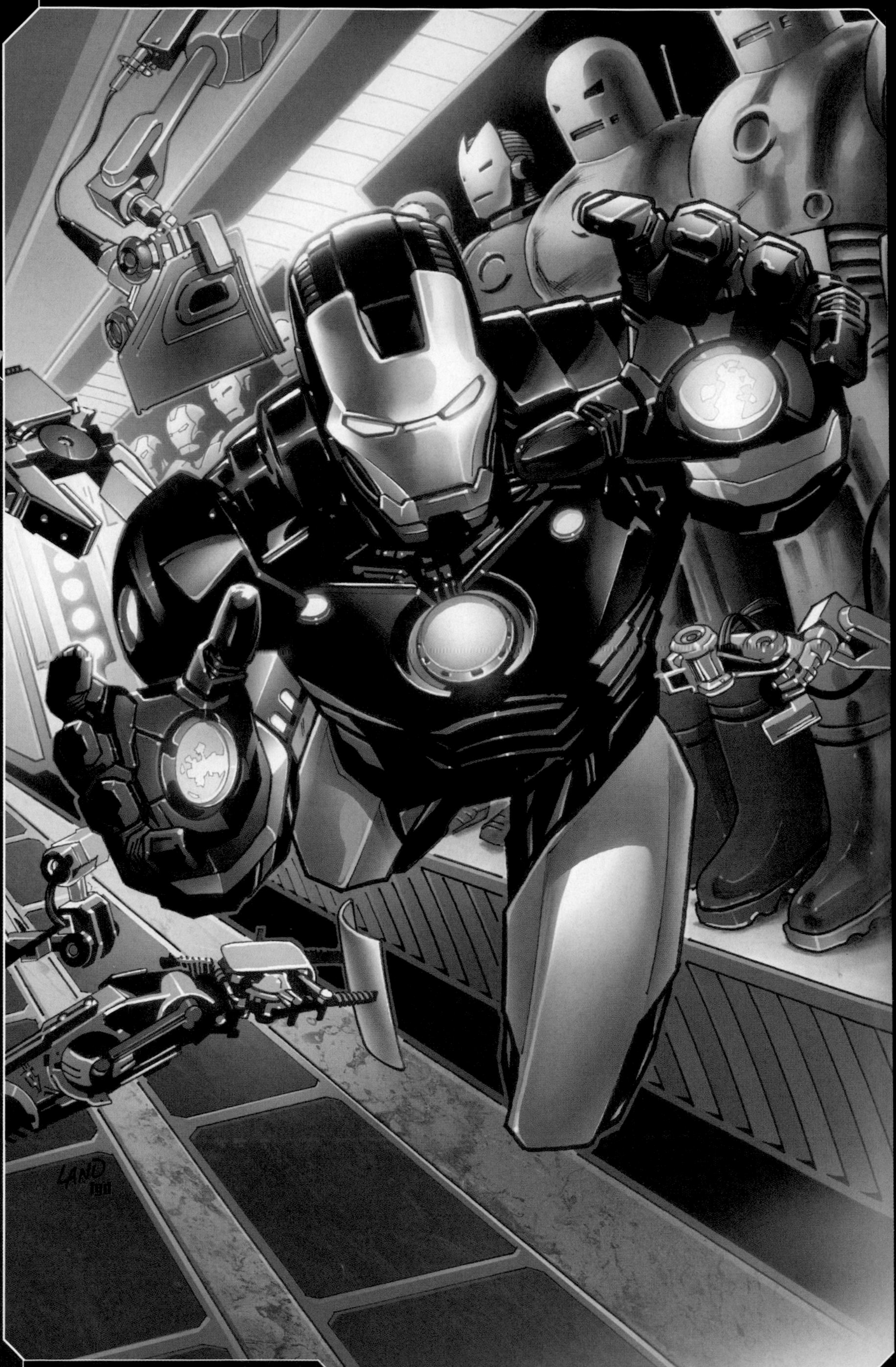

01 DEMONS AND GENIES

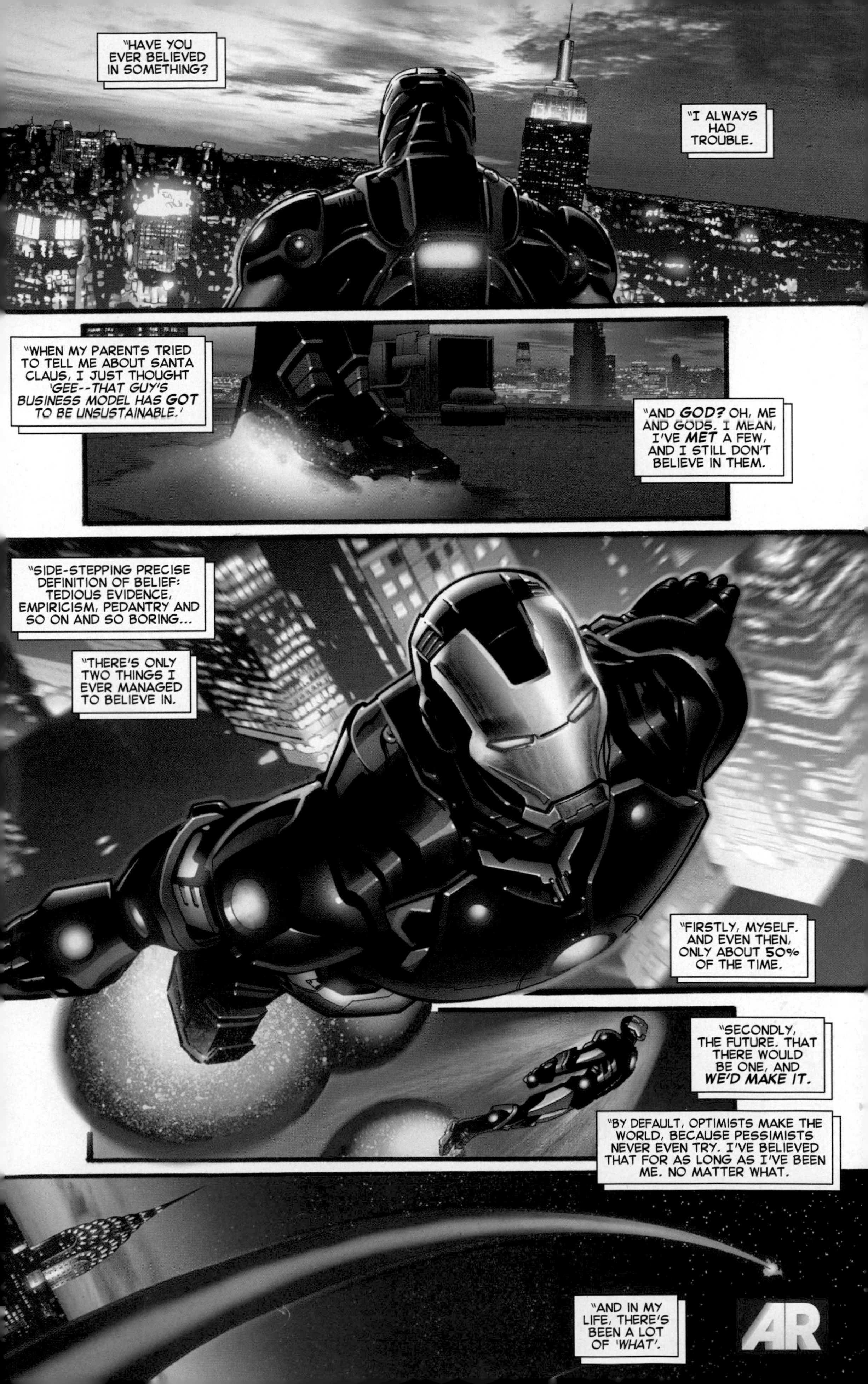
"HAVE YOU EVER BELIEVED IN SOMETHING?
"I ALWAYS HAD TROUBLE.
"WHEN MY PARENTS TRIED TO TELL ME ABOUT SANTA CLAUS, I JUST THOUGHT 'GEE--THAT GUY'S BUSINESS MODEL HAS GOT TO BE UNSUSTAINABLE.'
"AND GOD? OH, ME AND GODS. I MEAN, I'VE MET A FEW, AND I STILL DON'T BELIEVE IN THEM.
"SIDE-STEPPING PRECISE DEFINITION OF BELIEF: TEDIOUS EVIDENCE, EMPIRICISM, PEDANTRY AND SO ON AND SO BORING...
"THERE'S ONLY TWO THINGS I EVER MANAGED TO BELIEVE IN.
"FIRSTLY, MYSELF. AND EVEN THEN, ONLY ABOUT 50% OF THE TIME.
"SECONDLY, THE FUTURE. THAT THERE WOULD BE ONE, AND WE'D MAKE IT.
"BY DEFAULT, OPTIMISTS MAKE THE WORLD, BECAUSE PESSIMISTS NEVER EVEN TRY. I'VE BELIEVED THAT FOR AS LONG AS I'VE BEEN ME. NO MATTER WHAT.
"AND IN MY LIFE, THERE'S BEEN A LOT OF 'WHAT'.
AR

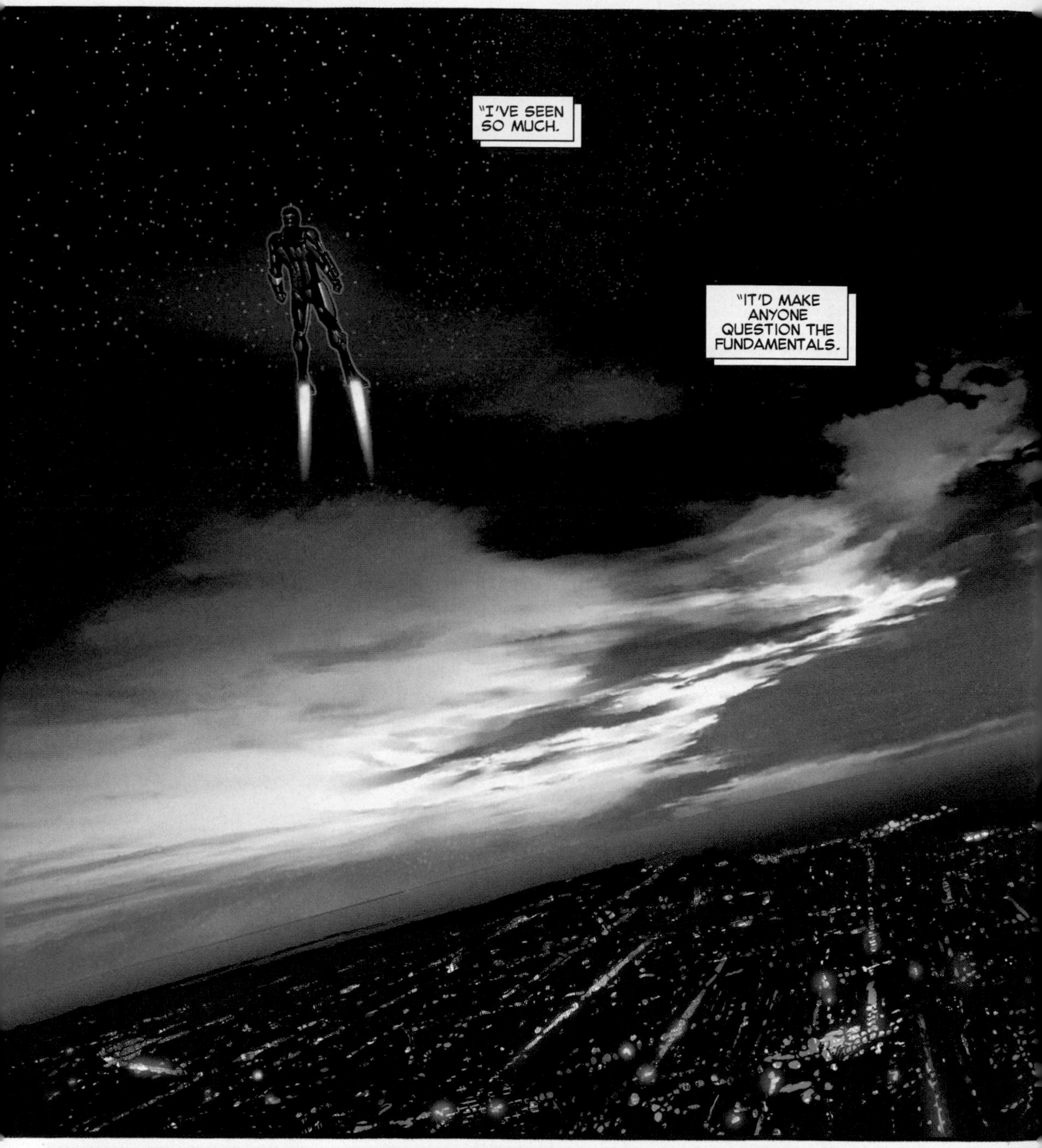
"I'VE SEEN SO MUCH.
"IT'D MAKE ANYONE QUESTION THE FUNDAMENTALS.

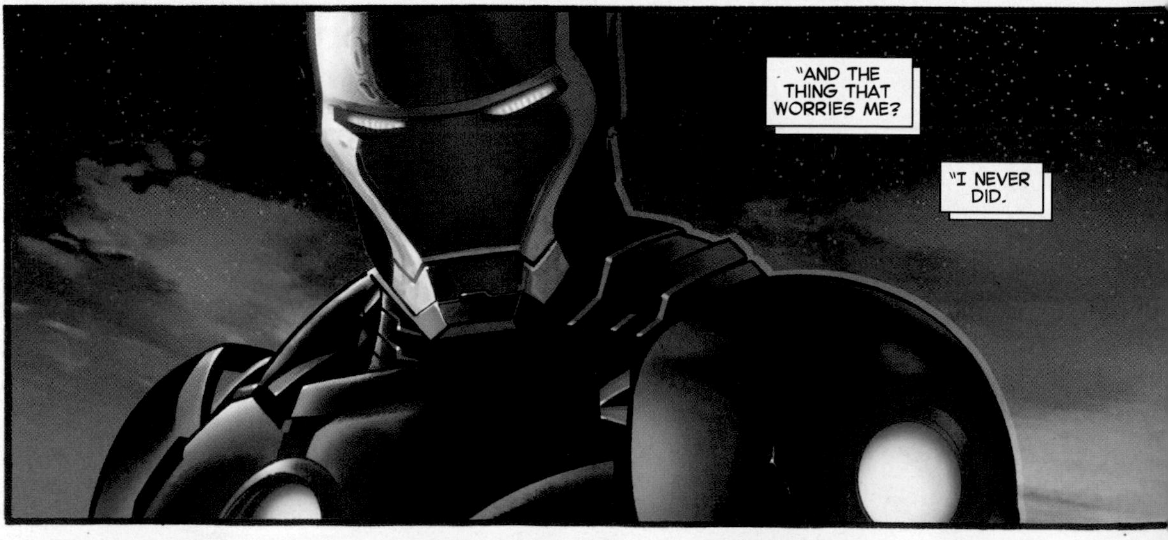
"AND THE THING THAT WORRIES ME?
"I NEVER DID.

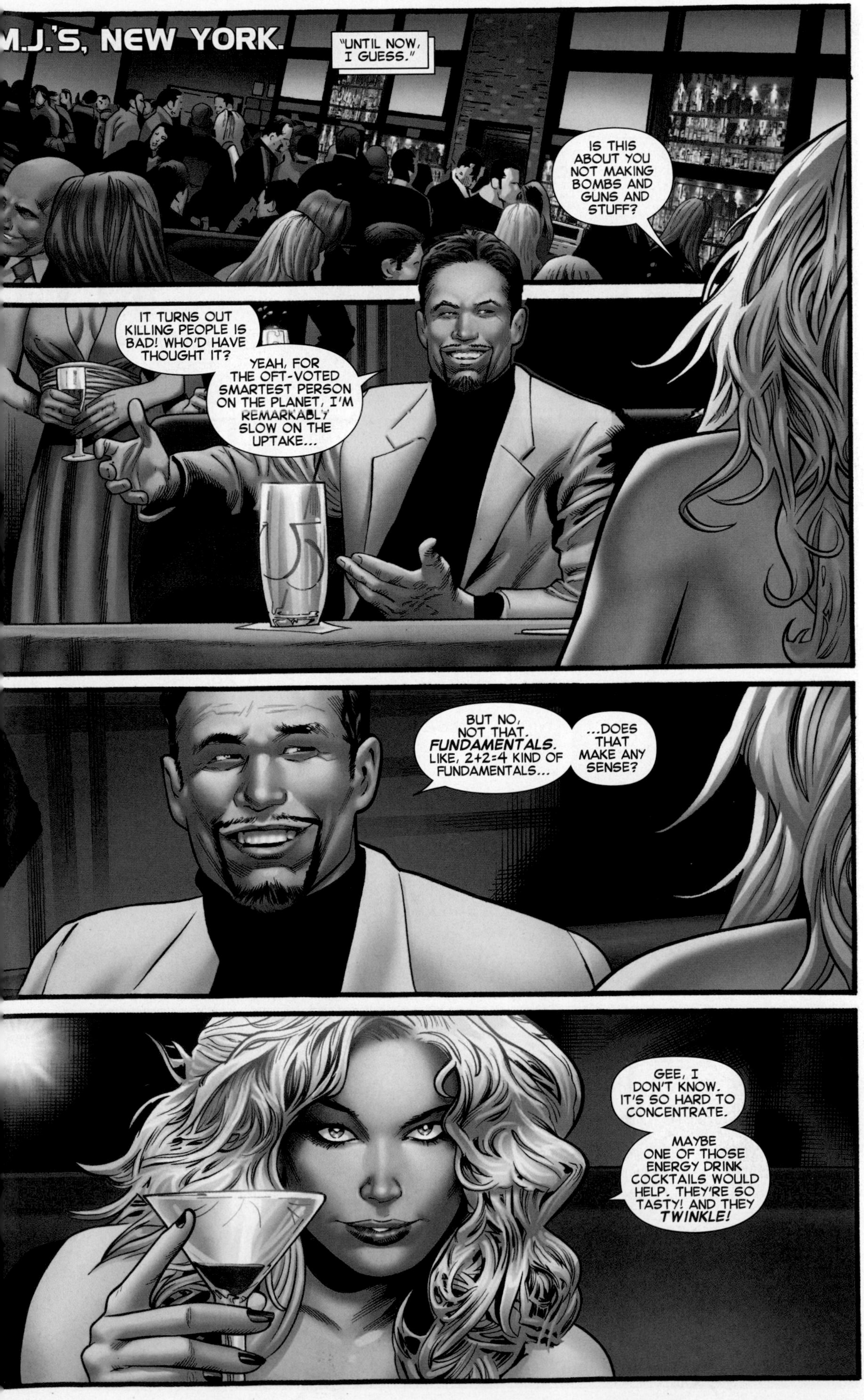
M.J.'S, NEW YORK.
"UNTIL NOW, I GUESS."
IS THIS ABOUT YOU NOT MAKING BOMBS AND GUNS AND STUFF?
IT TURNS OUT KILLING PEOPLE IS BAD! WHO'D HAVE THOUGHT IT?
YEAH, FOR THE OFT-VOTED SMARTEST PERSON ON THE PLANET, I'M REMARKABLY SLOW ON THE UPTAKE...
BUT NO, NOT THAT. FUNDAMENTALS. LIKE, 2+2=4 KIND OF FUNDAMENTALS...
...DOES THAT MAKE ANY SENSE?
GEE, I DON'T KNOW. IT'S SO HARD TO CONCENTRATE.
MAYBE ONE OF THOSE ENERGY DRINK COCKTAILS WOULD HELP. THEY'RE SO TASTY! AND THEY TWINKLE!

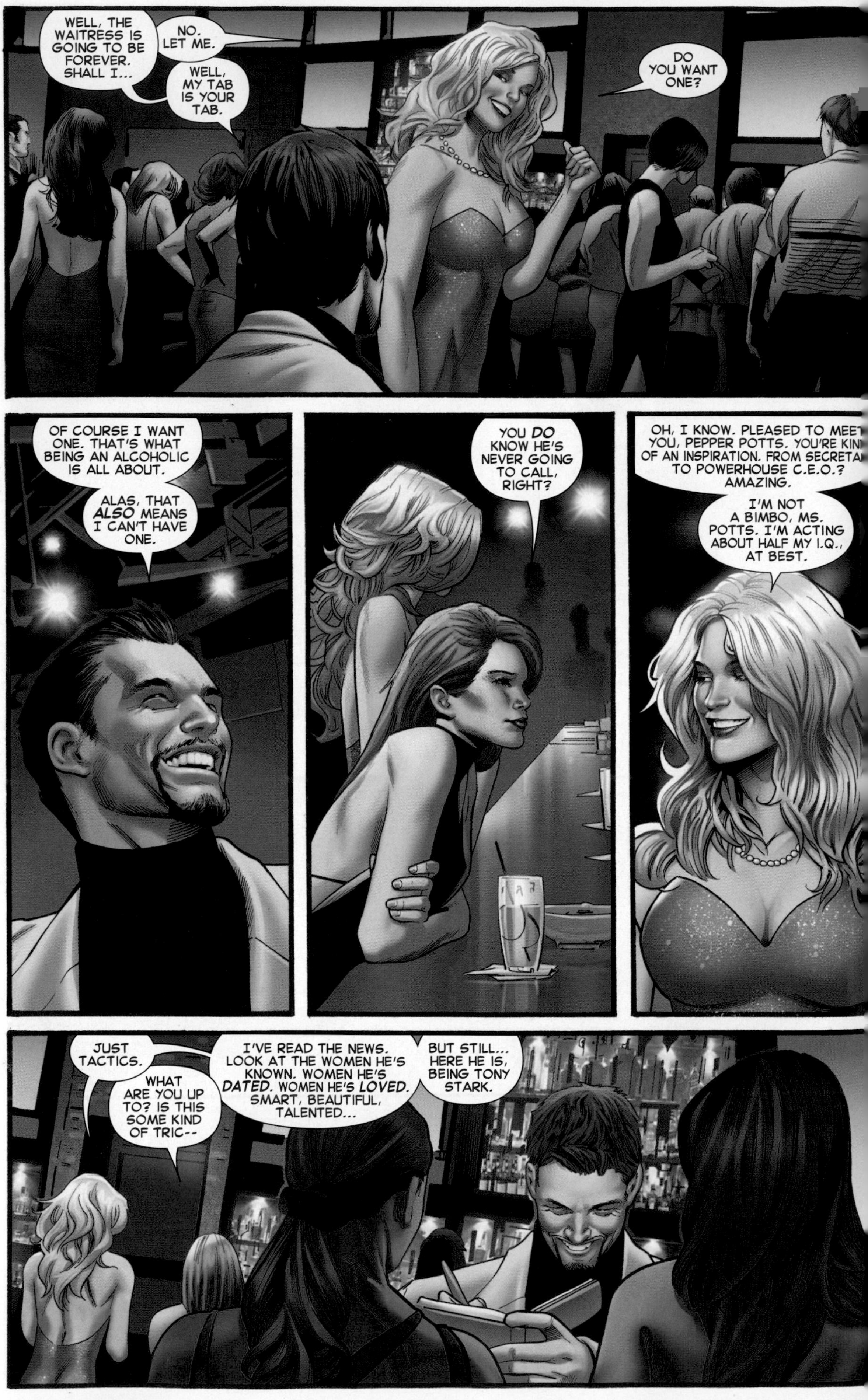
WELL, THE WAITRESS IS GOING TO BE FOREVER. SHALL I...
NO. LET ME.
WELL, MY TAB IS YOUR TAB.
DO YOU WANT ONE?
OF COURSE I WANT ONE. THAT'S WHAT BEING AN ALCOHOLIC IS ALL ABOUT.
ALAS, THAT *ALSO* MEANS I CAN'T HAVE ONE.
YOU *DO* KNOW HE'S NEVER GOING TO CALL, RIGHT?
OH, I KNOW. PLEASED TO MEET YOU, PEPPER POTTS. YOU'RE KIN OF AN INSPIRATION. FROM SECRETA TO POWERHOUSE C.E.O.? AMAZING.
I'M NOT A BIMBO, MS. POTTS. I'M ACTING ABOUT HALF MY I.Q., AT BEST.
JUST TACTICS.
WHAT ARE YOU UP TO? IS THIS SOME KIND OF TRIC--
I'VE READ THE NEWS. LOOK AT THE WOMEN HE'S KNOWN. WOMEN HE'S *DATED*. WOMEN HE'S *LOVED*. SMART, BEAUTIFUL, TALENTED...
BUT STILL... HERE HE IS, BEING TONY STARK.

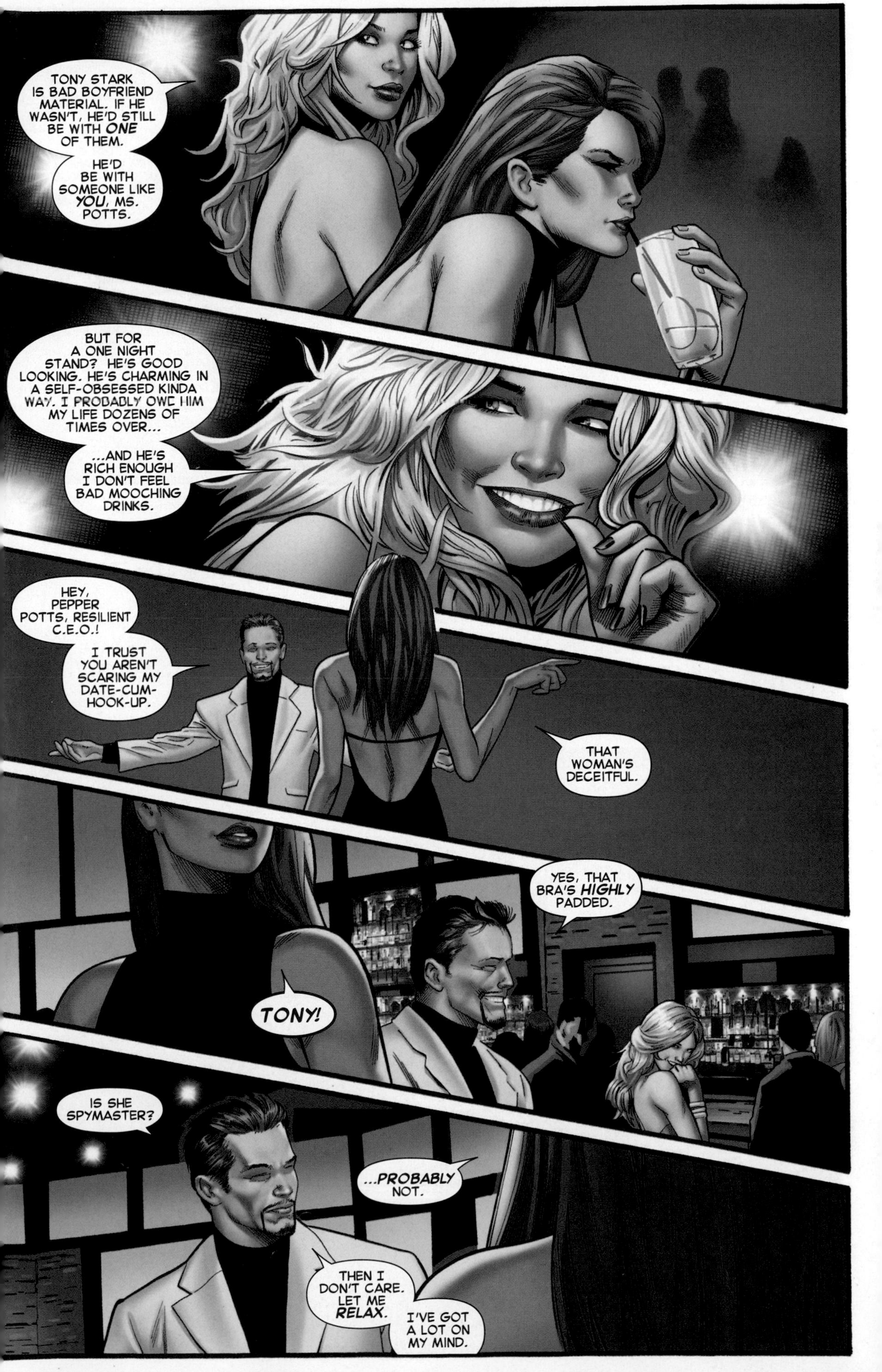

TONY STARK IS BAD BOYFRIEND MATERIAL. IF HE WASN'T, HE'D STILL BE WITH ONE OF THEM.
HE'D BE WITH SOMEONE LIKE YOU, MS. POTTS.
BUT FOR A ONE NIGHT STAND? HE'S GOOD LOOKING. HE'S CHARMING IN A SELF-OBSESSED KINDA WAY. I PROBABLY OWE HIM MY LIFE DOZENS OF TIMES OVER...
...AND HE'S RICH ENOUGH I DON'T FEEL BAD MOOCHING DRINKS.
HEY, PEPPER POTTS, RESILIENT C.E.O.!
I TRUST YOU AREN'T SCARING MY DATE-CUM-HOOK-UP.
THAT WOMAN'S DECEITFUL.
YES, THAT BRA'S HIGHLY PADDED.
TONY!
IS SHE SPYMASTER?
...PROBABLY NOT.
THEN I DON'T CARE. LET ME RELAX.
I'VE GOT A LOT ON MY MIND.

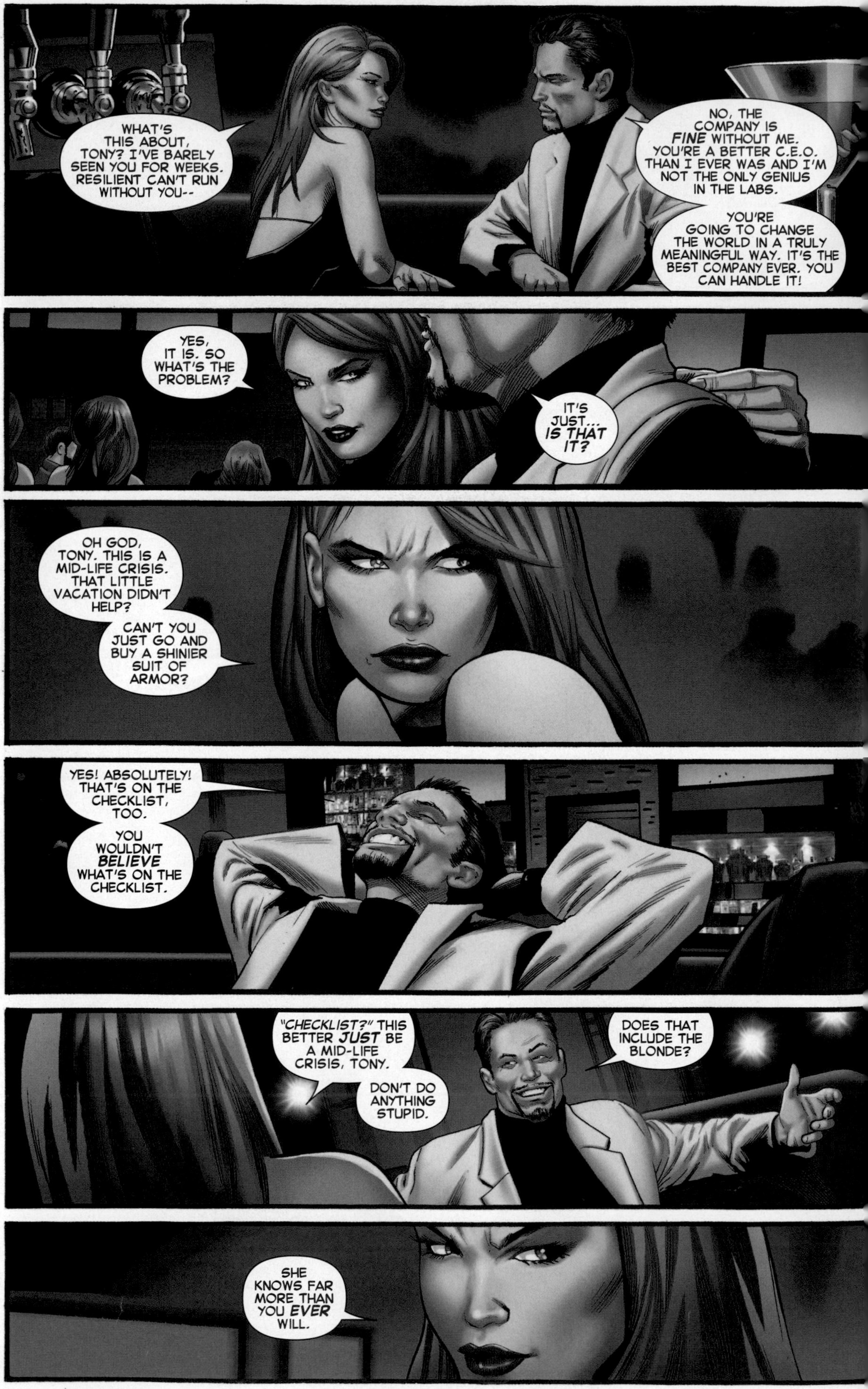
WHAT'S THIS ABOUT, TONY? I'VE BARELY SEEN YOU FOR WEEKS. RESILIENT CAN'T RUN WITHOUT YOU--
NO, THE COMPANY IS FINE WITHOUT ME. YOU'RE A BETTER C.E.O. THAN I EVER WAS AND I'M NOT THE ONLY GENIUS IN THE LABS.
YOU'RE GOING TO CHANGE THE WORLD IN A TRULY MEANINGFUL WAY. IT'S THE BEST COMPANY EVER. YOU CAN HANDLE IT!
YES, IT IS. SO WHAT'S THE PROBLEM?
IT'S JUST... IS THAT IT?
OH GOD, TONY. THIS IS A MID-LIFE CRISIS. THAT LITTLE VACATION DIDN'T HELP?
CAN'T YOU JUST GO AND BUY A SHINIER SUIT OF ARMOR?
YES! ABSOLUTELY! THAT'S ON THE CHECKLIST, TOO.
YOU WOULDN'T BELIEVE WHAT'S ON THE CHECKLIST.
"CHECKLIST?" THIS BETTER JUST BE A MID-LIFE CRISIS, TONY.
DON'T DO ANYTHING STUPID.
DOES THAT INCLUDE THE BLONDE?
SHE KNOWS FAR MORE THAN YOU EVER WILL.

BUENOS
AIRES,
ARGENTINA.

OH MY GOD.

OH MY GOD.

I NEED YOUR PHONE.

PLEASE. QUICKLY.

WH--

PLEASE!

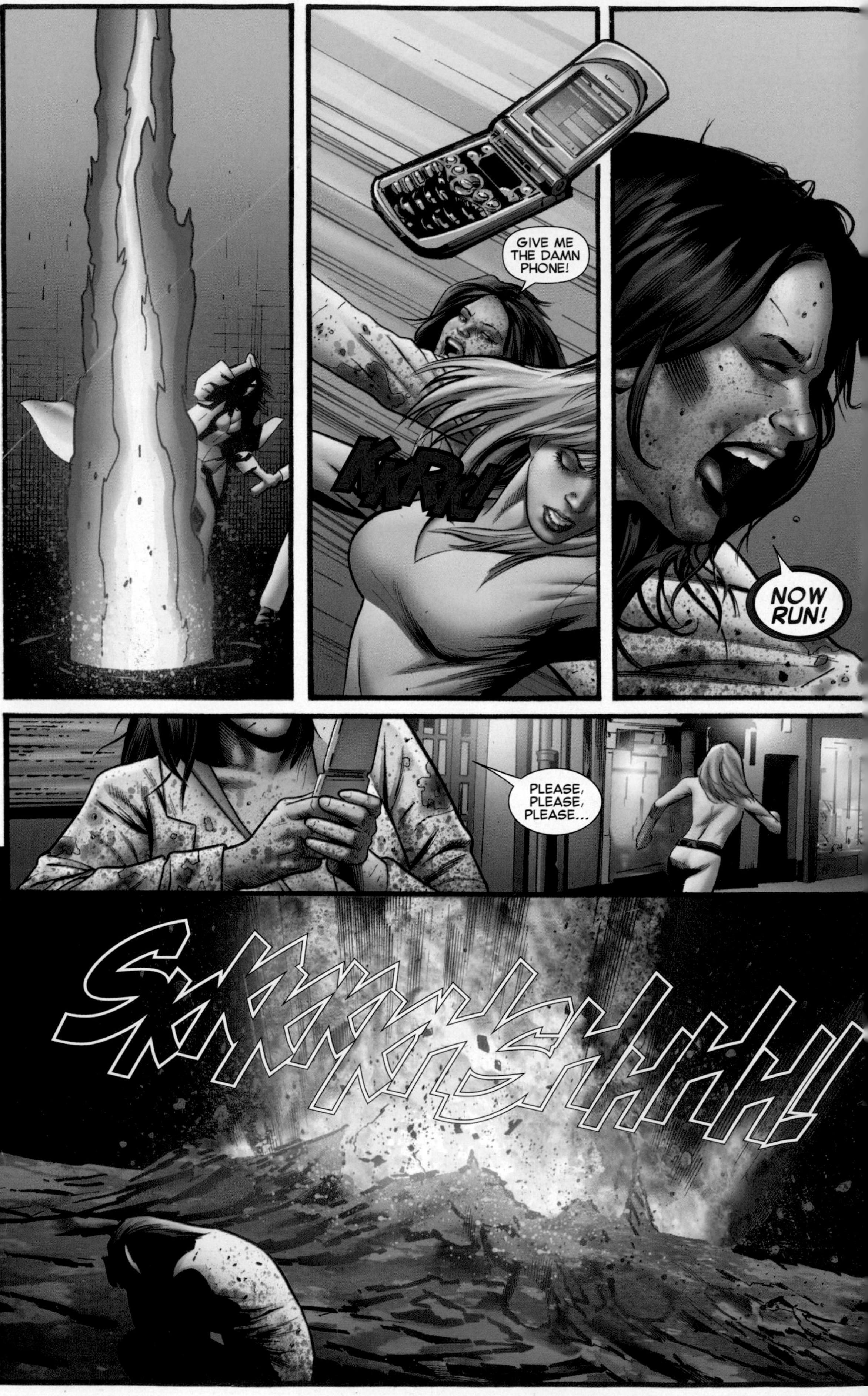
GIVE ME THE DAMN PHONE!
KKRRKK
NOW RUN!
PLEASE, PLEASE, PLEASE...
SPPPLLLLLAAAASSSHHH!

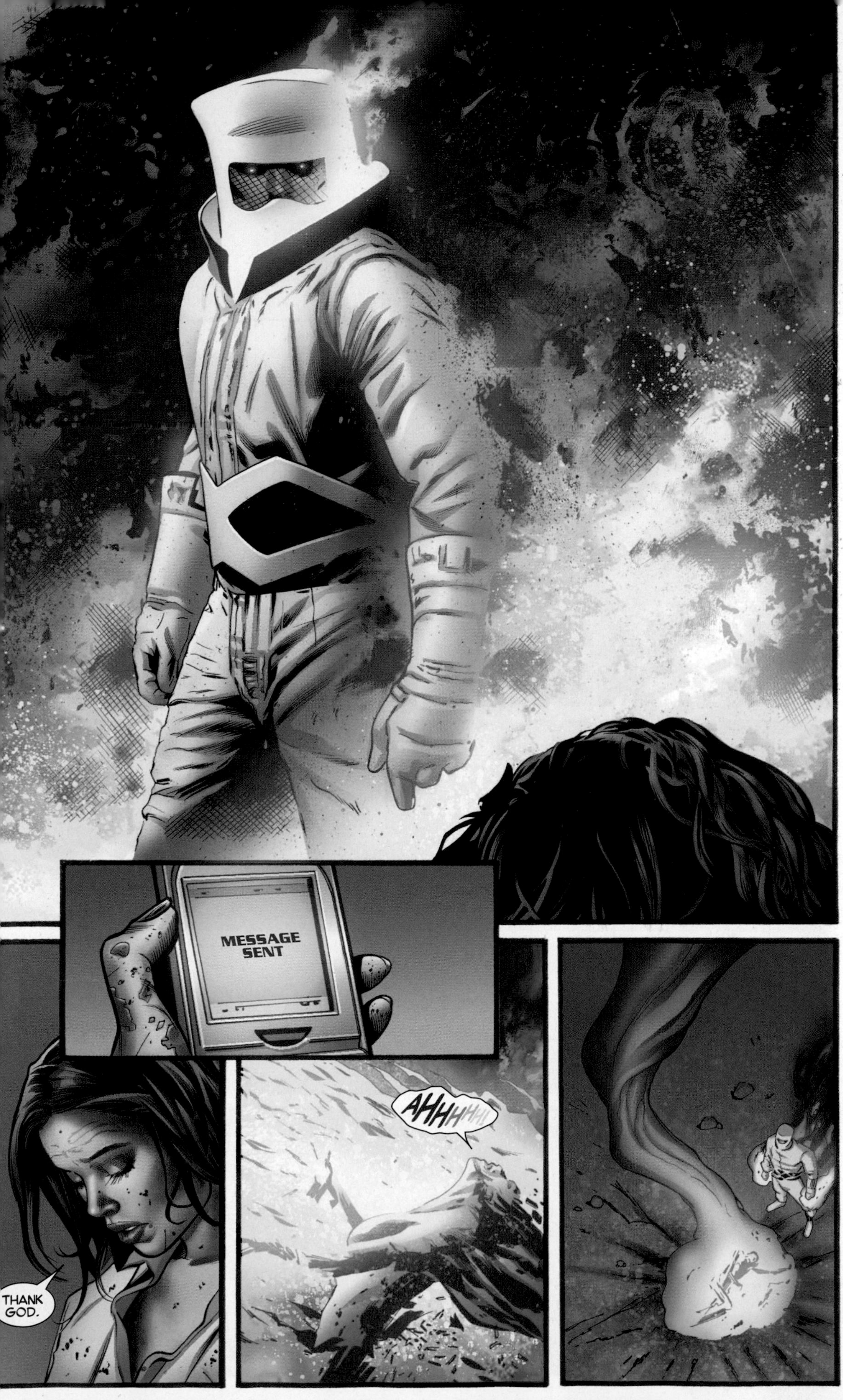
MESSAGE
SENT
THANK
GOD.
AHHHHH!

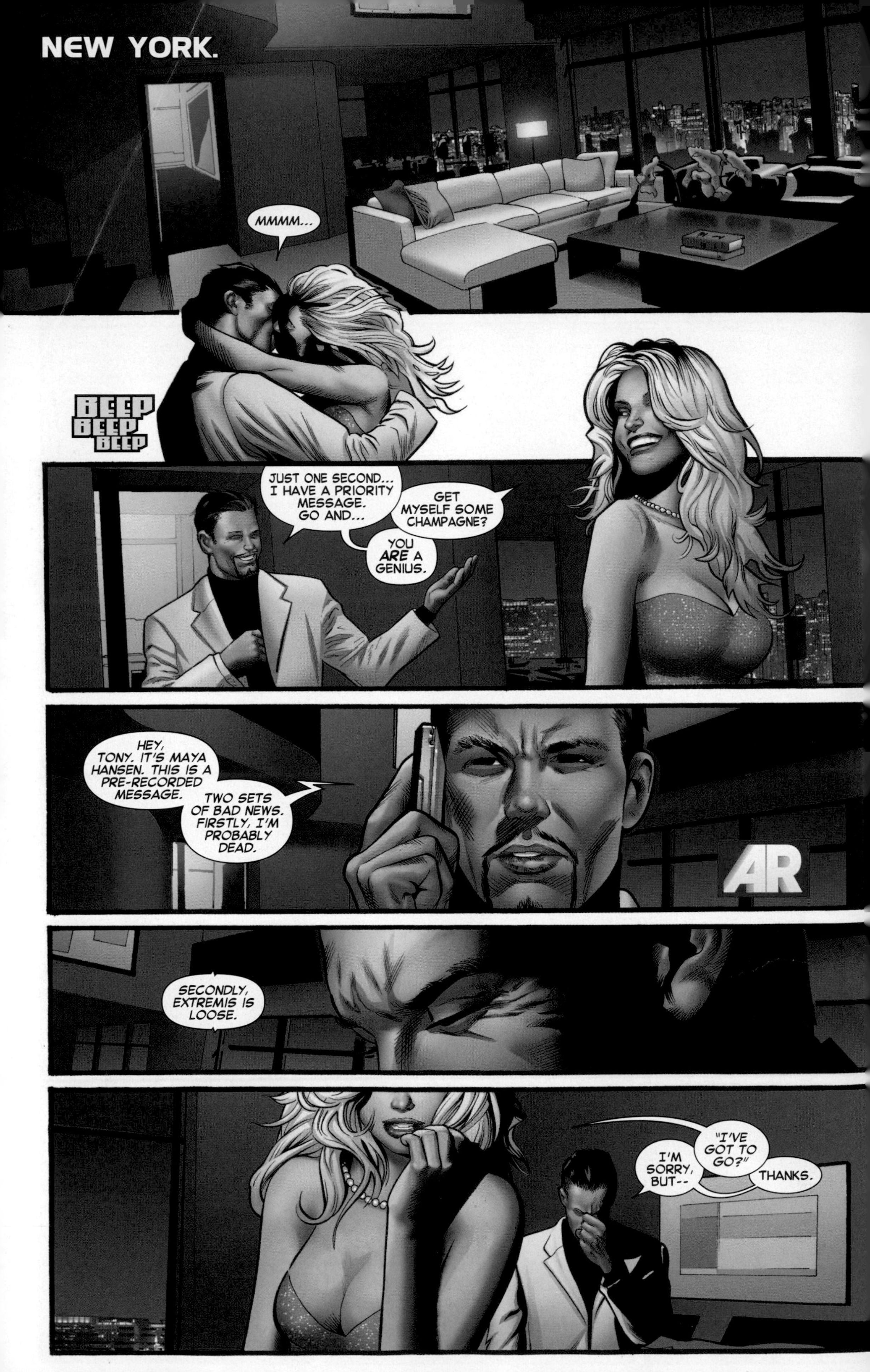
NEW YORK.
MMMM...
BEEP BEEP BEEP
JUST ONE SECOND... I HAVE A PRIORITY MESSAGE. GO AND...
GET MYSELF SOME CHAMPAGNE?
YOU ARE A GENIUS.
HEY, TONY. IT'S MAYA HANSEN. THIS IS A PRE-RECORDED MESSAGE.
TWO SETS OF BAD NEWS. FIRSTLY, I'M PROBABLY DEAD.
AR
SECONDLY, EXTREMIS IS LOOSE.
I'M SORRY, BUT--
"I'VE GOT TO GO?"
THANKS.

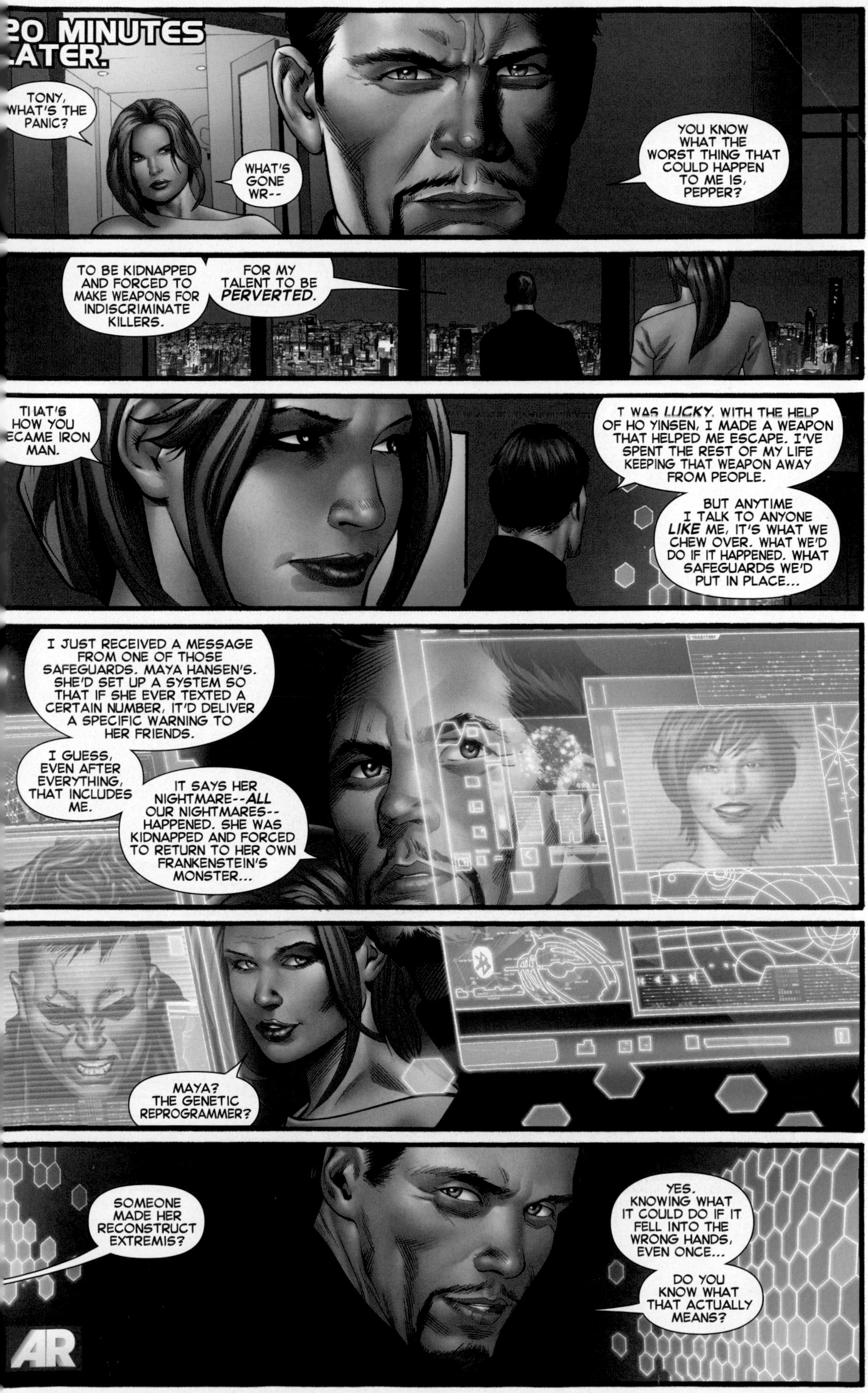
20 MINUTES LATER.
TONY, WHAT'S THE PANIC?
WHAT'S GONE WR--
YOU KNOW WHAT THE WORST THING THAT COULD HAPPEN TO ME IS, PEPPER?
TO BE KIDNAPPED AND FORCED TO MAKE WEAPONS FOR INDISCRIMINATE KILLERS.
FOR MY TALENT TO BE PERVERTED.
THAT'S HOW YOU BECAME IRON MAN.
I WAS LUCKY. WITH THE HELP OF HO YINSEN, I MADE A WEAPON THAT HELPED ME ESCAPE. I'VE SPENT THE REST OF MY LIFE KEEPING THAT WEAPON AWAY FROM PEOPLE.
BUT ANYTIME I TALK TO ANYONE LIKE ME, IT'S WHAT WE CHEW OVER. WHAT WE'D DO IF IT HAPPENED. WHAT SAFEGUARDS WE'D PUT IN PLACE...
I JUST RECEIVED A MESSAGE FROM ONE OF THOSE SAFEGUARDS. MAYA HANSEN'S. SHE'D SET UP A SYSTEM SO THAT IF SHE EVER TEXTED A CERTAIN NUMBER, IT'D DELIVER A SPECIFIC WARNING TO HER FRIENDS.
I GUESS, EVEN AFTER EVERYTHING, THAT INCLUDES ME.
IT SAYS HER NIGHTMARE--ALL OUR NIGHTMARES--HAPPENED. SHE WAS KIDNAPPED AND FORCED TO RETURN TO HER OWN FRANKENSTEIN'S MONSTER...
MAYA? THE GENETIC REPROGRAMMER?
SOMEONE MADE HER RECONSTRUCT EXTREMIS?
YES. KNOWING WHAT IT COULD DO IF IT FELL INTO THE WRONG HANDS, EVEN ONCE...
DO YOU KNOW WHAT THAT ACTUALLY MEANS?
AR

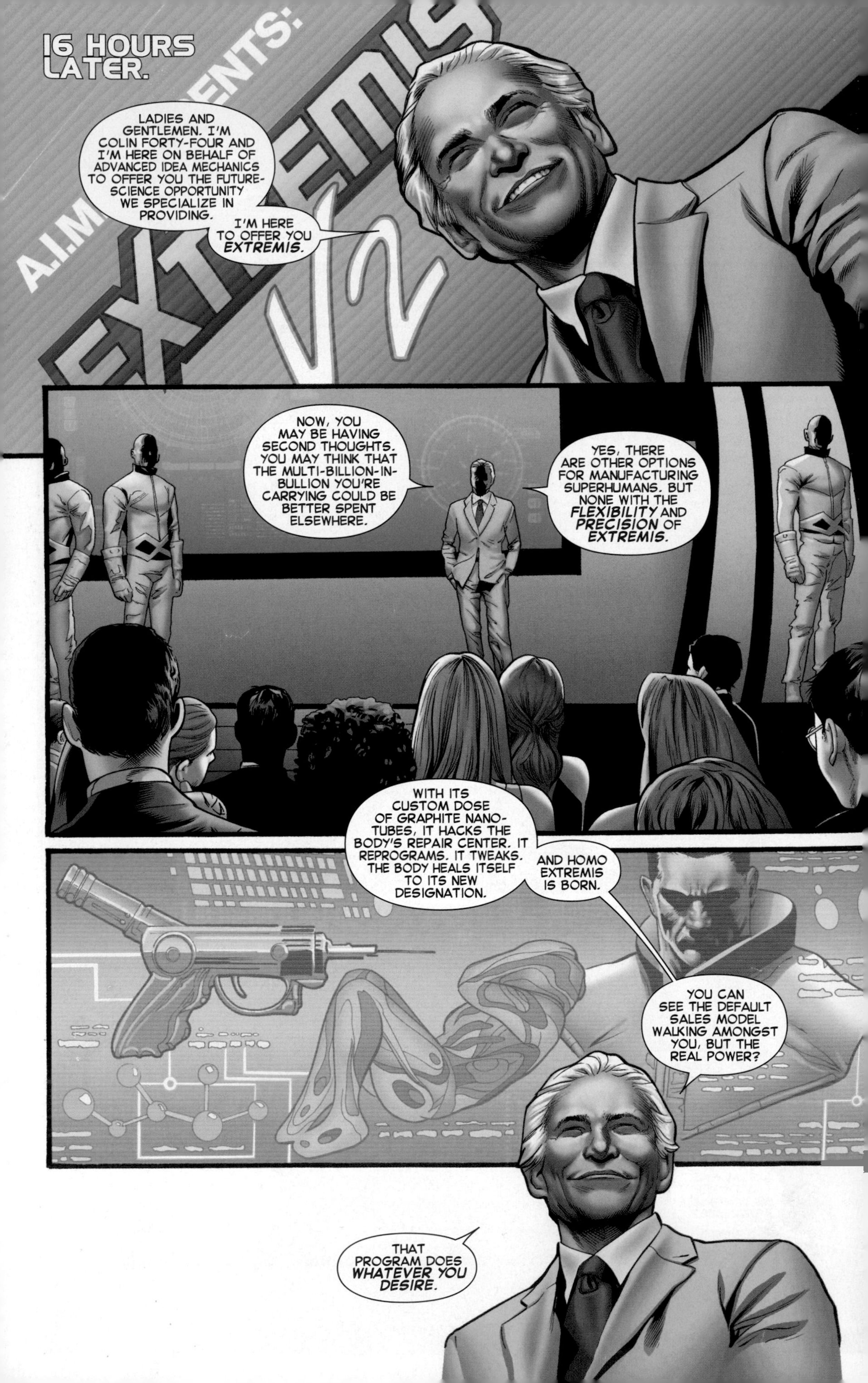
16 HOURS LATER.
A.I.M. PRESENTS: EXTREMIS V2
LADIES AND GENTLEMEN. I'M COLIN FORTY-FOUR AND I'M HERE ON BEHALF OF ADVANCED IDEA MECHANICS TO OFFER YOU THE FUTURE-SCIENCE OPPORTUNITY WE SPECIALIZE IN PROVIDING.
I'M HERE TO OFFER YOU *EXTREMIS.*
NOW, YOU MAY BE HAVING SECOND THOUGHTS. YOU MAY THINK THAT THE MULTI-BILLION-IN-BULLION YOU'RE CARRYING COULD BE BETTER SPENT ELSEWHERE.
YES, THERE ARE OTHER OPTIONS FOR MANUFACTURING SUPERHUMANS. BUT NONE WITH THE *FLEXIBILITY* AND *PRECISION* OF *EXTREMIS.*
WITH ITS CUSTOM DOSE OF GRAPHITE NANO-TUBES, IT HACKS THE BODY'S REPAIR CENTER. IT REPROGRAMS. IT TWEAKS. THE BODY HEALS ITSELF TO ITS NEW DESIGNATION.
AND HOMO EXTREMIS IS BORN.
YOU CAN SEE THE DEFAULT SALES MODEL WALKING AMONGST YOU, BUT THE REAL POWER?
THAT PROGRAM DOES *WHATEVER YOU DESIRE.*

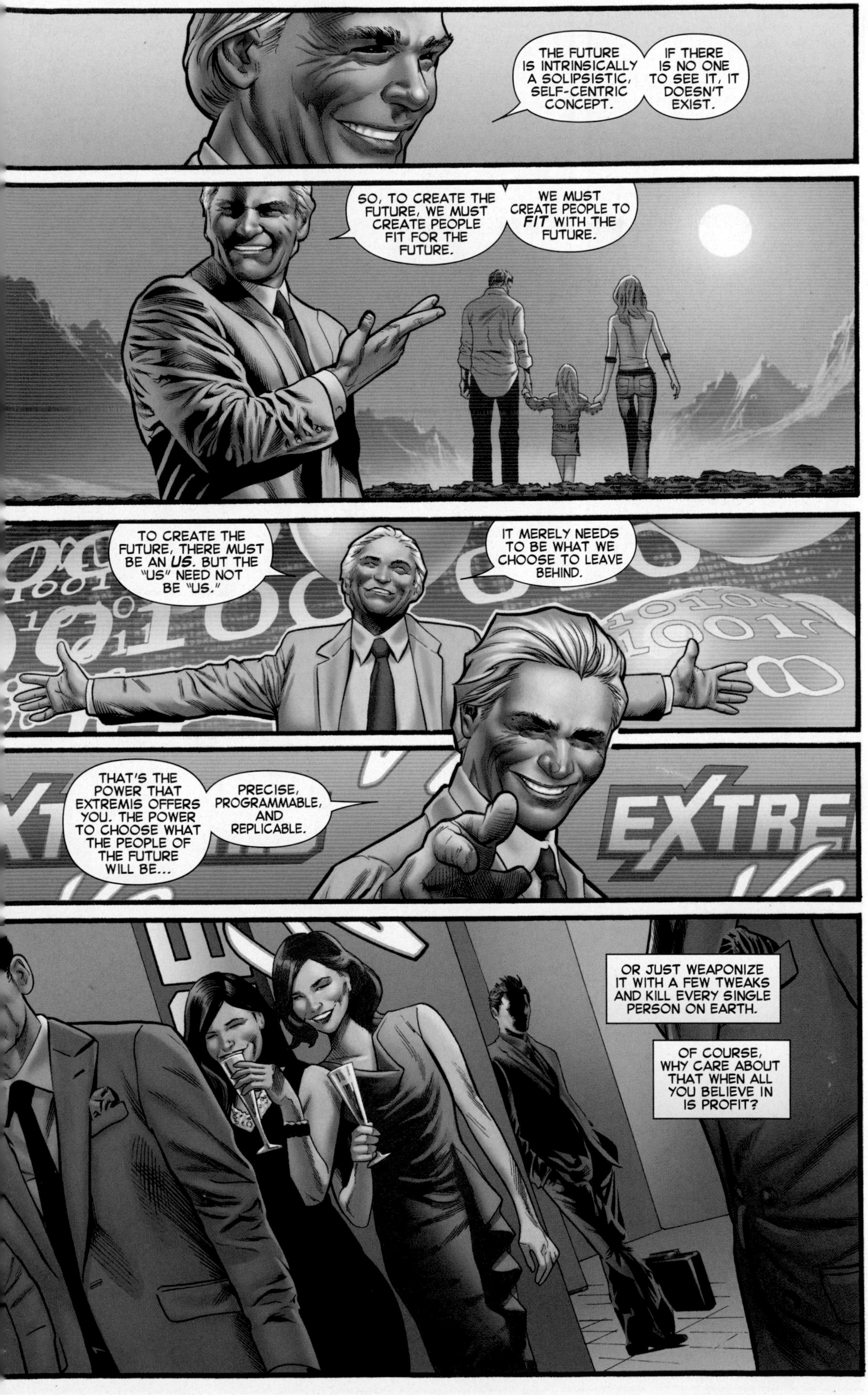
THE FUTURE IS INTRINSICALLY A SOLIPSISTIC, SELF-CENTRIC CONCEPT.
IF THERE IS NO ONE TO SEE IT, IT DOESN'T EXIST.
SO, TO CREATE THE FUTURE, WE MUST CREATE PEOPLE FIT FOR THE FUTURE.
WE MUST CREATE PEOPLE TO *FIT* WITH THE FUTURE.
TO CREATE THE FUTURE, THERE MUST BE AN *US*. BUT THE "US" NEED NOT BE "US."
IT MERELY NEEDS TO BE WHAT WE CHOOSE TO LEAVE BEHIND.
THAT'S THE POWER THAT EXTREMIS OFFERS YOU. THE POWER TO CHOOSE WHAT THE PEOPLE OF THE FUTURE WILL BE...
PRECISE, PROGRAMMABLE, AND REPLICABLE.
EXTRE
OR JUST WEAPONIZE IT WITH A FEW TWEAKS AND KILL EVERY SINGLE PERSON ON EARTH.
OF COURSE, WHY CARE ABOUT THAT WHEN ALL YOU BELIEVE IN IS PROFIT?

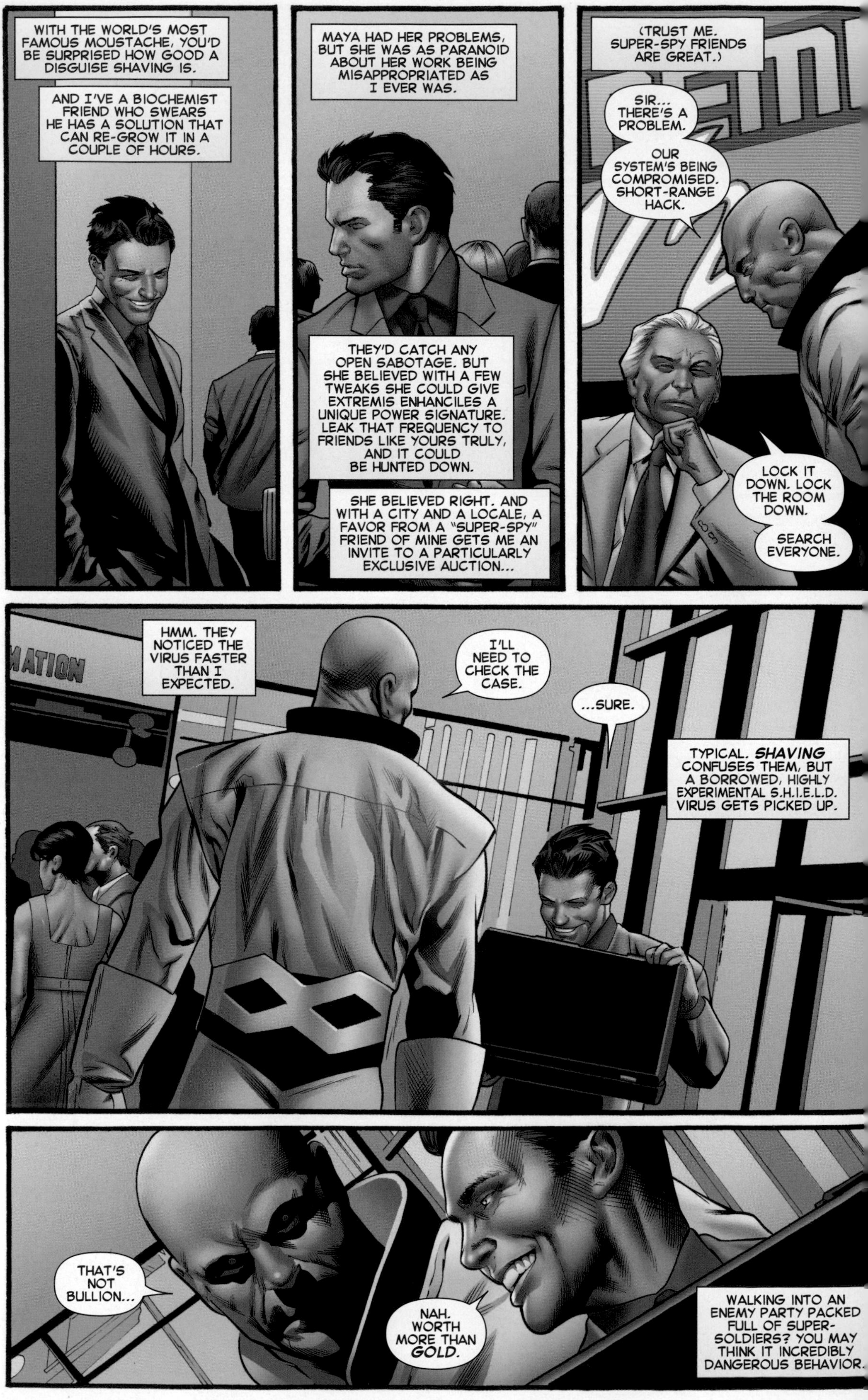
WITH THE WORLD'S MOST FAMOUS MOUSTACHE, YOU'D BE SURPRISED HOW GOOD A DISGUISE SHAVING IS.
AND I'VE A BIOCHEMIST FRIEND WHO SWEARS HE HAS A SOLUTION THAT CAN RE-GROW IT IN A COUPLE OF HOURS.
MAYA HAD HER PROBLEMS, BUT SHE WAS AS PARANOID ABOUT HER WORK BEING MISAPPROPRIATED AS I EVER WAS.
THEY'D CATCH ANY OPEN SABOTAGE. BUT SHE BELIEVED WITH A FEW TWEAKS SHE COULD GIVE EXTREMIS ENHANCILES A UNIQUE POWER SIGNATURE. LEAK THAT FREQUENCY TO FRIENDS LIKE YOURS TRULY, AND IT COULD BE HUNTED DOWN.
SHE BELIEVED RIGHT. AND WITH A CITY AND A LOCALE, A FAVOR FROM A "SUPER-SPY" FRIEND OF MINE GETS ME AN INVITE TO A PARTICULARLY EXCLUSIVE AUCTION...
(TRUST ME. SUPER-SPY FRIENDS ARE GREAT.)
SIR... THERE'S A PROBLEM.
OUR SYSTEM'S BEING COMPROMISED. SHORT-RANGE HACK.
LOCK IT DOWN. LOCK THE ROOM DOWN.
SEARCH EVERYONE.
HMM. THEY NOTICED THE VIRUS FASTER THAN I EXPECTED.
MATION
I'LL NEED TO CHECK THE CASE.
...SURE.
TYPICAL. SHAVING CONFUSES THEM, BUT A BORROWED, HIGHLY EXPERIMENTAL S.H.I.E.L.D. VIRUS GETS PICKED UP.
THAT'S NOT BULLION...
NAH. WORTH MORE THAN GOLD.
WALKING INTO AN ENEMY PARTY PACKED FULL OF SUPER-SOLDIERS? YOU MAY THINK IT INCREDIBLY DANGEROUS BEHAVIOR.

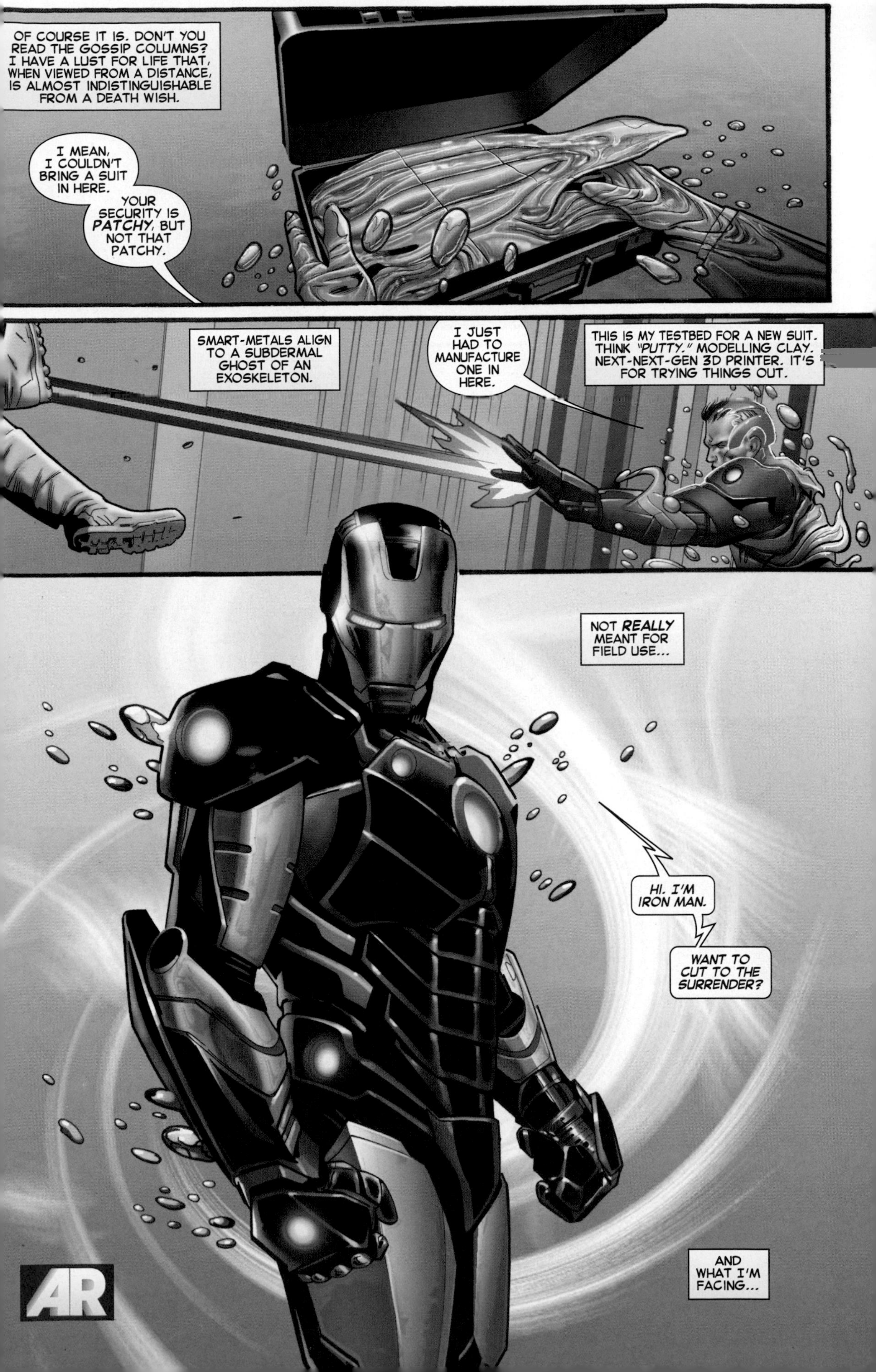
OF COURSE IT IS. DON'T YOU READ THE GOSSIP COLUMNS? I HAVE A LUST FOR LIFE THAT, WHEN VIEWED FROM A DISTANCE, IS ALMOST INDISTINGUISHABLE FROM A DEATH WISH.
I MEAN, I COULDN'T BRING A SUIT IN HERE.
YOUR SECURITY IS *PATCHY*, BUT NOT THAT PATCHY.
SMART-METALS ALIGN TO A SUBDERMAL GHOST OF AN EXOSKELETON.
I JUST HAD TO MANUFACTURE ONE IN HERE.
THIS IS MY TESTBED FOR A NEW SUIT. THINK "PUTTY." MODELLING CLAY. NEXT-NEXT-GEN 3D PRINTER. IT'S FOR TRYING THINGS OUT.
NOT *REALLY* MEANT FOR FIELD USE...
HI. I'M IRON MAN.
WANT TO CUT TO THE SURRENDER?
AND WHAT I'M FACING...
AR

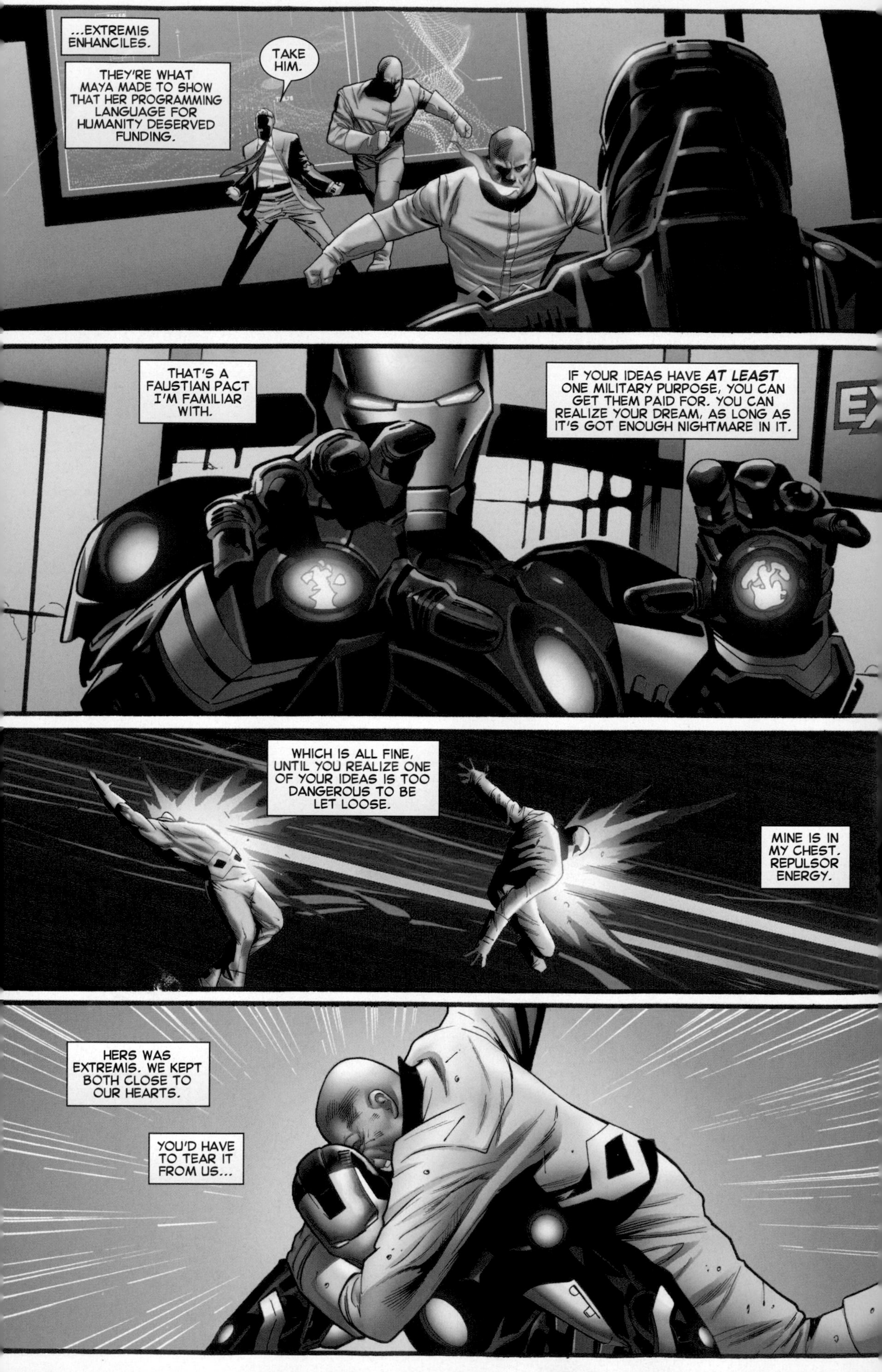
...EXTREMIS ENHANCILES.
THEY'RE WHAT MAYA MADE TO SHOW THAT HER PROGRAMMING LANGUAGE FOR HUMANITY DESERVED FUNDING.
TAKE HIM.
THAT'S A FAUSTIAN PACT I'M FAMILIAR WITH.
IF YOUR IDEAS HAVE AT LEAST ONE MILITARY PURPOSE, YOU CAN GET THEM PAID FOR. YOU CAN REALIZE YOUR DREAM, AS LONG AS IT'S GOT ENOUGH NIGHTMARE IN IT.
WHICH IS ALL FINE, UNTIL YOU REALIZE ONE OF YOUR IDEAS IS TOO DANGEROUS TO BE LET LOOSE.
MINE IS IN MY CHEST. REPULSOR ENERGY.
HERS WAS EXTREMIS. WE KEPT BOTH CLOSE TO OUR HEARTS.
YOU'D HAVE TO TEAR IT FROM US...

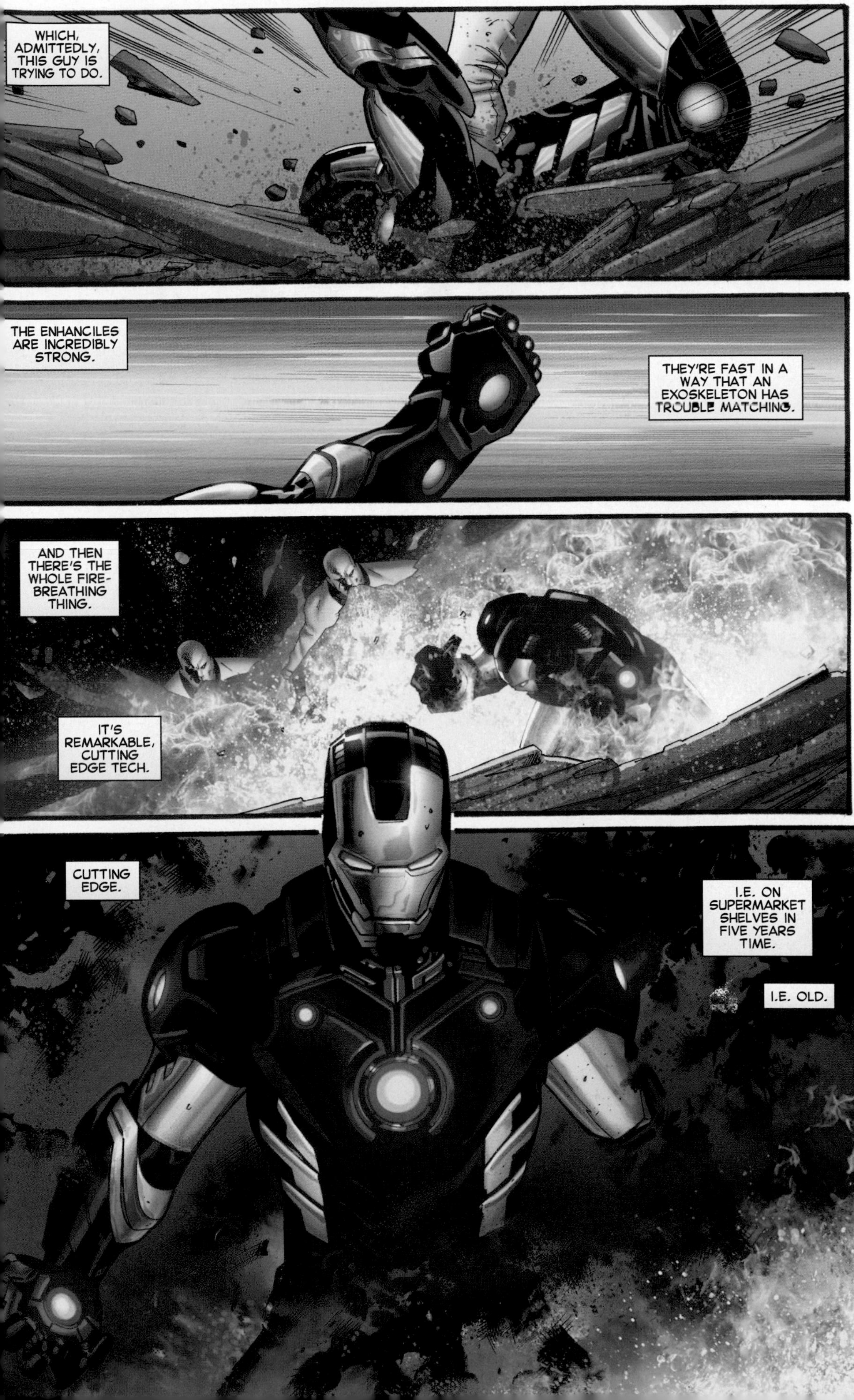
WHICH, ADMITTEDLY, THIS GUY IS TRYING TO DO.
THE ENHANCILES ARE INCREDIBLY STRONG.
THEY'RE FAST IN A WAY THAT AN EXOSKELETON HAS TROUBLE MATCHING.
AND THEN THERE'S THE WHOLE FIRE-BREATHING THING.
IT'S REMARKABLE, CUTTING EDGE TECH.
CUTTING EDGE.
I.E. ON SUPERMARKET SHELVES IN FIVE YEARS TIME.
I.E. OLD.

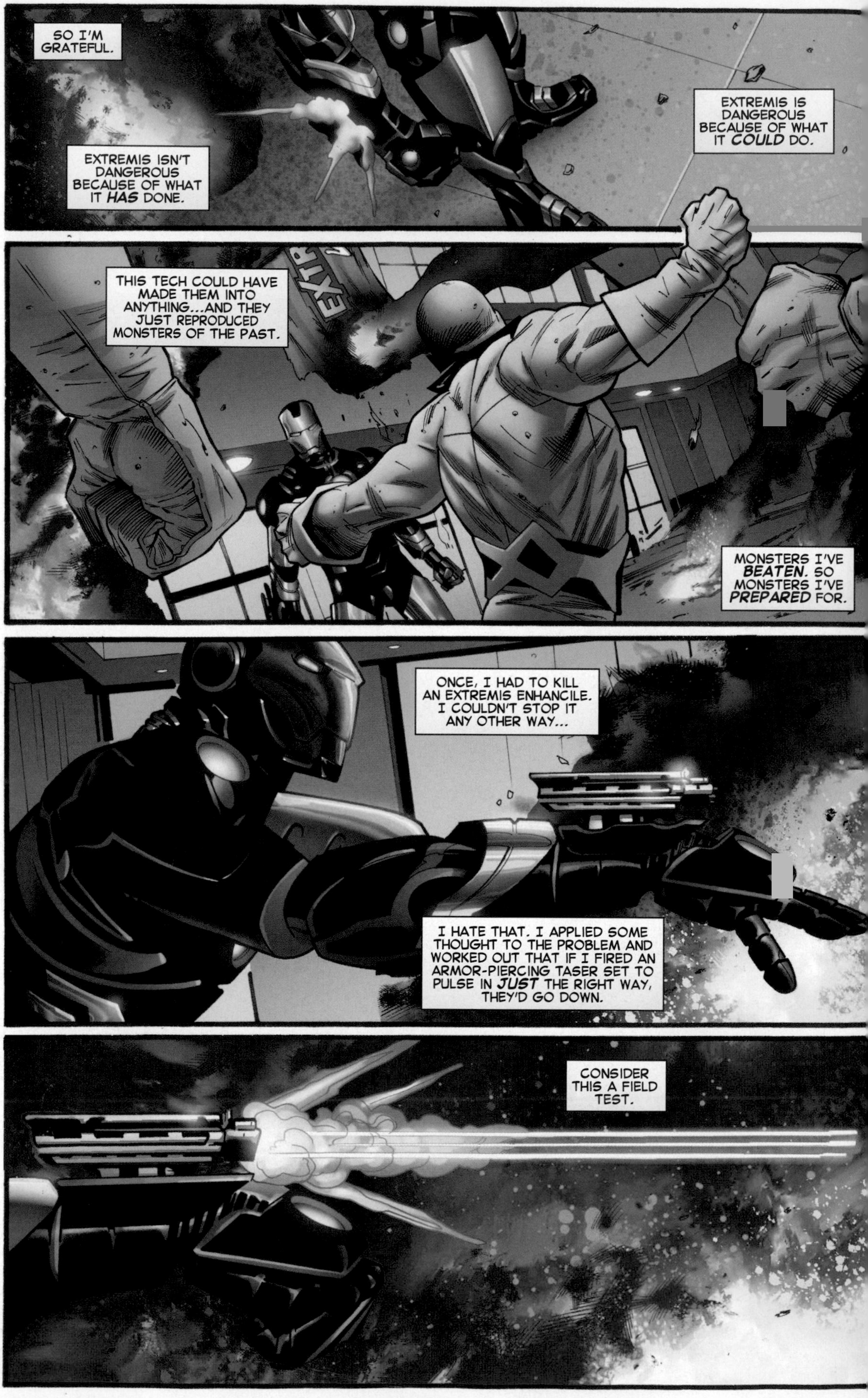
SO I'M GRATEFUL.
EXTREMIS ISN'T DANGEROUS BECAUSE OF WHAT IT HAS DONE.
EXTREMIS IS DANGEROUS BECAUSE OF WHAT IT COULD DO.
THIS TECH COULD HAVE MADE THEM INTO ANYTHING...AND THEY JUST REPRODUCED MONSTERS OF THE PAST.
MONSTERS I'VE BEATEN. SO MONSTERS I'VE PREPARED FOR.
ONCE, I HAD TO KILL AN EXTREMIS ENHANCILE. I COULDN'T STOP IT ANY OTHER WAY...
I HATE THAT. I APPLIED SOME THOUGHT TO THE PROBLEM AND WORKED OUT THAT IF I FIRED AN ARMOR-PIERCING TASER SET TO PULSE IN JUST THE RIGHT WAY, THEY'D GO DOWN.
CONSIDER THIS A FIELD TEST.

THERE IS NOTHING LIKE BEING RIGHT.

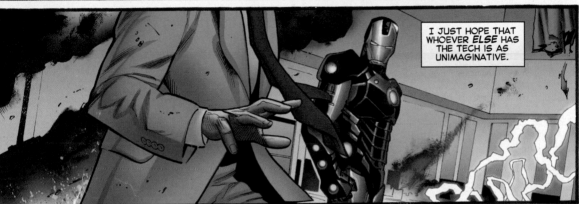

I JUST HOPE THAT WHOEVER *ELSE* HAS THE TECH IS AS UNIMAGINATIVE.

SO...HOW MANY PEOPLE ALREADY HAVE THE KIT?

DO YOU REALLY THINK I'M GOING TO TALK?

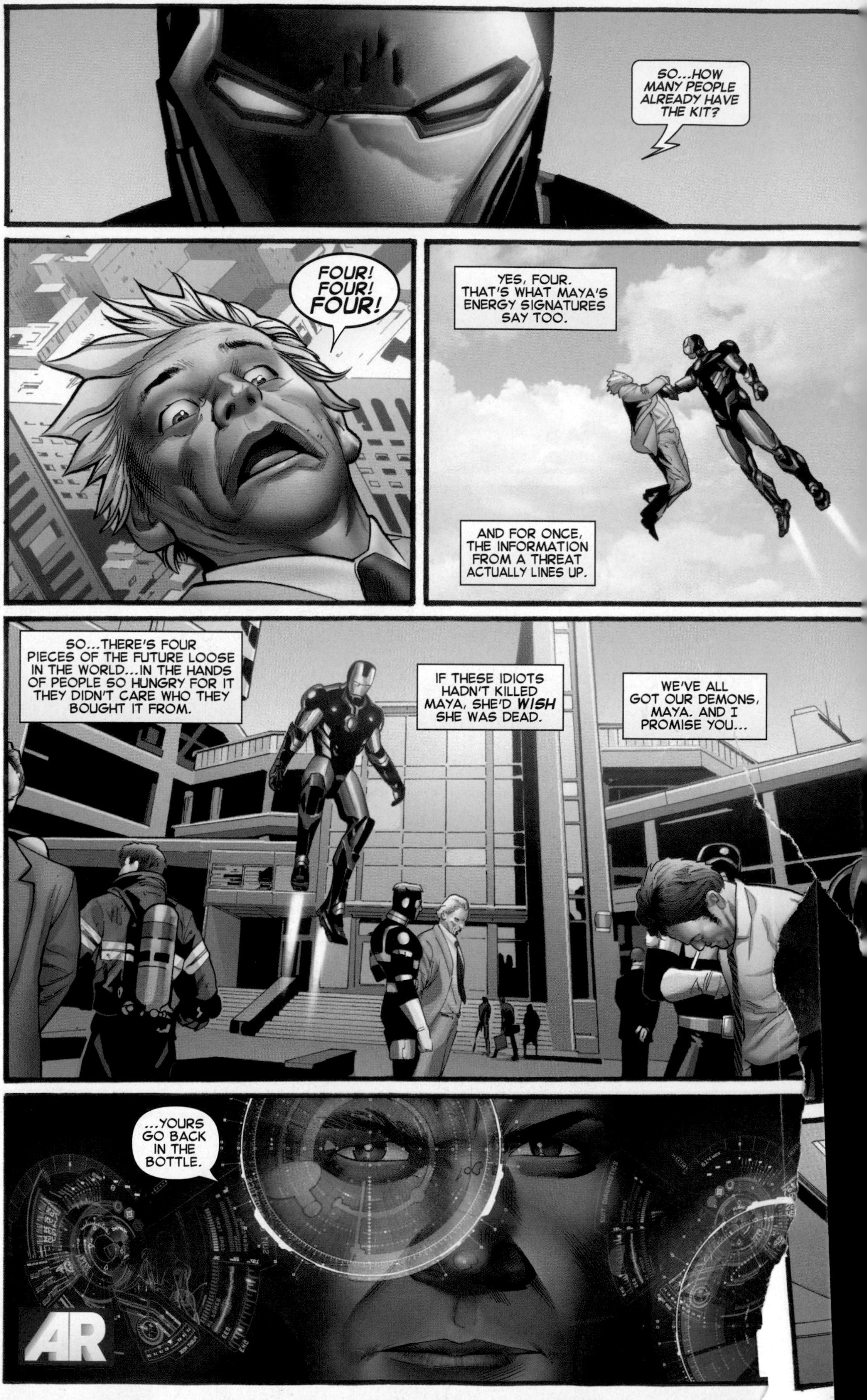

SO...HOW MANY PEOPLE ALREADY HAVE THE KIT?
FOUR! FOUR! FOUR!
YES, FOUR. THAT'S WHAT MAYA'S ENERGY SIGNATURES SAY TOO.
AND FOR ONCE, THE INFORMATION FROM A THREAT ACTUALLY LINES UP.
SO...THERE'S FOUR PIECES OF THE FUTURE LOOSE IN THE WORLD...IN THE HANDS OF PEOPLE SO HUNGRY FOR IT THEY DIDN'T CARE WHO THEY BOUGHT IT FROM.
IF THESE IDIOTS HADN'T KILLED MAYA, SHE'D WISH SHE WAS DEAD.
WE'VE ALL GOT OUR DEMONS, MAYA. AND I PROMISE YOU...
...YOURS GO BACK IN THE BOTTLE.
AR

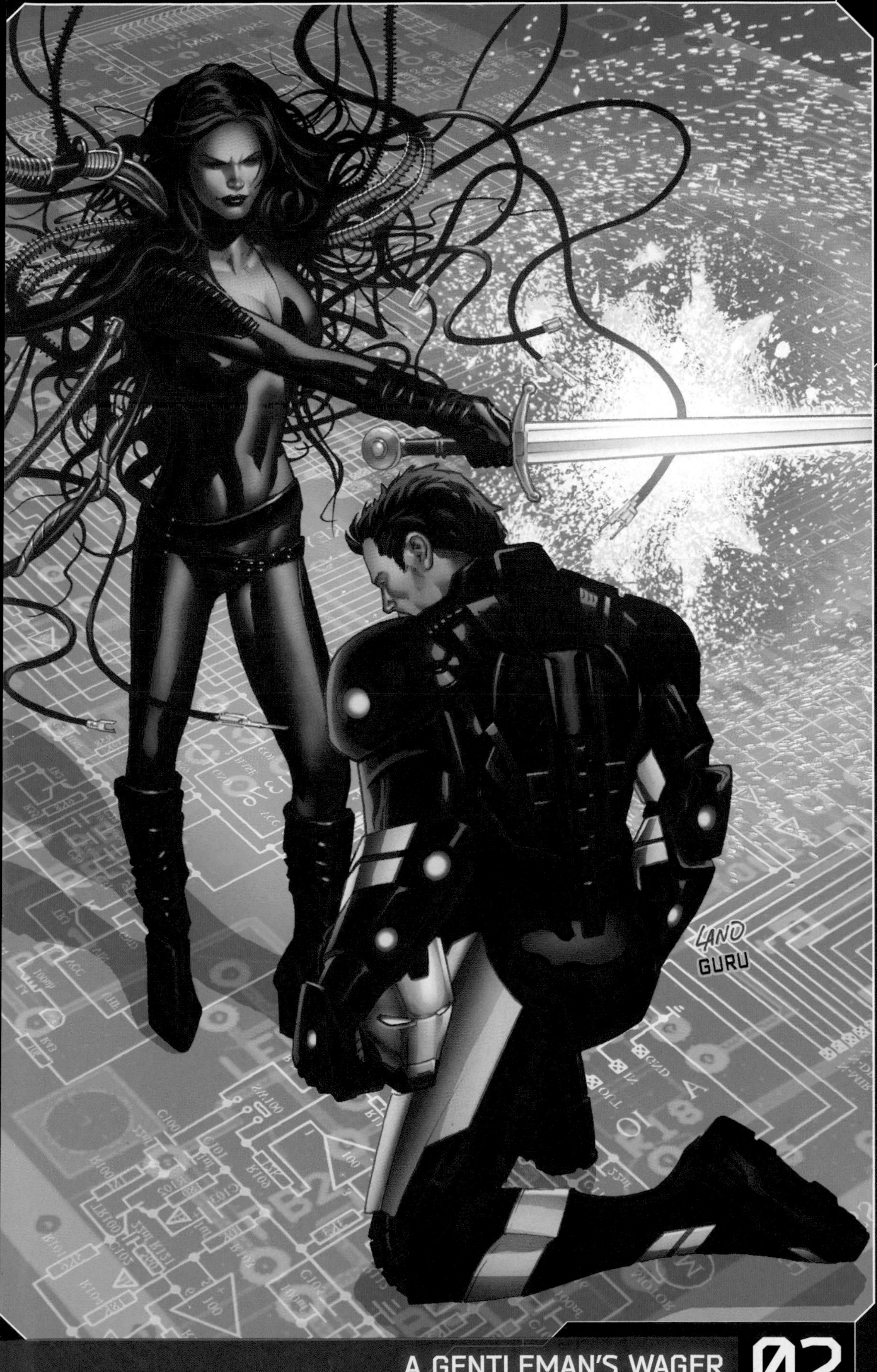
LAND
GURU

A GENTLEMAN'S WAGER 02

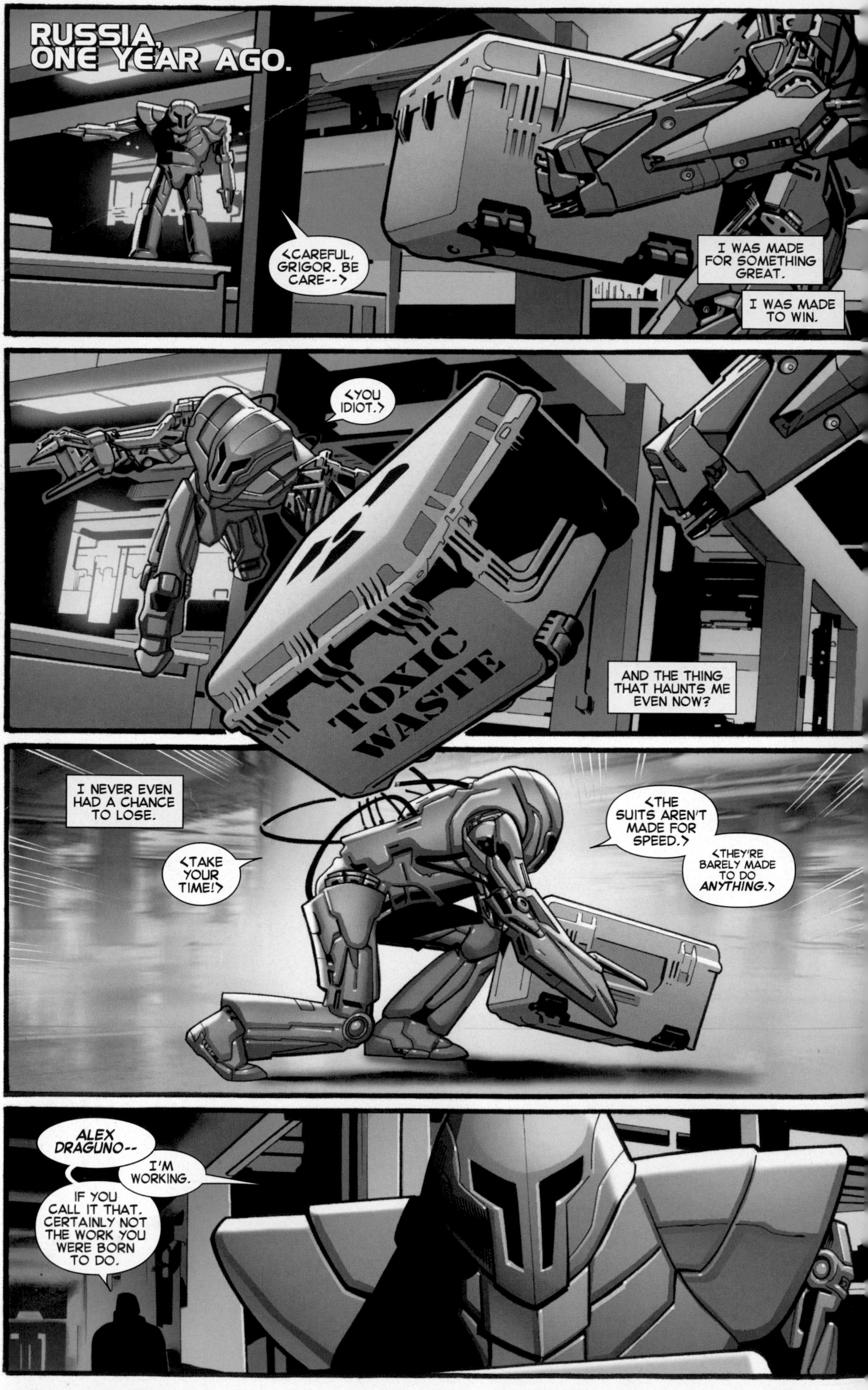
RUSSIA, ONE YEAR AGO.
<CAREFUL, GRIGOR. BE CARE-->
I WAS MADE FOR SOMETHING GREAT.
I WAS MADE TO WIN.
<YOU IDIOT.>
TOXIC WASTE
AND THE THING THAT HAUNTS ME EVEN NOW?
I NEVER EVEN HAD A CHANCE TO LOSE.
<TAKE YOUR TIME!>
<THE SUITS AREN'T MADE FOR SPEED.>
<THEY'RE BARELY MADE TO DO ANYTHING.>
ALEX DRAGUNO--
I'M WORKING.
IF YOU CALL IT THAT. CERTAINLY NOT THE WORK YOU WERE BORN TO DO.

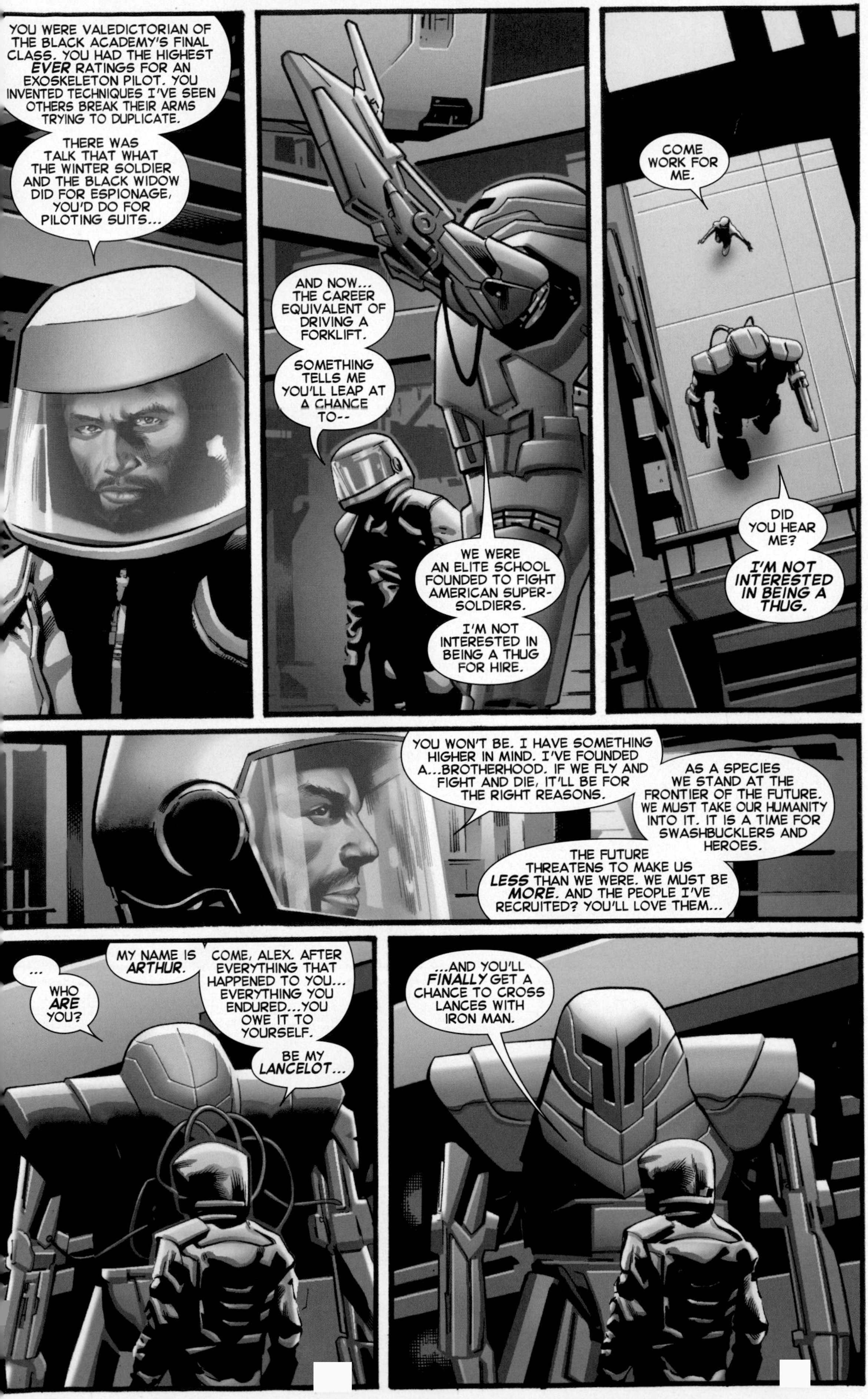
YOU WERE VALEDICTORIAN OF THE BLACK ACADEMY'S FINAL CLASS. YOU HAD THE HIGHEST EVER RATINGS FOR AN EXOSKELETON PILOT. YOU INVENTED TECHNIQUES I'VE SEEN OTHERS BREAK THEIR ARMS TRYING TO DUPLICATE.
THERE WAS TALK THAT WHAT THE WINTER SOLDIER AND THE BLACK WIDOW DID FOR ESPIONAGE, YOU'D DO FOR PILOTING SUITS...
AND NOW... THE CAREER EQUIVALENT OF DRIVING A FORKLIFT.
SOMETHING TELLS ME YOU'LL LEAP AT A CHANCE TO--
WE WERE AN ELITE SCHOOL FOUNDED TO FIGHT AMERICAN SUPER-SOLDIERS.
I'M NOT INTERESTED IN BEING A THUG FOR HIRE.
COME WORK FOR ME.
DID YOU HEAR ME?
I'M NOT INTERESTED IN BEING A THUG.
YOU WON'T BE. I HAVE SOMETHING HIGHER IN MIND. I'VE FOUNDED A...BROTHERHOOD. IF WE FLY AND FIGHT AND DIE, IT'LL BE FOR THE RIGHT REASONS.
AS A SPECIES WE STAND AT THE FRONTIER OF THE FUTURE. WE MUST TAKE OUR HUMANITY INTO IT. IT IS A TIME FOR SWASHBUCKLERS AND HEROES.
THE FUTURE THREATENS TO MAKE US LESS THAN WE WERE. WE MUST BE MORE. AND THE PEOPLE I'VE RECRUITED? YOU'LL LOVE THEM...
... WHO ARE YOU?
MY NAME IS ARTHUR.
COME, ALEX. AFTER EVERYTHING THAT HAPPENED TO YOU... EVERYTHING YOU ENDURED...YOU OWE IT TO YOURSELF.
BE MY LANCELOT...
...AND YOU'LL FINALLY GET A CHANCE TO CROSS LANCES WITH IRON MAN.

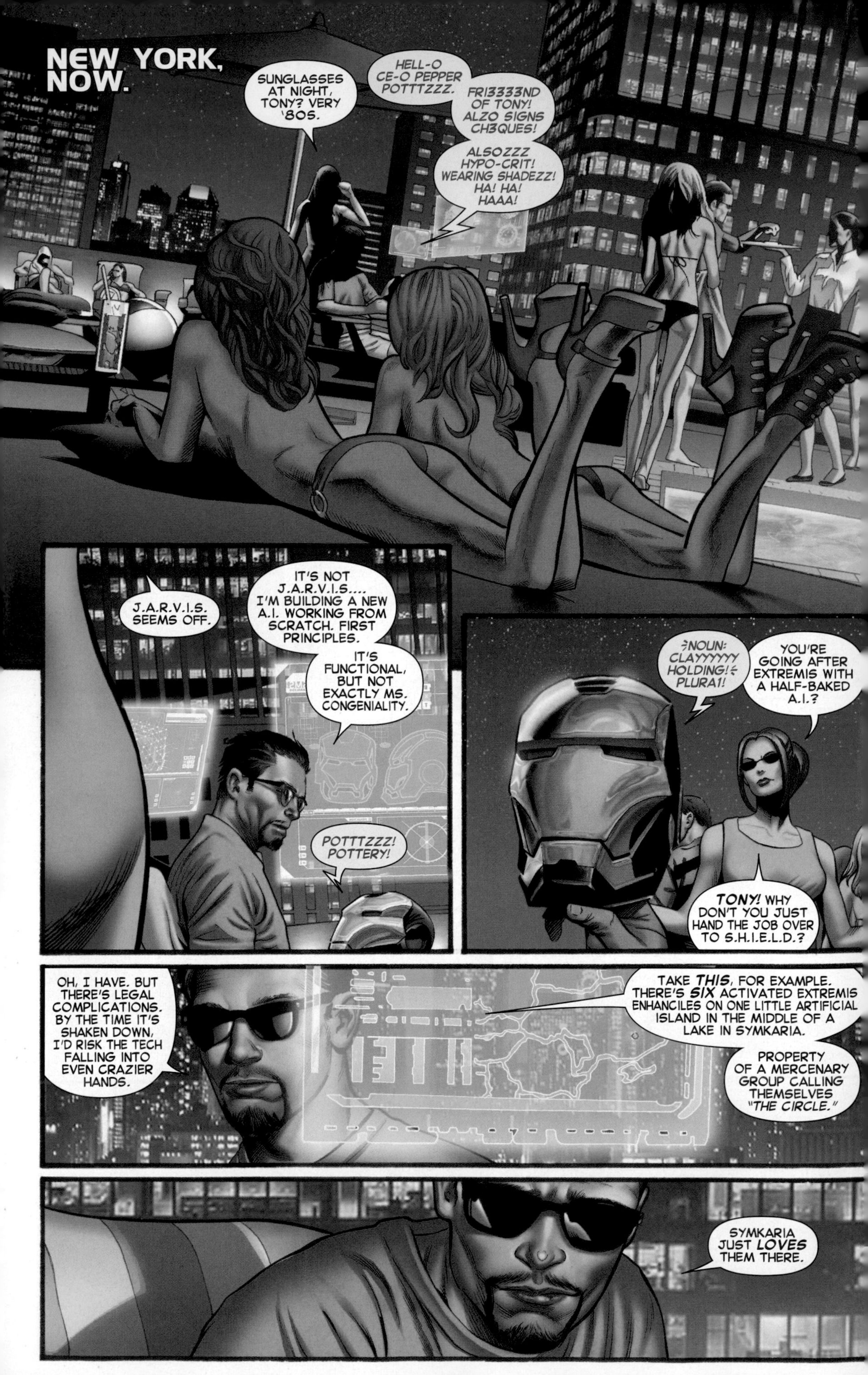
NEW YORK, NOW.
SUNGLASSES AT NIGHT, TONY? VERY '80S.
HELL-O CE-O PEPPER POTTTZZZ.
FRI3333ND OF TONY! ALZO SIGNS CH3QUES!
ALSOZZZ HYPO-CRIT! WEARING SHADEZZ! HA! HA! HAAA!
J.A.R.V.I.S. SEEMS OFF.
IT'S NOT J.A.R.V.I.S.... I'M BUILDING A NEW A.I. WORKING FROM SCRATCH. FIRST PRINCIPLES.
IT'S FUNCTIONAL, BUT NOT EXACTLY MS. CONGENIALITY.
POTTTZZZ! POTTERY!
NOUN: CLAYYYYYY HOLDING! PLURA1!
YOU'RE GOING AFTER EXTREMIS WITH A HALF-BAKED A.I.?
TONY! WHY DON'T YOU JUST HAND THE JOB OVER TO S.H.I.E.L.D.?
OH, I HAVE. BUT THERE'S LEGAL COMPLICATIONS. BY THE TIME IT'S SHAKEN DOWN, I'D RISK THE TECH FALLING INTO EVEN CRAZIER HANDS.
TAKE THIS, FOR EXAMPLE. THERE'S SIX ACTIVATED EXTREMIS ENHANCILES ON ONE LITTLE ARTIFICIAL ISLAND IN THE MIDDLE OF A LAKE IN SYMKARIA.
PROPERTY OF A MERCENARY GROUP CALLING THEMSELVES "THE CIRCLE."
SYMKARIA JUST LOVES THEM THERE.

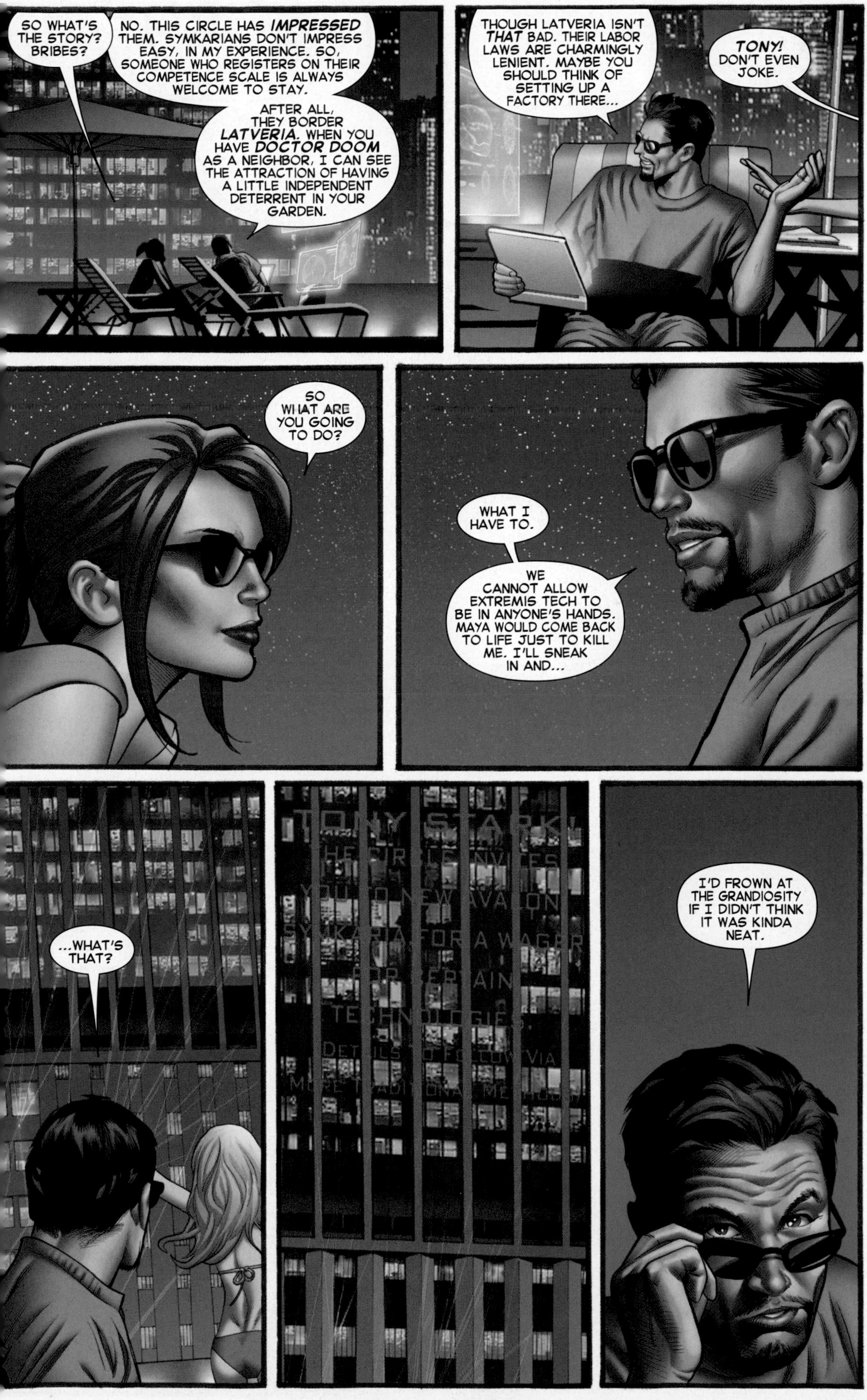
SO WHAT'S THE STORY? BRIBES?
NO. THIS CIRCLE HAS IMPRESSED THEM. SYMKARIANS DON'T IMPRESS EASY, IN MY EXPERIENCE. SO, SOMEONE WHO REGISTERS ON THEIR COMPETENCE SCALE IS ALWAYS WELCOME TO STAY.
AFTER ALL, THEY BORDER LATVERIA. WHEN YOU HAVE DOCTOR DOOM AS A NEIGHBOR, I CAN SEE THE ATTRACTION OF HAVING A LITTLE INDEPENDENT DETERRENT IN YOUR GARDEN.
THOUGH LATVERIA ISN'T THAT BAD. THEIR LABOR LAWS ARE CHARMINGLY LENIENT. MAYBE YOU SHOULD THINK OF SETTING UP A FACTORY THERE...
TONY! DON'T EVEN JOKE.
SO WHAT ARE YOU GOING TO DO?
WHAT I HAVE TO.
WE CANNOT ALLOW EXTREMIS TECH TO BE IN ANYONE'S HANDS. MAYA WOULD COME BACK TO LIFE JUST TO KILL ME. I'LL SNEAK IN AND...
...WHAT'S THAT?
TONY STARK!
I'D FROWN AT THE GRANDIOSITY IF I DIDN'T THINK IT WAS KINDA NEAT.

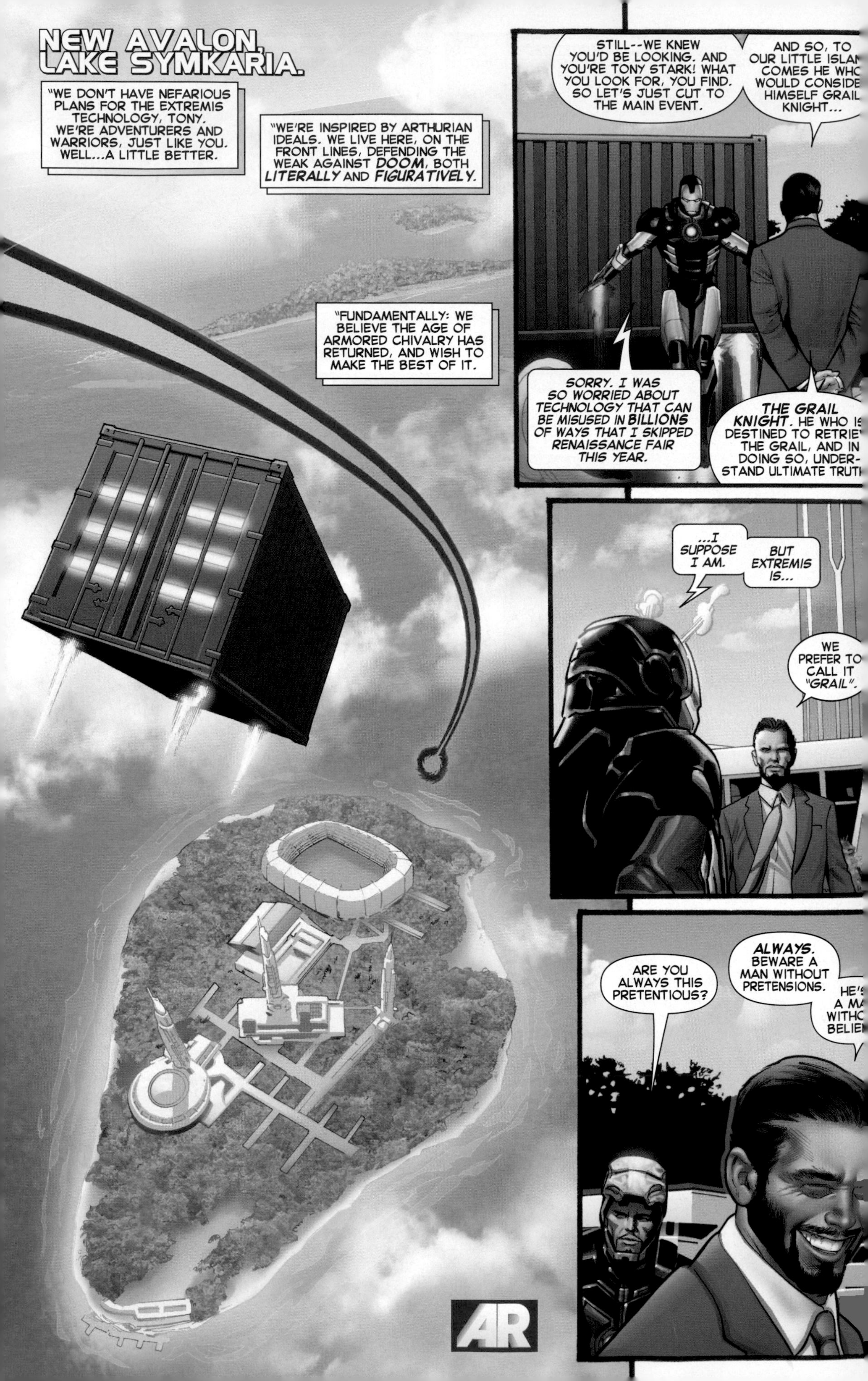

NEW AVALON, LAKE SYMKARIA.
"WE DON'T HAVE NEFARIOUS PLANS FOR THE EXTREMIS TECHNOLOGY, TONY. WE'RE ADVENTURERS AND WARRIORS, JUST LIKE YOU. WELL...A LITTLE BETTER.
"WE'RE INSPIRED BY ARTHURIAN IDEALS. WE LIVE HERE, ON THE FRONT LINES, DEFENDING THE WEAK AGAINST DOOM, BOTH LITERALLY AND FIGURATIVELY.
"FUNDAMENTALLY: WE BELIEVE THE AGE OF ARMORED CHIVALRY HAS RETURNED, AND WISH TO MAKE THE BEST OF IT.
STILL--WE KNEW YOU'D BE LOOKING. AND YOU'RE TONY STARK! WHAT YOU LOOK FOR, YOU FIND. SO LET'S JUST CUT TO THE MAIN EVENT.
AND SO, TO OUR LITTLE ISLAN COMES HE WHO WOULD CONSIDE HIMSELF GRAIL KNIGHT...
SORRY. I WAS SO WORRIED ABOUT TECHNOLOGY THAT CAN BE MISUSED IN BILLIONS OF WAYS THAT I SKIPPED RENAISSANCE FAIR THIS YEAR.
THE GRAIL KNIGHT. HE WHO IS DESTINED TO RETRIE THE GRAIL, AND IN DOING SO, UNDER-STAND ULTIMATE TRUT
...I SUPPOSE I AM.
BUT EXTREMIS IS...
WE PREFER TO CALL IT "GRAIL".
ARE YOU ALWAYS THIS PRETENTIOUS?
ALWAYS. BEWARE A MAN WITHOUT PRETENSIONS.
HE'S A MA WITHO BELIE
AR

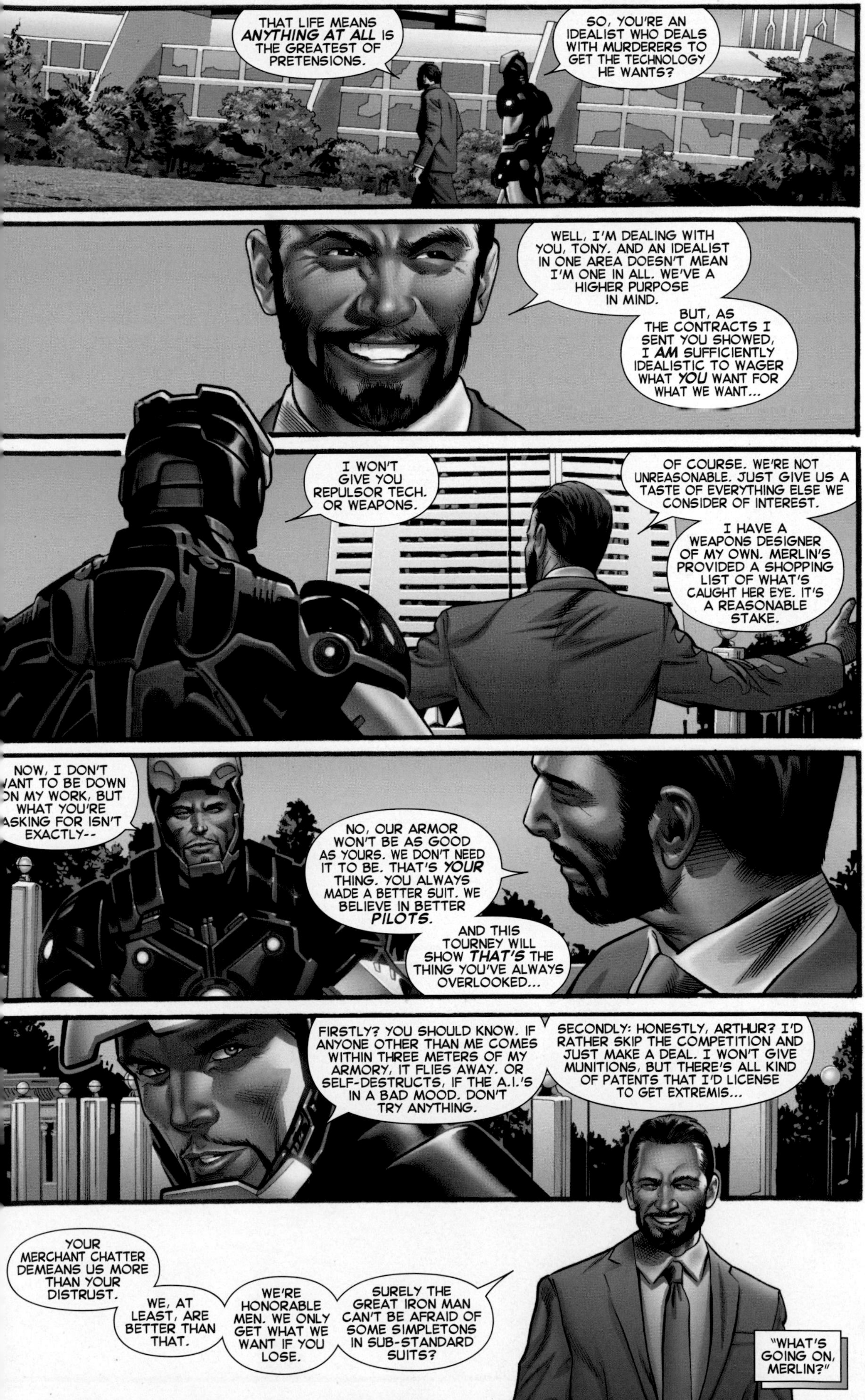
THAT LIFE MEANS ANYTHING AT ALL IS THE GREATEST OF PRETENSIONS.
SO, YOU'RE AN IDEALIST WHO DEALS WITH MURDERERS TO GET THE TECHNOLOGY HE WANTS?
WELL, I'M DEALING WITH YOU, TONY. AND AN IDEALIST IN ONE AREA DOESN'T MEAN I'M ONE IN ALL. WE'VE A HIGHER PURPOSE IN MIND.
BUT, AS THE CONTRACTS I SENT YOU SHOWED, I AM SUFFICIENTLY IDEALISTIC TO WAGER WHAT YOU WANT FOR WHAT WE WANT...
I WON'T GIVE YOU REPULSOR TECH. OR WEAPONS.
OF COURSE. WE'RE NOT UNREASONABLE. JUST GIVE US A TASTE OF EVERYTHING ELSE WE CONSIDER OF INTEREST.
I HAVE A WEAPONS DESIGNER OF MY OWN. MERLIN'S PROVIDED A SHOPPING LIST OF WHAT'S CAUGHT HER EYE. IT'S A REASONABLE STAKE.
NOW, I DON'T WANT TO BE DOWN ON MY WORK, BUT WHAT YOU'RE ASKING FOR ISN'T EXACTLY--
NO, OUR ARMOR WON'T BE AS GOOD AS YOURS. WE DON'T NEED IT TO BE. THAT'S YOUR THING. YOU ALWAYS MADE A BETTER SUIT. WE BELIEVE IN BETTER PILOTS.
AND THIS TOURNEY WILL SHOW THAT'S THE THING YOU'VE ALWAYS OVERLOOKED...
FIRSTLY? YOU SHOULD KNOW. IF ANYONE OTHER THAN ME COMES WITHIN THREE METERS OF MY ARMORY, IT FLIES AWAY. OR SELF-DESTRUCTS, IF THE A.I.'S IN A BAD MOOD. DON'T TRY ANYTHING.
SECONDLY: HONESTLY, ARTHUR? I'D RATHER SKIP THE COMPETITION AND JUST MAKE A DEAL. I WON'T GIVE MUNITIONS, BUT THERE'S ALL KIND OF PATENTS THAT I'D LICENSE TO GET EXTREMIS...
YOUR MERCHANT CHATTER DEMEANS US MORE THAN YOUR DISTRUST.
WE, AT LEAST, ARE BETTER THAN THAT.
WE'RE HONORABLE MEN. WE ONLY GET WHAT WE WANT IF YOU LOSE.
SURELY THE GREAT IRON MAN CAN'T BE AFRAID OF SOME SIMPLETONS IN SUB-STANDARD SUITS?
"WHAT'S GOING ON, MERLIN?"

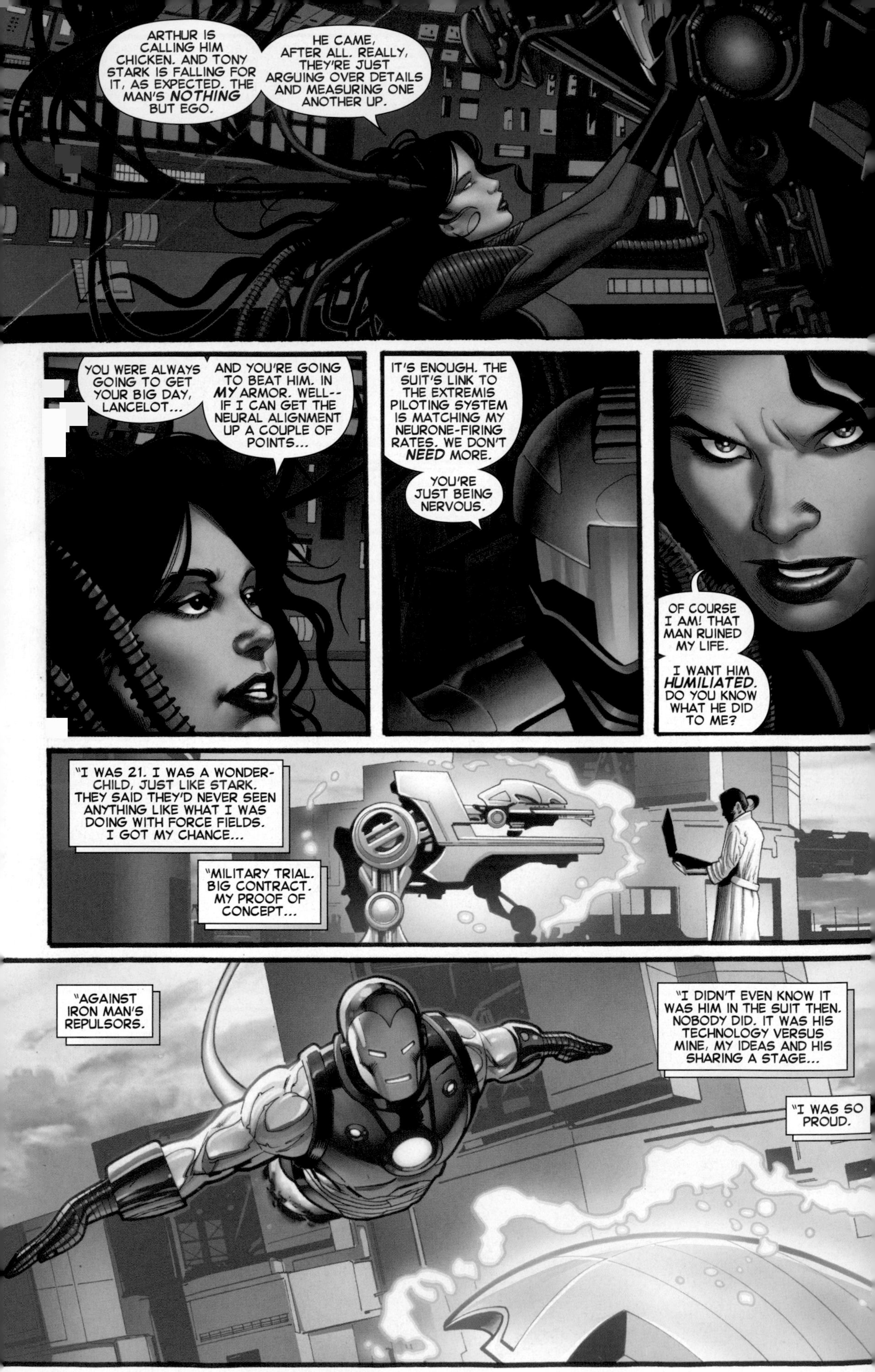
ARTHUR IS CALLING HIM CHICKEN. AND TONY STARK IS FALLING FOR IT, AS EXPECTED. THE MAN'S NOTHING BUT EGO.
HE CAME, AFTER ALL. REALLY, THEY'RE JUST ARGUING OVER DETAILS AND MEASURING ONE ANOTHER UP.
YOU WERE ALWAYS GOING TO GET YOUR BIG DAY, LANCELOT...
AND YOU'RE GOING TO BEAT HIM. IN MY ARMOR. WELL--IF I CAN GET THE NEURAL ALIGNMENT UP A COUPLE OF POINTS...
IT'S ENOUGH. THE SUIT'S LINK TO THE EXTREMIS PILOTING SYSTEM IS MATCHING MY NEURONE-FIRING RATES. WE DON'T NEED MORE.
YOU'RE JUST BEING NERVOUS.
OF COURSE I AM! THAT MAN RUINED MY LIFE.
I WANT HIM HUMILIATED. DO YOU KNOW WHAT HE DID TO ME?
"I WAS 21. I WAS A WONDER-CHILD, JUST LIKE STARK. THEY SAID THEY'D NEVER SEEN ANYTHING LIKE WHAT I WAS DOING WITH FORCE FIELDS. I GOT MY CHANCE...
"MILITARY TRIAL. BIG CONTRACT. MY PROOF OF CONCEPT...
"AGAINST IRON MAN'S REPULSORS.
"I DIDN'T EVEN KNOW IT WAS HIM IN THE SUIT THEN. NOBODY DID. IT WAS HIS TECHNOLOGY VERSUS MINE, MY IDEAS AND HIS SHARING A STAGE...
"I WAS SO PROUD.

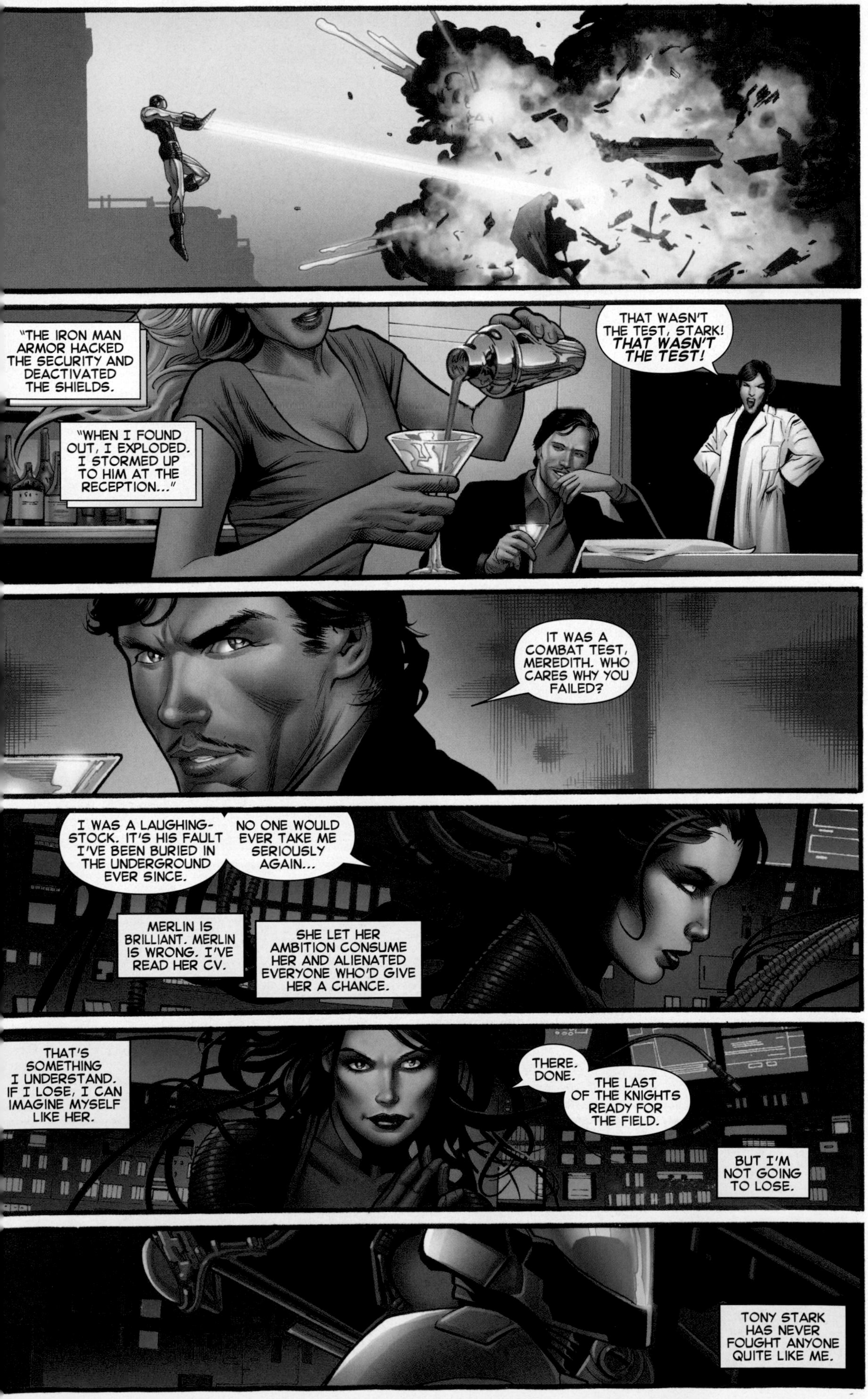
"THE IRON MAN ARMOR HACKED THE SECURITY AND DEACTIVATED THE SHIELDS.
"WHEN I FOUND OUT, I EXPLODED. I STORMED UP TO HIM AT THE RECEPTION..."
THAT WASN'T THE TEST, STARK! THAT WASN'T THE TEST!
IT WAS A COMBAT TEST, MEREDITH. WHO CARES WHY YOU FAILED?
I WAS A LAUGHING-STOCK. IT'S HIS FAULT I'VE BEEN BURIED IN THE UNDERGROUND EVER SINCE.
NO ONE WOULD EVER TAKE ME SERIOUSLY AGAIN...
MERLIN IS BRILLIANT. MERLIN IS WRONG. I'VE READ HER CV.
SHE LET HER AMBITION CONSUME HER AND ALIENATED EVERYONE WHO'D GIVE HER A CHANCE.
THAT'S SOMETHING I UNDERSTAND. IF I LOSE, I CAN IMAGINE MYSELF LIKE HER.
THERE. DONE.
THE LAST OF THE KNIGHTS READY FOR THE FIELD.
BUT I'M NOT GOING TO LOSE.
TONY STARK HAS NEVER FOUGHT ANYONE QUITE LIKE ME.

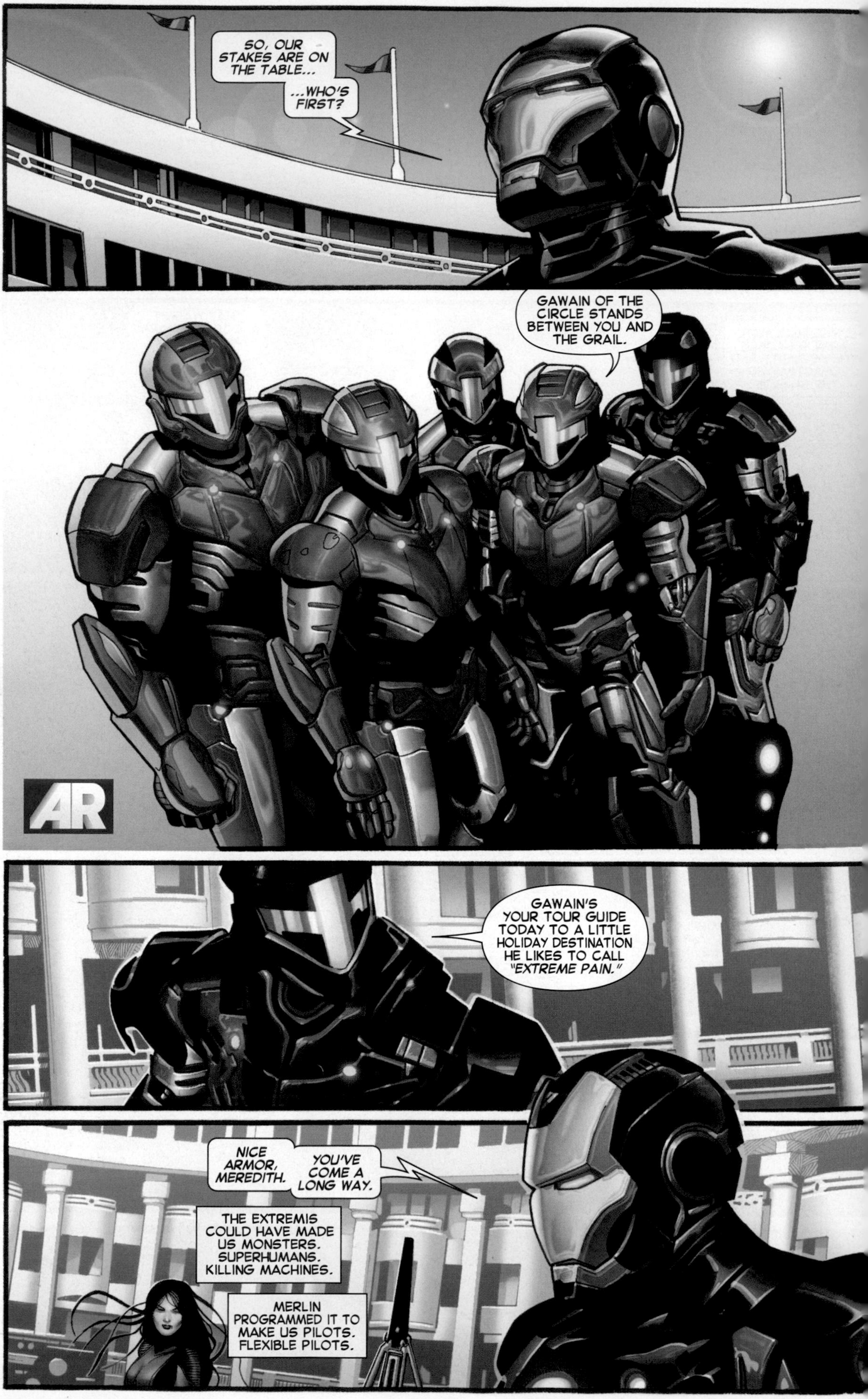

SO, OUR STAKES ARE ON THE TABLE...
...WHO'S FIRST?
GAWAIN OF THE CIRCLE STANDS BETWEEN YOU AND THE GRAIL.
AR
GAWAIN'S YOUR TOUR GUIDE TODAY TO A LITTLE HOLIDAY DESTINATION HE LIKES TO CALL "EXTREME PAIN."
NICE ARMOR, MEREDITH.
YOU'VE COME A LONG WAY.
THE EXTREMIS COULD HAVE MADE US MONSTERS. SUPERHUMANS. KILLING MACHINES.
MERLIN PROGRAMMED IT TO MAKE US PILOTS. FLEXIBLE PILOTS.

WE ARE NOW LIVING CONTROL SYSTEMS, DIRECTLY CONNECTED TO WHATEVER SUITS MERLIN BUILDS. IT'S FUTURE-PROOFED. THE SUITS CAN IMPROVE WHILE THE PILOTS ARE AS GOOD AS THEY CAN GET WHILE STILL REMAINING HUMANS.

WELL, MOSTLY HUMAN. SOME MINOR BOOSTS. G-TOLERANCE AND SO ON, BUT THEY'RE NOT THE SORT OF THINGS THAT GET YOU INTO THE AVENGERS.

COMPUTER?

YZZ?

DEPLOY THE ARMORY.

YZZ!

GIVE ME A SINGLE-OPPONENT LOAD-OUT. THROW THE LATEST REPULSOR IN THERE. THE MARK IVa.

IT'S ABOUT FLEXIBILITY.

AFFIRMIYES!

THANKS.

STARK'S THINKING ON SIMILARLY MODULAR LINES. IT'S IMPRESSIVE. ARTHUR DOUBTS STARK'S CALIBER AS A PILOT, BUT NO ONE IS STUPID ENOUGH TO QUESTION HIM AS A TECHNOLOGIST.

READY WHEN YOU ARE, WAYNE.

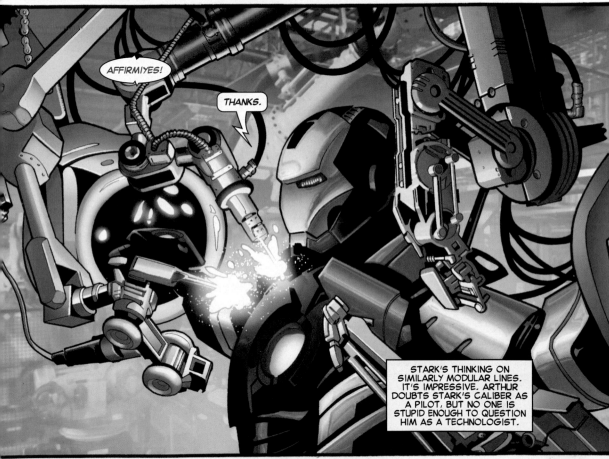

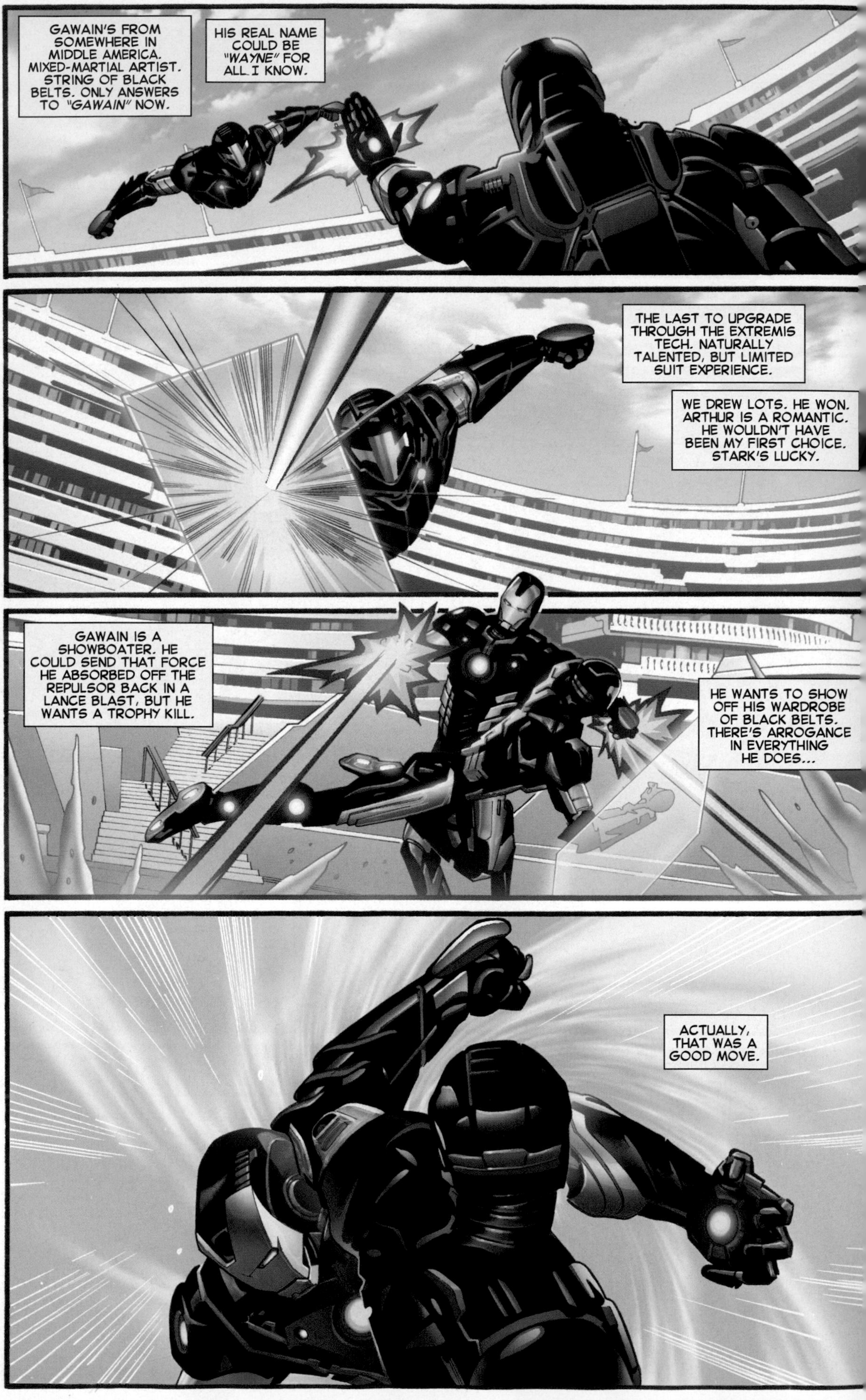
GAWAIN'S FROM SOMEWHERE IN MIDDLE AMERICA. MIXED-MARTIAL ARTIST. STRING OF BLACK BELTS. ONLY ANSWERS TO "GAWAIN" NOW.
HIS REAL NAME COULD BE "WAYNE" FOR ALL I KNOW.
THE LAST TO UPGRADE THROUGH THE EXTREMIS TECH. NATURALLY TALENTED, BUT LIMITED SUIT EXPERIENCE.
WE DREW LOTS. HE WON. ARTHUR IS A ROMANTIC. HE WOULDN'T HAVE BEEN MY FIRST CHOICE. STARK'S LUCKY.
GAWAIN IS A SHOWBOATER. HE COULD SEND THAT FORCE HE ABSORBED OFF THE REPULSOR BACK IN A LANCE BLAST, BUT HE WANTS A TROPHY KILL.
HE WANTS TO SHOW OFF HIS WARDROBE OF BLACK BELTS. THERE'S ARROGANCE IN EVERYTHING HE DOES...
ACTUALLY, THAT WAS A GOOD MOVE.

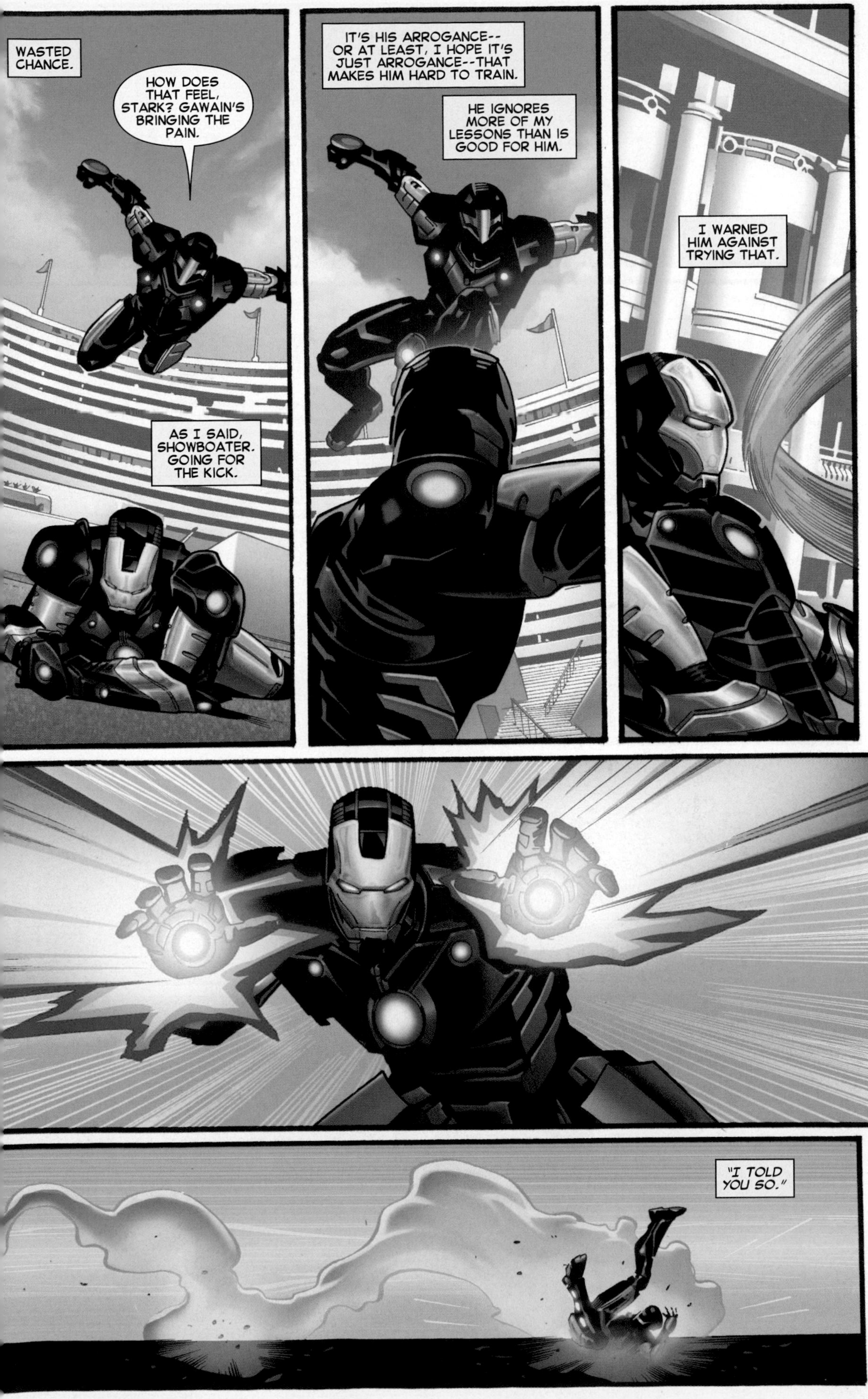
WASTED CHANCE.
HOW DOES THAT FEEL, STARK? GAWAIN'S BRINGING THE PAIN.
AS I SAID, SHOWBOATER. GOING FOR THE KICK.
IT'S HIS ARROGANCE-- OR AT LEAST, I HOPE IT'S JUST ARROGANCE--THAT MAKES HIM HARD TO TRAIN.
HE IGNORES MORE OF MY LESSONS THAN IS GOOD FOR HIM.
I WARNED HIM AGAINST TRYING THAT.
"I TOLD YOU SO."

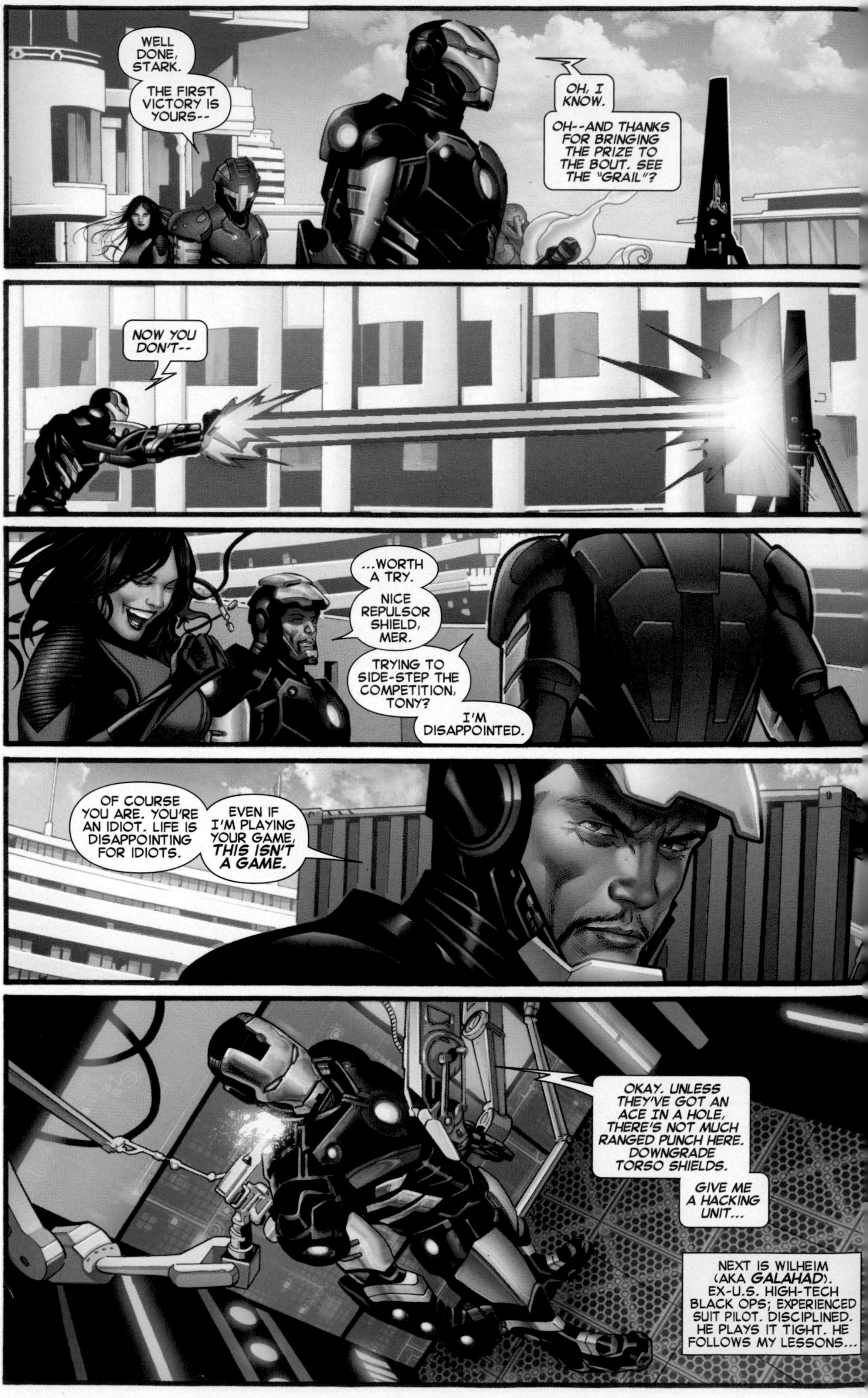
WELL DONE, STARK.
THE FIRST VICTORY IS YOURS--
OH, I KNOW.
OH--AND THANKS FOR BRINGING THE PRIZE TO THE BOUT. SEE THE "GRAIL"?
NOW YOU DON'T--
...WORTH A TRY.
NICE REPULSOR SHIELD, MER.
TRYING TO SIDE-STEP THE COMPETITION, TONY?
I'M DISAPPOINTED.
OF COURSE YOU ARE. YOU'RE AN IDIOT. LIFE IS DISAPPOINTING FOR IDIOTS.
EVEN IF I'M PLAYING YOUR GAME, THIS ISN'T A GAME.
OKAY. UNLESS THEY'VE GOT AN ACE IN A HOLE, THERE'S NOT MUCH RANGED PUNCH HERE. DOWNGRADE TORSO SHIELDS.
GIVE ME A HACKING UNIT...
NEXT IS WILHEIM (AKA GALAHAD). EX-U.S. HIGH-TECH BLACK OPS; EXPERIENCED SUIT PILOT. DISCIPLINED. HE PLAYS IT TIGHT. HE FOLLOWS MY LESSONS...

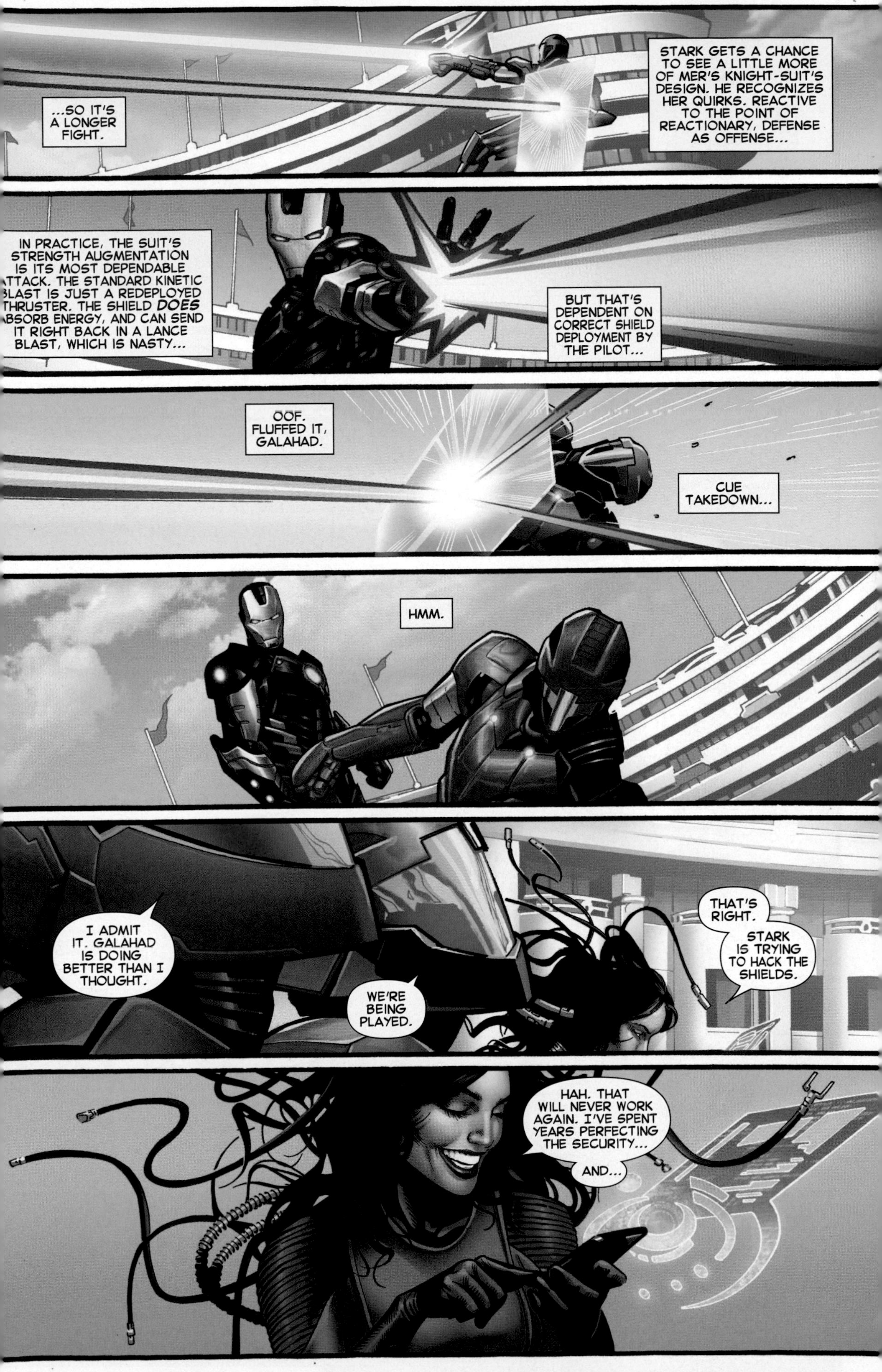

...SO IT'S A LONGER FIGHT.
STARK GETS A CHANCE TO SEE A LITTLE MORE OF MER'S KNIGHT-SUIT'S DESIGN. HE RECOGNIZES HER QUIRKS. REACTIVE TO THE POINT OF REACTIONARY, DEFENSE AS OFFENSE...
IN PRACTICE, THE SUIT'S STRENGTH AUGMENTATION IS ITS MOST DEPENDABLE TTACK. THE STANDARD KINETIC LAST IS JUST A REDEPLOYED HRUSTER. THE SHIELD *DOES* BSORB ENERGY, AND CAN SEND IT RIGHT BACK IN A LANCE BLAST, WHICH IS NASTY...
BUT THAT'S DEPENDENT ON CORRECT SHIELD DEPLOYMENT BY THE PILOT...
OOF. FLUFFED IT, GALAHAD.
CUE TAKEDOWN...
HMM.
I ADMIT IT. GALAHAD IS DOING BETTER THAN I THOUGHT.
WE'RE BEING PLAYED.
THAT'S RIGHT.
STARK IS TRYING TO HACK THE SHIELDS.
HAH. THAT WILL NEVER WORK AGAIN. I'VE SPENT YEARS PERFECTING THE SECURITY...
AND...

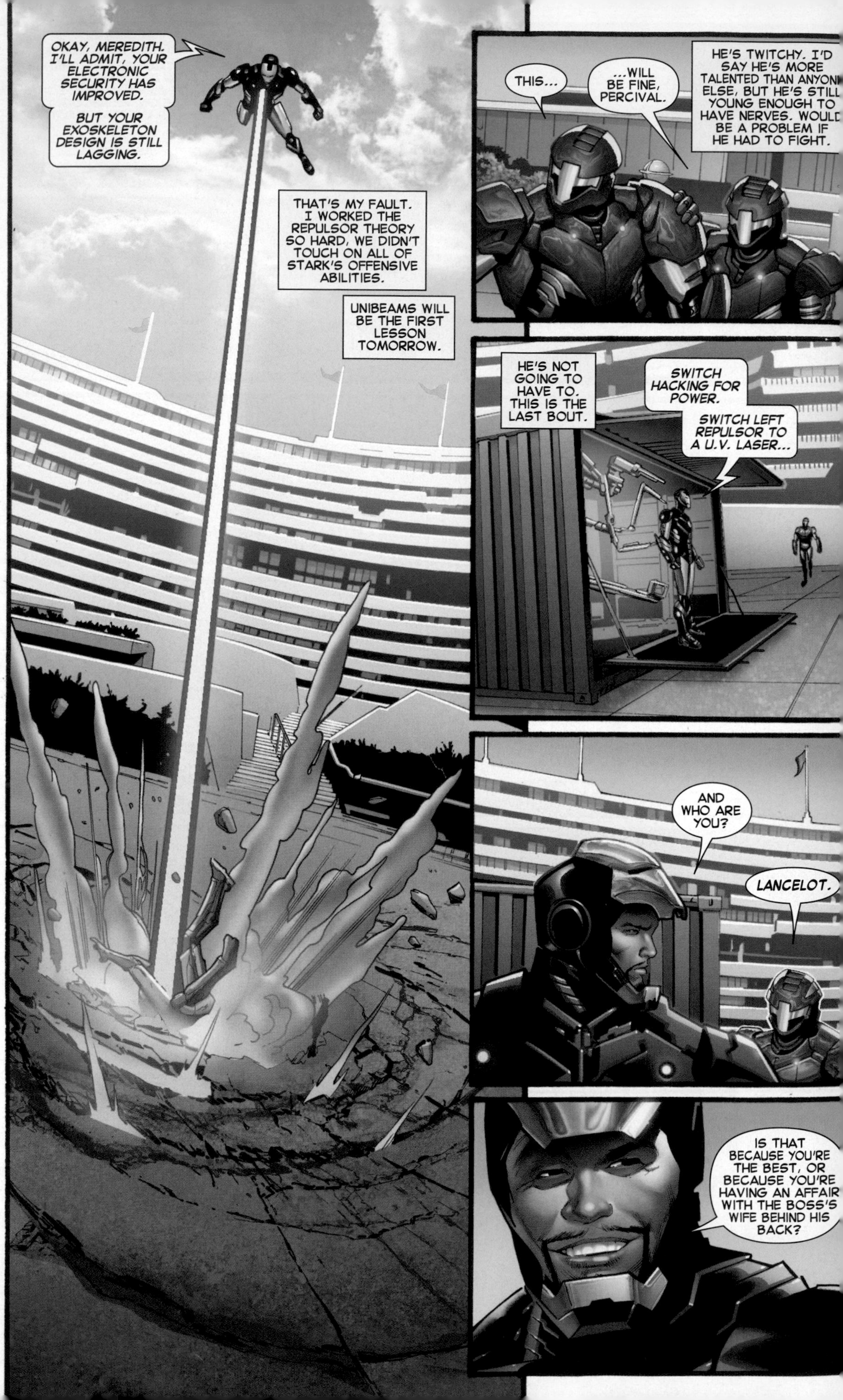
OKAY, MEREDITH. I'LL ADMIT, YOUR ELECTRONIC SECURITY HAS IMPROVED.
BUT YOUR EXOSKELETON DESIGN IS STILL LAGGING.
THAT'S MY FAULT. I WORKED THE REPULSOR THEORY SO HARD, WE DIDN'T TOUCH ON ALL OF STARK'S OFFENSIVE ABILITIES.
UNIBEAMS WILL BE THE FIRST LESSON TOMORROW.
THIS...
...WILL BE FINE, PERCIVAL.
HE'S TWITCHY. I'D SAY HE'S MORE TALENTED THAN ANYONE ELSE, BUT HE'S STILL YOUNG ENOUGH TO HAVE NERVES. WOULD BE A PROBLEM IF HE HAD TO FIGHT.
HE'S NOT GOING TO HAVE TO. THIS IS THE LAST BOUT.
SWITCH HACKING FOR POWER.
SWITCH LEFT REPULSOR TO A U.V. LASER...
AND WHO ARE YOU?
LANCELOT.
IS THAT BECAUSE YOU'RE THE BEST, OR BECAUSE YOU'RE HAVING AN AFFAIR WITH THE BOSS'S WIFE BEHIND HIS BACK?

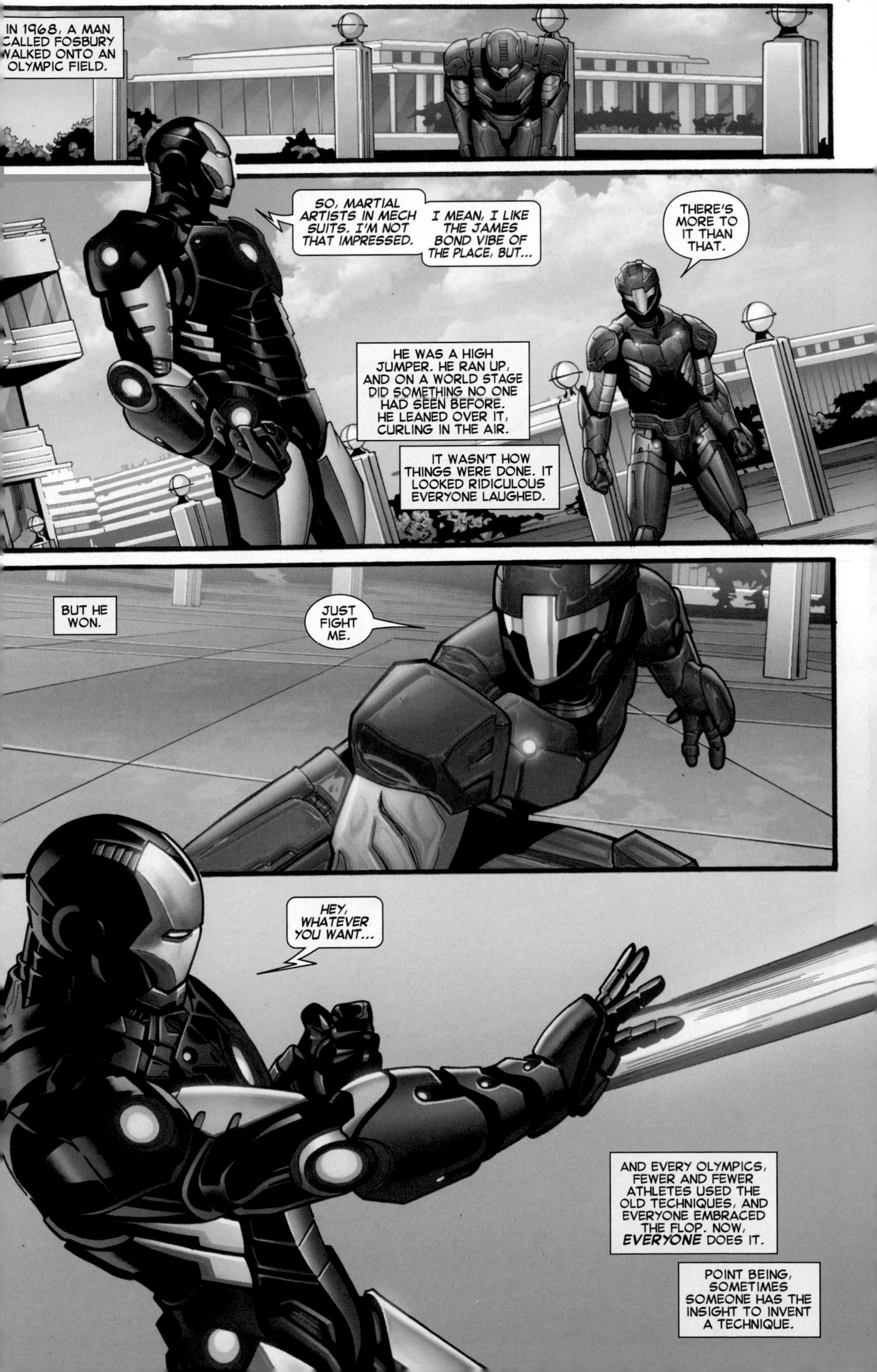
IN 1968, A MAN CALLED FOSBURY WALKED ONTO AN OLYMPIC FIELD.
SO, MARTIAL ARTISTS IN MECH SUITS. I'M NOT THAT IMPRESSED.
I MEAN, I LIKE THE JAMES BOND VIBE OF THE PLACE, BUT...
THERE'S MORE TO IT THAN THAT.
HE WAS A HIGH JUMPER. HE RAN UP, AND ON A WORLD STAGE DID SOMETHING NO ONE HAD SEEN BEFORE. HE LEANED OVER IT, CURLING IN THE AIR.
IT WASN'T HOW THINGS WERE DONE. IT LOOKED RIDICULOUS EVERYONE LAUGHED.
BUT HE WON.
JUST FIGHT ME.
HEY, WHATEVER YOU WANT...
AND EVERY OLYMPICS, FEWER AND FEWER ATHLETES USED THE OLD TECHNIQUES, AND EVERYONE EMBRACED THE FLOP. NOW, EVERYONE DOES IT.
POINT BEING, SOMETIMES SOMEONE HAS THE INSIGHT TO INVENT A TECHNIQUE.

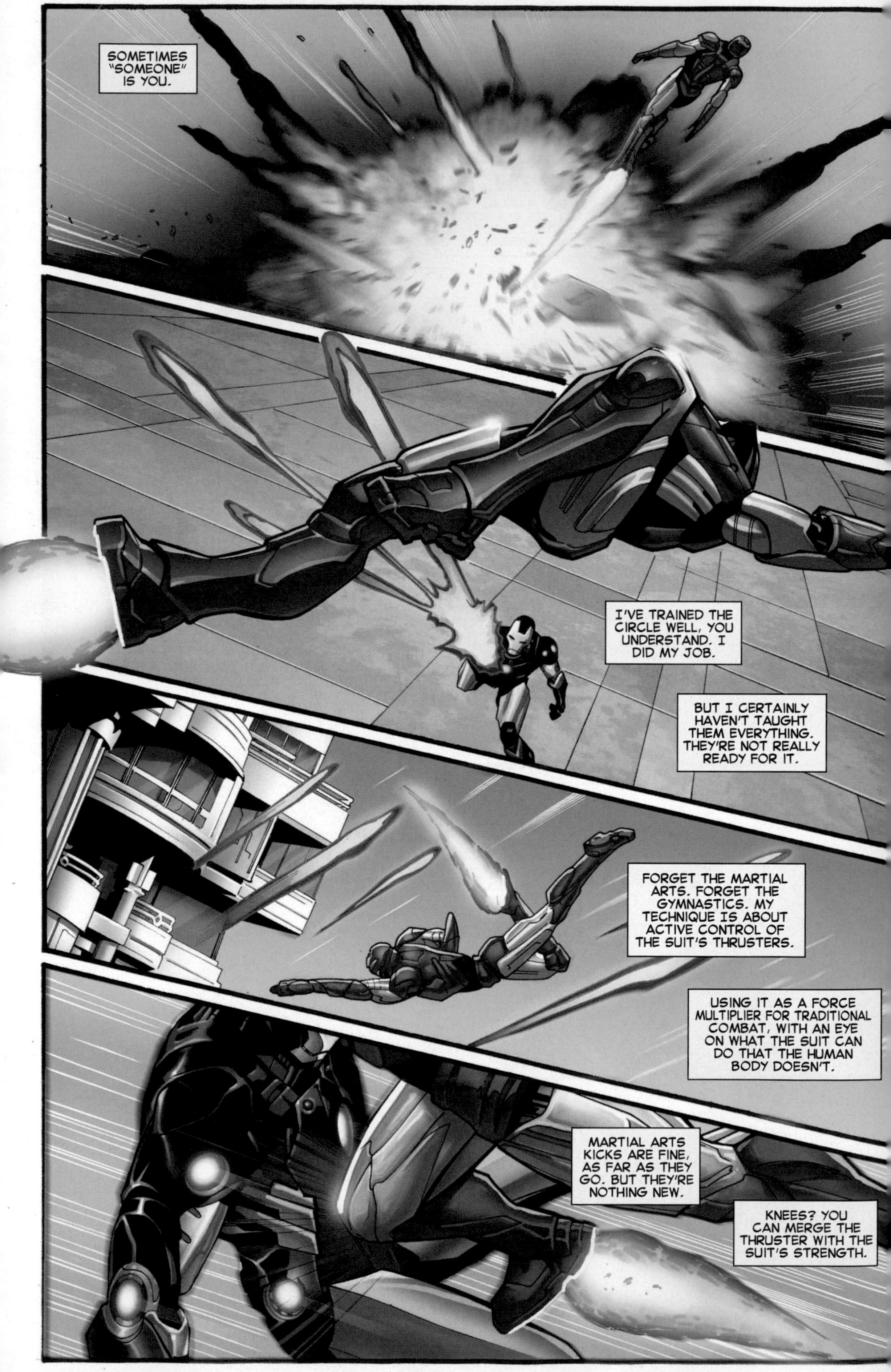
SOMETIMES "SOMEONE" IS YOU.
I'VE TRAINED THE CIRCLE WELL, YOU UNDERSTAND. I DID MY JOB.
BUT I CERTAINLY HAVEN'T TAUGHT THEM EVERYTHING. THEY'RE NOT REALLY READY FOR IT.
FORGET THE MARTIAL ARTS. FORGET THE GYMNASTICS. MY TECHNIQUE IS ABOUT ACTIVE CONTROL OF THE SUIT'S THRUSTERS.
USING IT AS A FORCE MULTIPLIER FOR TRADITIONAL COMBAT, WITH AN EYE ON WHAT THE SUIT CAN DO THAT THE HUMAN BODY DOESN'T.
MARTIAL ARTS KICKS ARE FINE, AS FAR AS THEY GO. BUT THEY'RE NOTHING NEW.
KNEES? YOU CAN MERGE THE THRUSTER WITH THE SUIT'S STRENGTH.

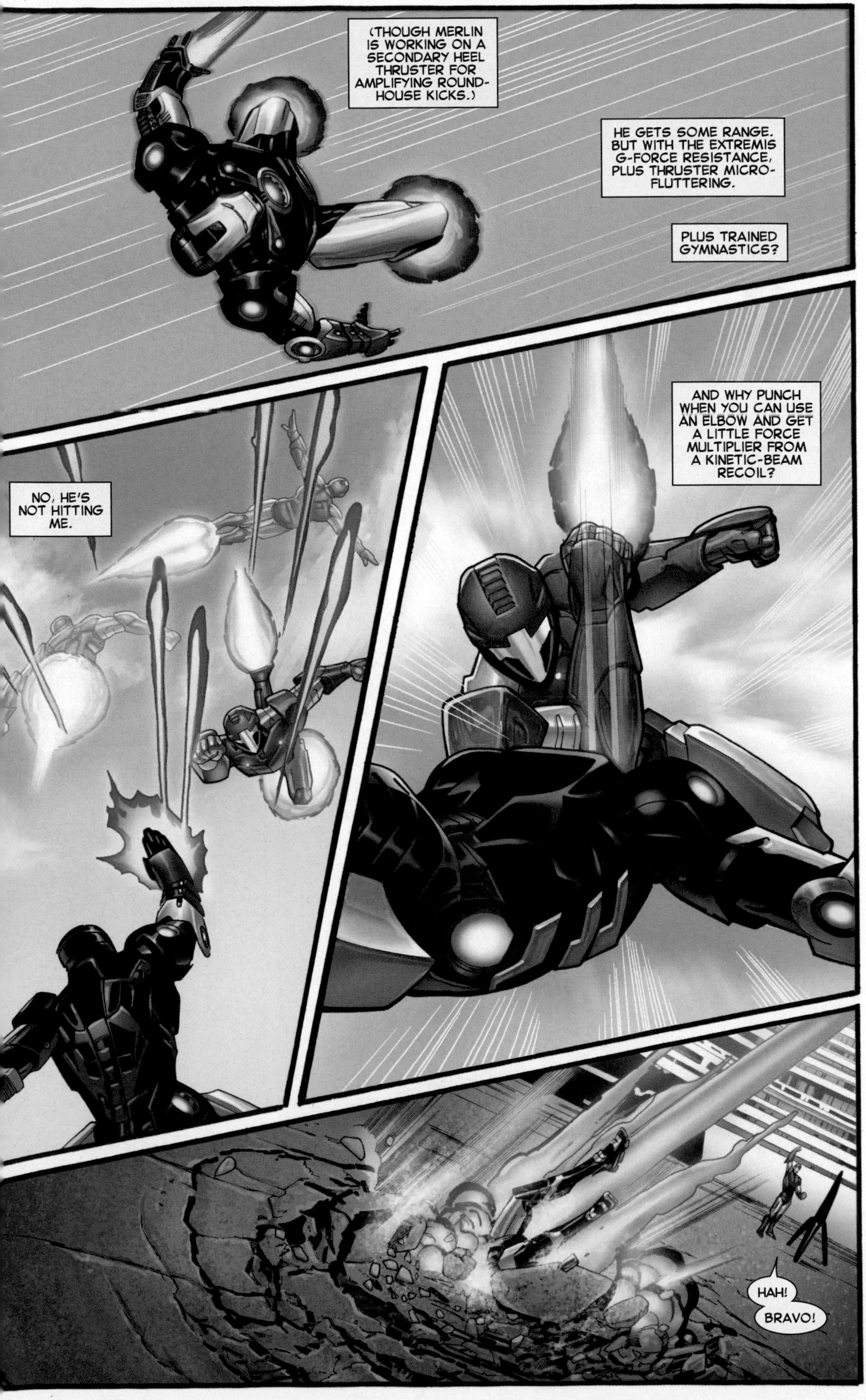
(THOUGH MERLIN IS WORKING ON A SECONDARY HEEL THRUSTER FOR AMPLIFYING ROUND-HOUSE KICKS.)
HE GETS SOME RANGE. BUT WITH THE EXTREMIS G-FORCE RESISTANCE, PLUS THRUSTER MICRO-FLUTTERING.
PLUS TRAINED GYMNASTICS?
NO, HE'S NOT HITTING ME.
AND WHY PUNCH WHEN YOU CAN USE AN ELBOW AND GET A LITTLE FORCE MULTIPLIER FROM A KINETIC-BEAM RECOIL?
HAH!
BRAVO!

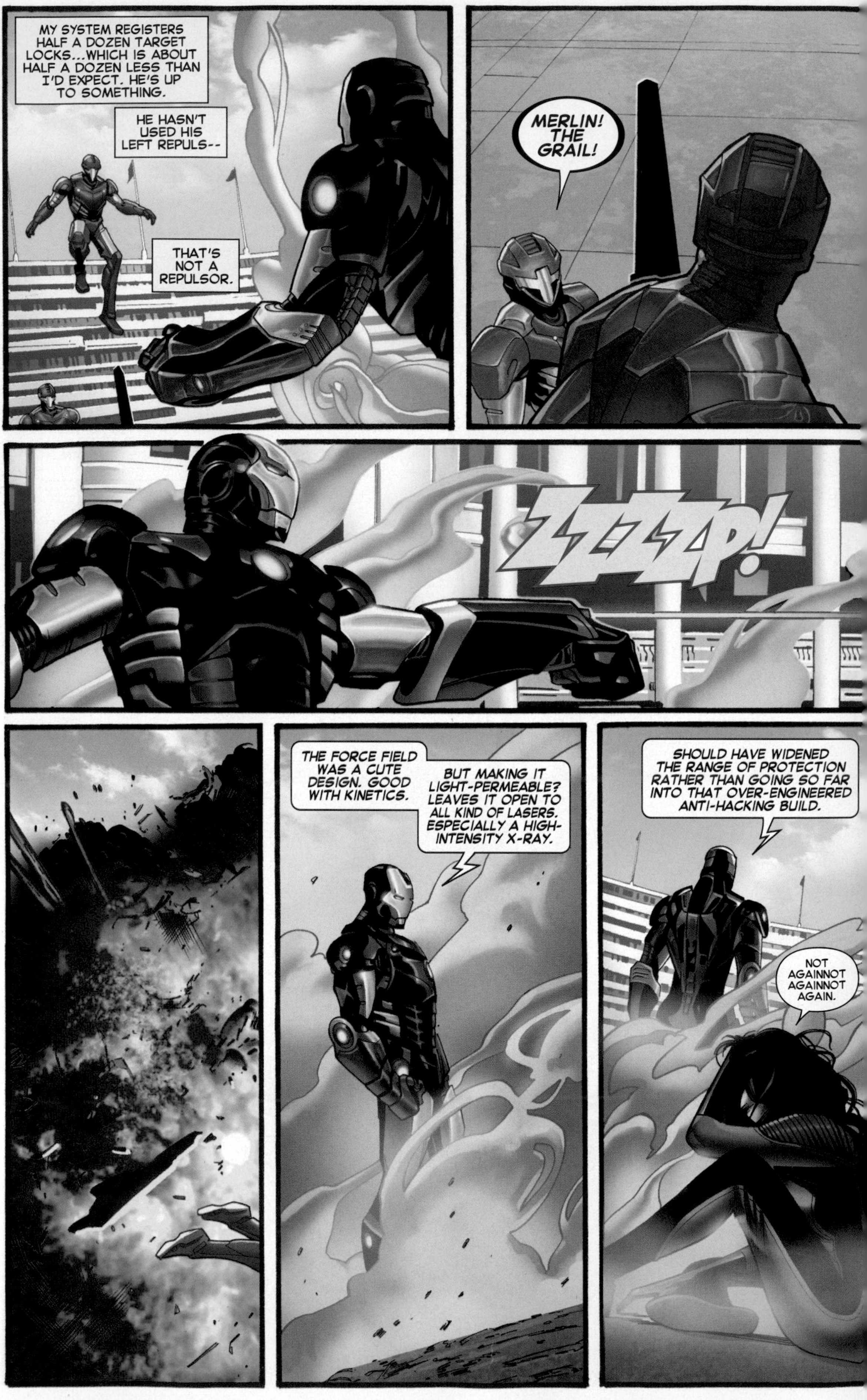
MY SYSTEM REGISTERS HALF A DOZEN TARGET LOCKS...WHICH IS ABOUT HALF A DOZEN LESS THAN I'D EXPECT. HE'S UP TO SOMETHING.
HE HASN'T USED HIS LEFT REPULS--
THAT'S NOT A REPULSOR.
MERLIN! THE GRAIL!
ZZZZP!
THE FORCE FIELD WAS A CUTE DESIGN. GOOD WITH KINETICS.
BUT MAKING IT LIGHT-PERMEABLE? LEAVES IT OPEN TO ALL KIND OF LASERS. ESPECIALLY A HIGH-INTENSITY X-RAY.
SHOULD HAVE WIDENED THE RANGE OF PROTECTION RATHER THAN GOING SO FAR INTO THAT OVER-ENGINEERED ANTI-HACKING BUILD.
NOT AGAINNOT AGAINNOT AGAIN.

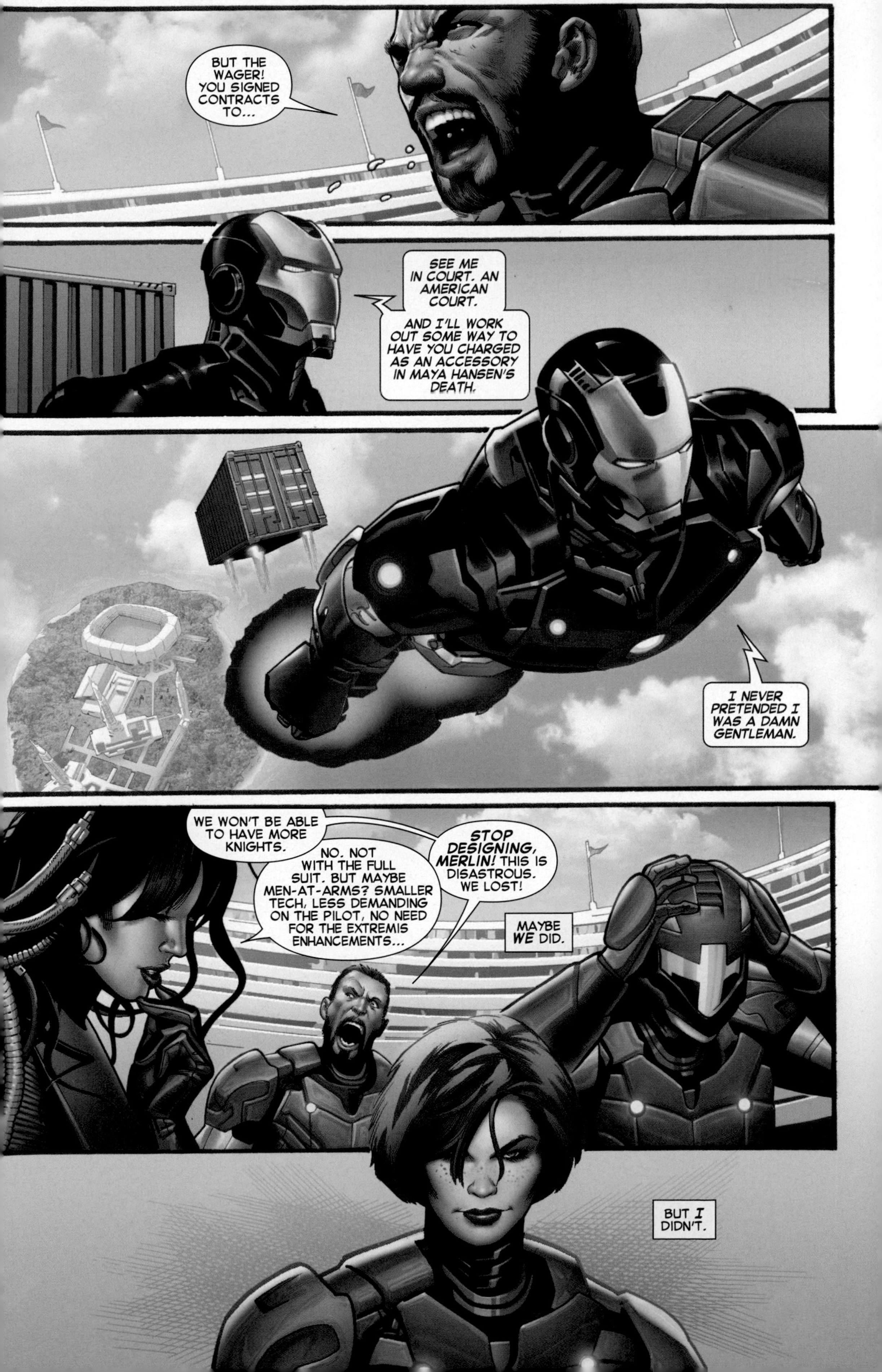
BUT THE WAGER! YOU SIGNED CONTRACTS TO...
SEE ME IN COURT. AN AMERICAN COURT.
AND I'LL WORK OUT SOME WAY TO HAVE YOU CHARGED AS AN ACCESSORY IN MAYA HANSEN'S DEATH.
I NEVER PRETENDED I WAS A DAMN GENTLEMAN.
WE WON'T BE ABLE TO HAVE MORE KNIGHTS.
NO. NOT WITH THE FULL SUIT. BUT MAYBE MEN-AT-ARMS? SMALLER TECH, LESS DEMANDING ON THE PILOT, NO NEED FOR THE EXTREMIS ENHANCEMENTS...
STOP DESIGNING, MERLIN! THIS IS DISASTROUS. WE LOST!
MAYBE WE DID.
BUT I DIDN'T.

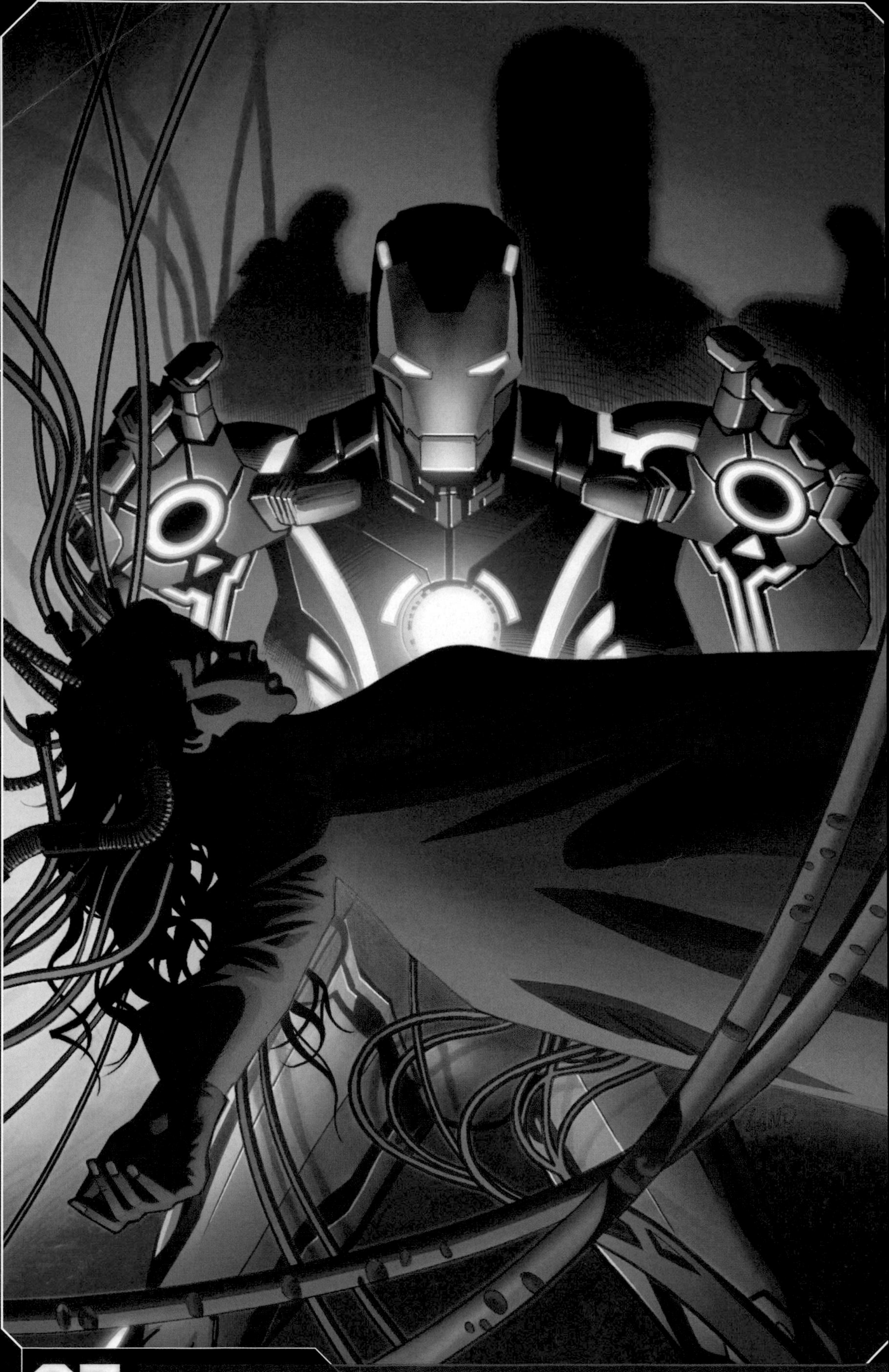

03 IT MAKES US STRONGER

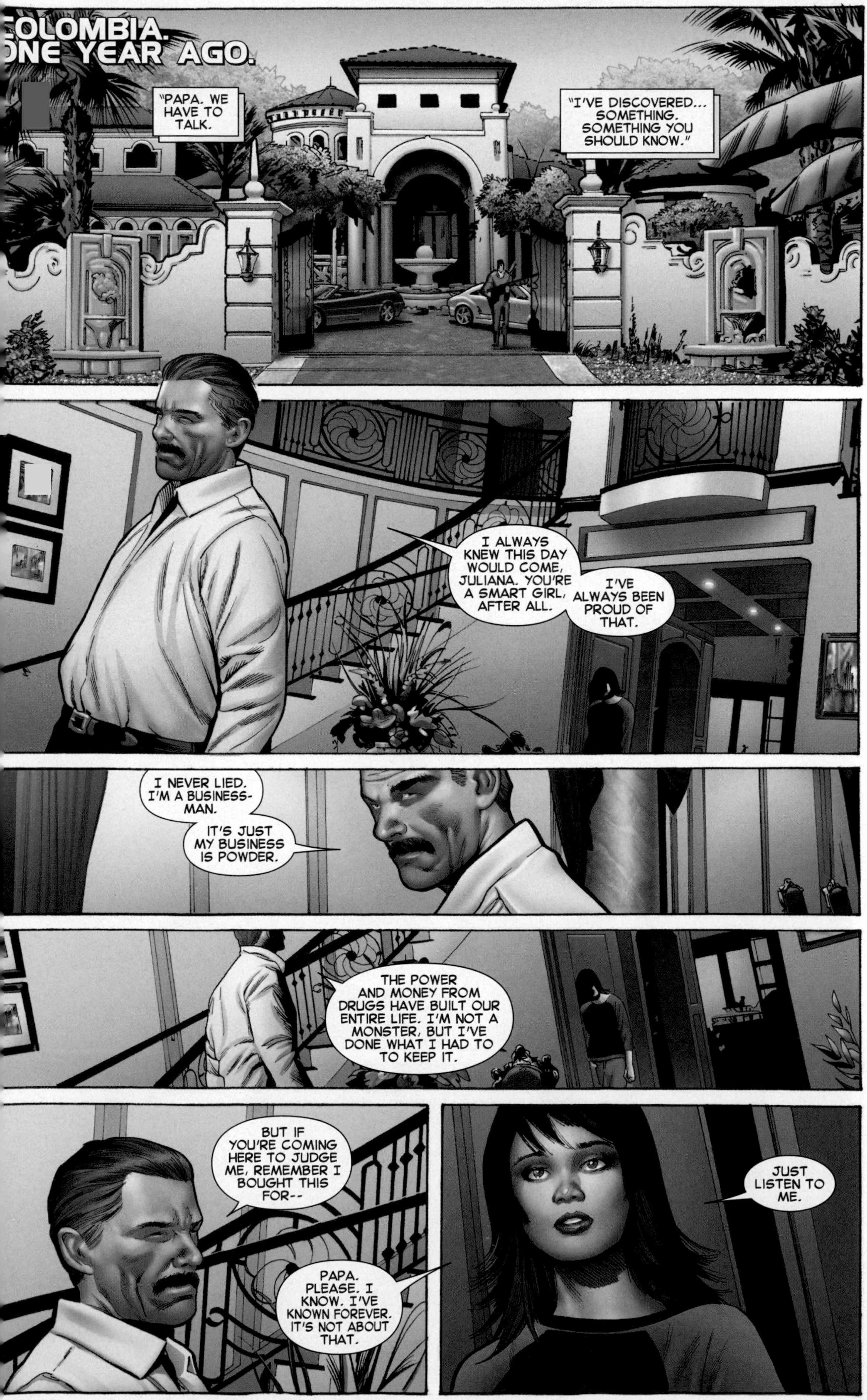
COLOMBIA. ONE YEAR AGO.
"PAPA. WE HAVE TO TALK.
"I'VE DISCOVERED... SOMETHING. SOMETHING YOU SHOULD KNOW."
I ALWAYS KNEW THIS DAY WOULD COME, JULIANA. YOU'RE A SMART GIRL, AFTER ALL.
I'VE ALWAYS BEEN PROUD OF THAT.
I NEVER LIED. I'M A BUSINESS-MAN.
IT'S JUST MY BUSINESS IS POWDER.
THE POWER AND MONEY FROM DRUGS HAVE BUILT OUR ENTIRE LIFE. I'M NOT A MONSTER, BUT I'VE DONE WHAT I HAD TO TO KEEP IT.
BUT IF YOU'RE COMING HERE TO JUDGE ME, REMEMBER I BOUGHT THIS FOR--
PAPA. PLEASE. I KNOW. I'VE KNOWN FOREVER. IT'S NOT ABOUT THAT.
JUST LISTEN TO ME.

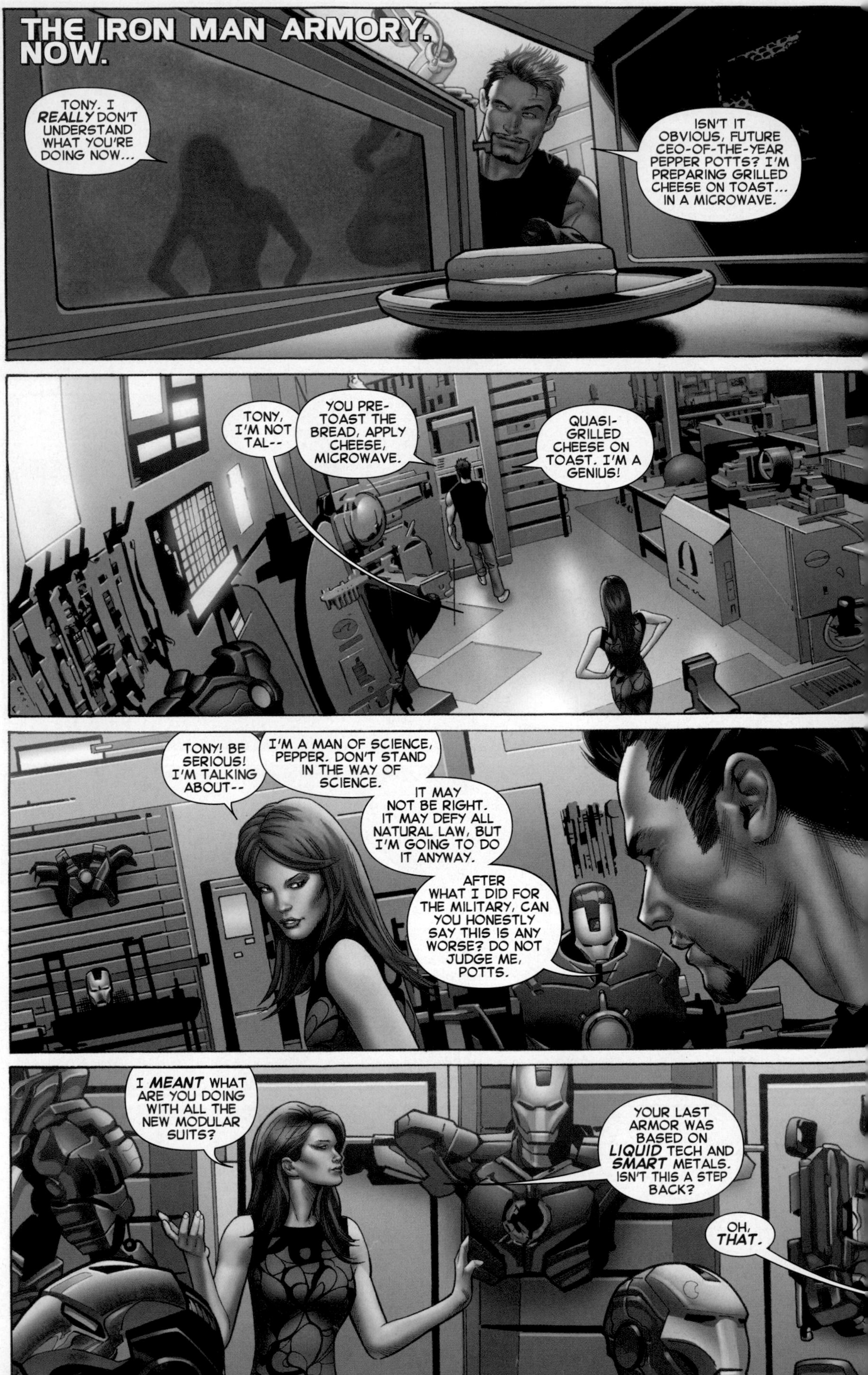
THE IRON MAN ARMORY. NOW.
TONY. I REALLY DON'T UNDERSTAND WHAT YOU'RE DOING NOW...
ISN'T IT OBVIOUS, FUTURE CEO-OF-THE-YEAR PEPPER POTTS? I'M PREPARING GRILLED CHEESE ON TOAST... IN A MICROWAVE.
TONY, I'M NOT TAL--
YOU PRE-TOAST THE BREAD, APPLY CHEESE, MICROWAVE.
QUASI-GRILLED CHEESE ON TOAST. I'M A GENIUS!
TONY! BE SERIOUS! I'M TALKING ABOUT--
I'M A MAN OF SCIENCE, PEPPER. DON'T STAND IN THE WAY OF SCIENCE.
IT MAY NOT BE RIGHT. IT MAY DEFY ALL NATURAL LAW, BUT I'M GOING TO DO IT ANYWAY.
AFTER WHAT I DID FOR THE MILITARY, CAN YOU HONESTLY SAY THIS IS ANY WORSE? DO NOT JUDGE ME, POTTS.
I MEANT WHAT ARE YOU DOING WITH ALL THE NEW MODULAR SUITS?
YOUR LAST ARMOR WAS BASED ON LIQUID TECH AND SMART METALS. ISN'T THIS A STEP BACK?
OH, THAT.

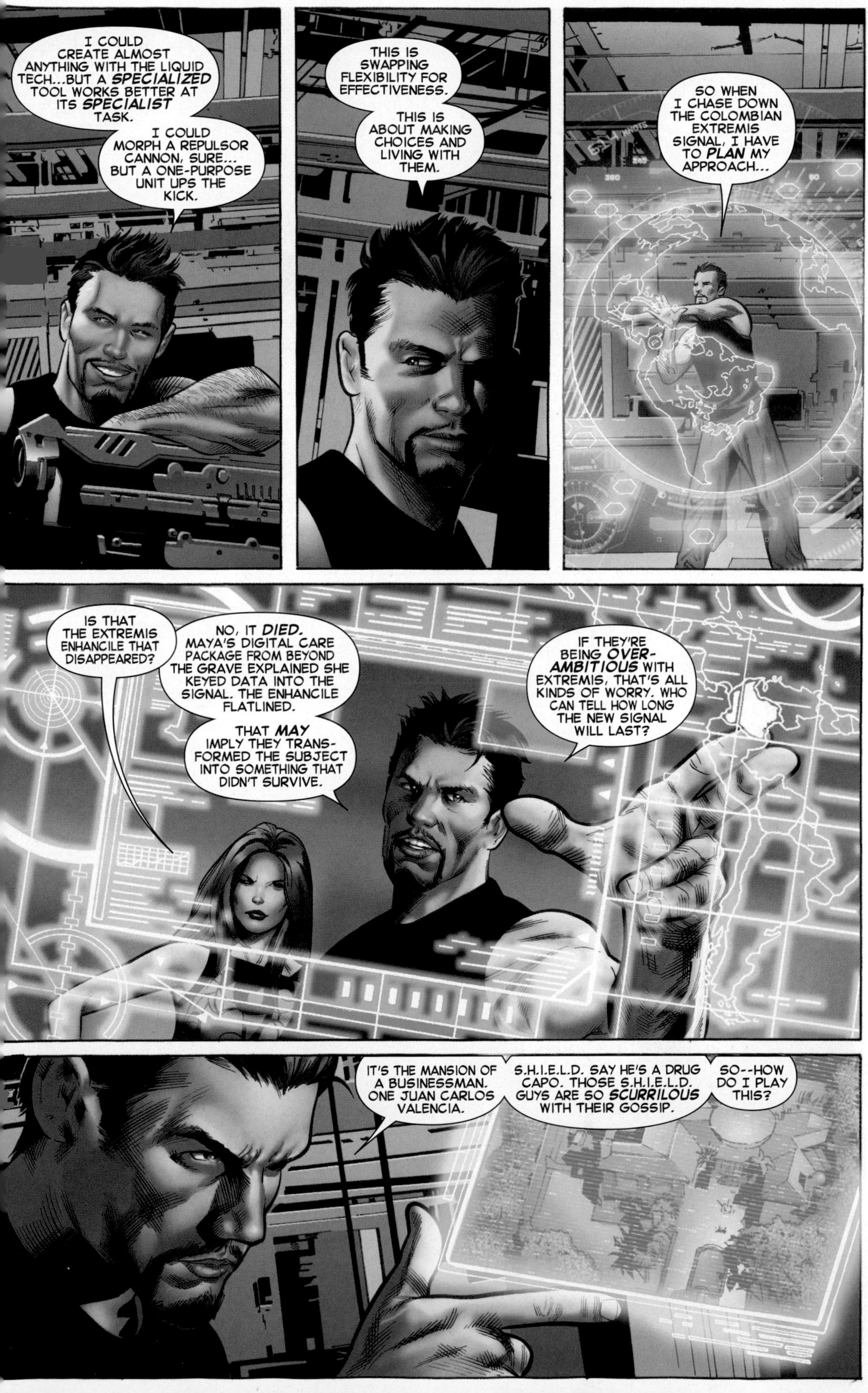
I COULD CREATE ALMOST ANYTHING WITH THE LIQUID TECH...BUT A SPECIALIZED TOOL WORKS BETTER AT ITS SPECIALIST TASK.
I COULD MORPH A REPULSOR CANNON, SURE... BUT A ONE-PURPOSE UNIT UPS THE KICK.
THIS IS SWAPPING FLEXIBILITY FOR EFFECTIVENESS.
THIS IS ABOUT MAKING CHOICES AND LIVING WITH THEM.
SO WHEN I CHASE DOWN THE COLOMBIAN EXTREMIS SIGNAL, I HAVE TO PLAN MY APPROACH...
IS THAT THE EXTREMIS ENHANCILE THAT DISAPPEARED?
NO, IT DIED. MAYA'S DIGITAL CARE PACKAGE FROM BEYOND THE GRAVE EXPLAINED SHE KEYED DATA INTO THE SIGNAL. THE ENHANCILE FLATLINED.
THAT MAY IMPLY THEY TRANSFORMED THE SUBJECT INTO SOMETHING THAT DIDN'T SURVIVE.
IF THEY'RE BEING OVER-AMBITIOUS WITH EXTREMIS, THAT'S ALL KINDS OF WORRY. WHO CAN TELL HOW LONG THE NEW SIGNAL WILL LAST?
IT'S THE MANSION OF A BUSINESSMAN. ONE JUAN CARLOS VALENCIA.
S.H.I.E.L.D. SAY HE'S A DRUG CAPO. THOSE S.H.I.E.L.D. GUYS ARE SO SCURRILOUS WITH THEIR GOSSIP.
SO--HOW DO I PLAY THIS?

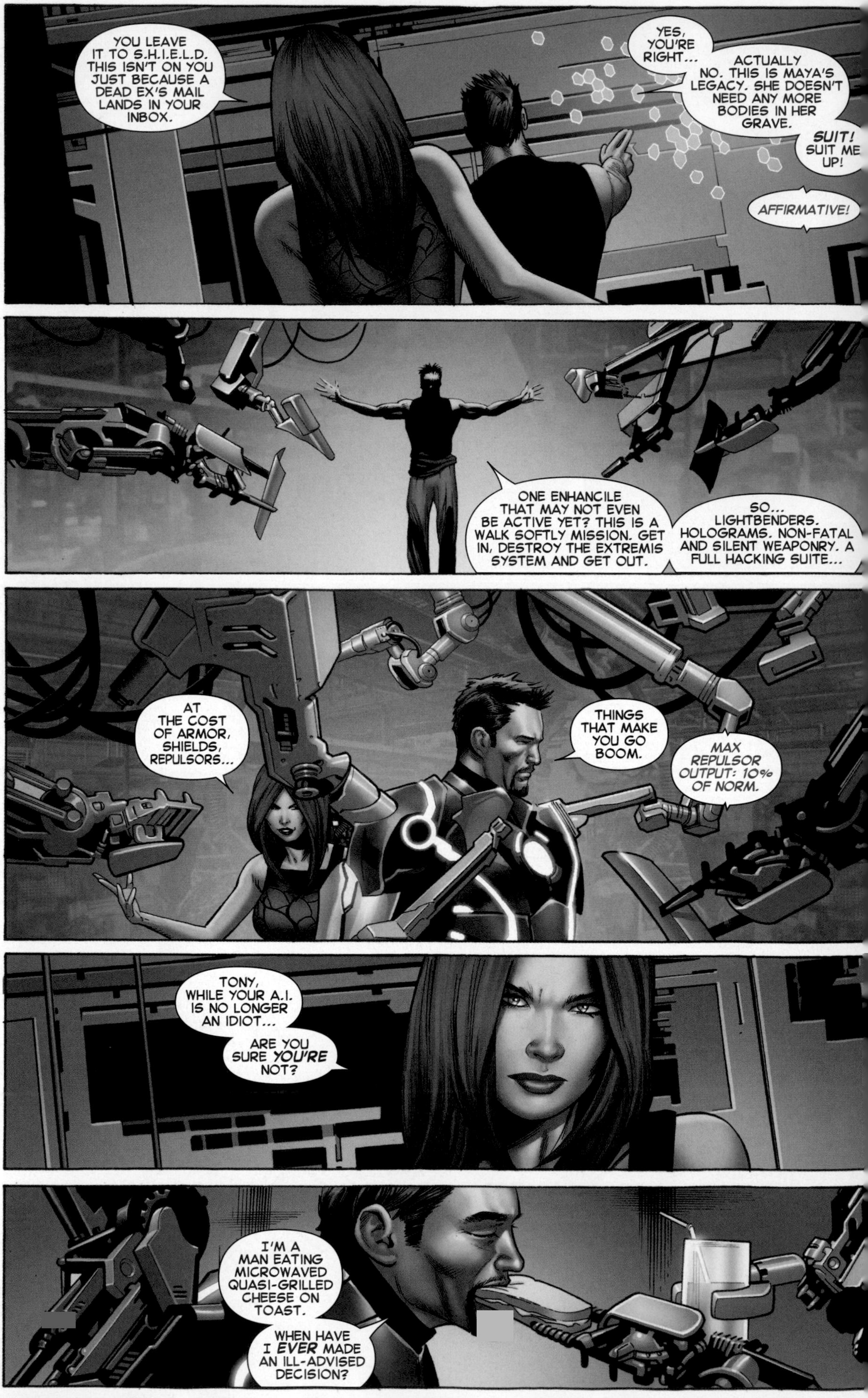
YOU LEAVE IT TO S.H.I.E.L.D. THIS ISN'T ON YOU JUST BECAUSE A DEAD EX'S MAIL LANDS IN YOUR INBOX.
YES, YOU'RE RIGHT...
ACTUALLY NO. THIS IS MAYA'S LEGACY. SHE DOESN'T NEED ANY MORE BODIES IN HER GRAVE.
SUIT! SUIT ME UP!
AFFIRMATIVE!
ONE ENHANCILE THAT MAY NOT EVEN BE ACTIVE YET? THIS IS A WALK SOFTLY MISSION. GET IN, DESTROY THE EXTREMIS SYSTEM AND GET OUT.
SO... LIGHTBENDERS. HOLOGRAMS. NON-FATAL AND SILENT WEAPONRY. A FULL HACKING SUITE...
AT THE COST OF ARMOR, SHIELDS, REPULSORS...
THINGS THAT MAKE YOU GO BOOM.
MAX REPULSOR OUTPUT: 10% OF NORM.
TONY, WHILE YOUR A.I. IS NO LONGER AN IDIOT...
ARE YOU SURE YOU'RE NOT?
I'M A MAN EATING MICROWAVED QUASI-GRILLED CHEESE ON TOAST.
WHEN HAVE I EVER MADE AN ILL-ADVISED DECISION?

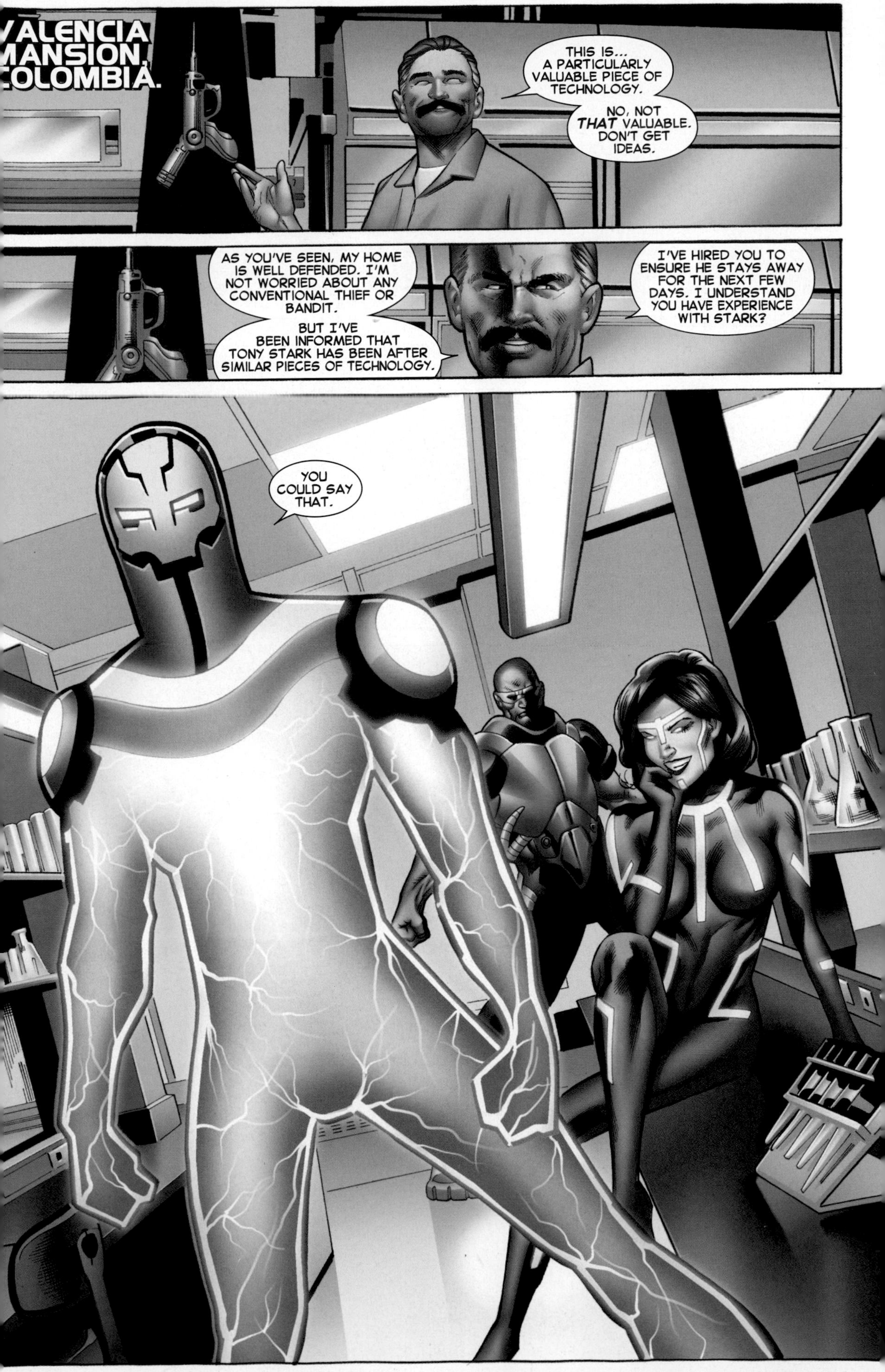
VALENCIA MANSION. COLOMBIA.
THIS IS... A PARTICULARLY VALUABLE PIECE OF TECHNOLOGY.
NO, NOT THAT VALUABLE. DON'T GET IDEAS.
AS YOU'VE SEEN, MY HOME IS WELL DEFENDED. I'M NOT WORRIED ABOUT ANY CONVENTIONAL THIEF OR BANDIT.
BUT I'VE BEEN INFORMED THAT TONY STARK HAS BEEN AFTER SIMILAR PIECES OF TECHNOLOGY.
I'VE HIRED YOU TO ENSURE HE STAYS AWAY FOR THE NEXT FEW DAYS. I UNDERSTAND YOU HAVE EXPERIENCE WITH STARK?
YOU COULD SAY THAT.

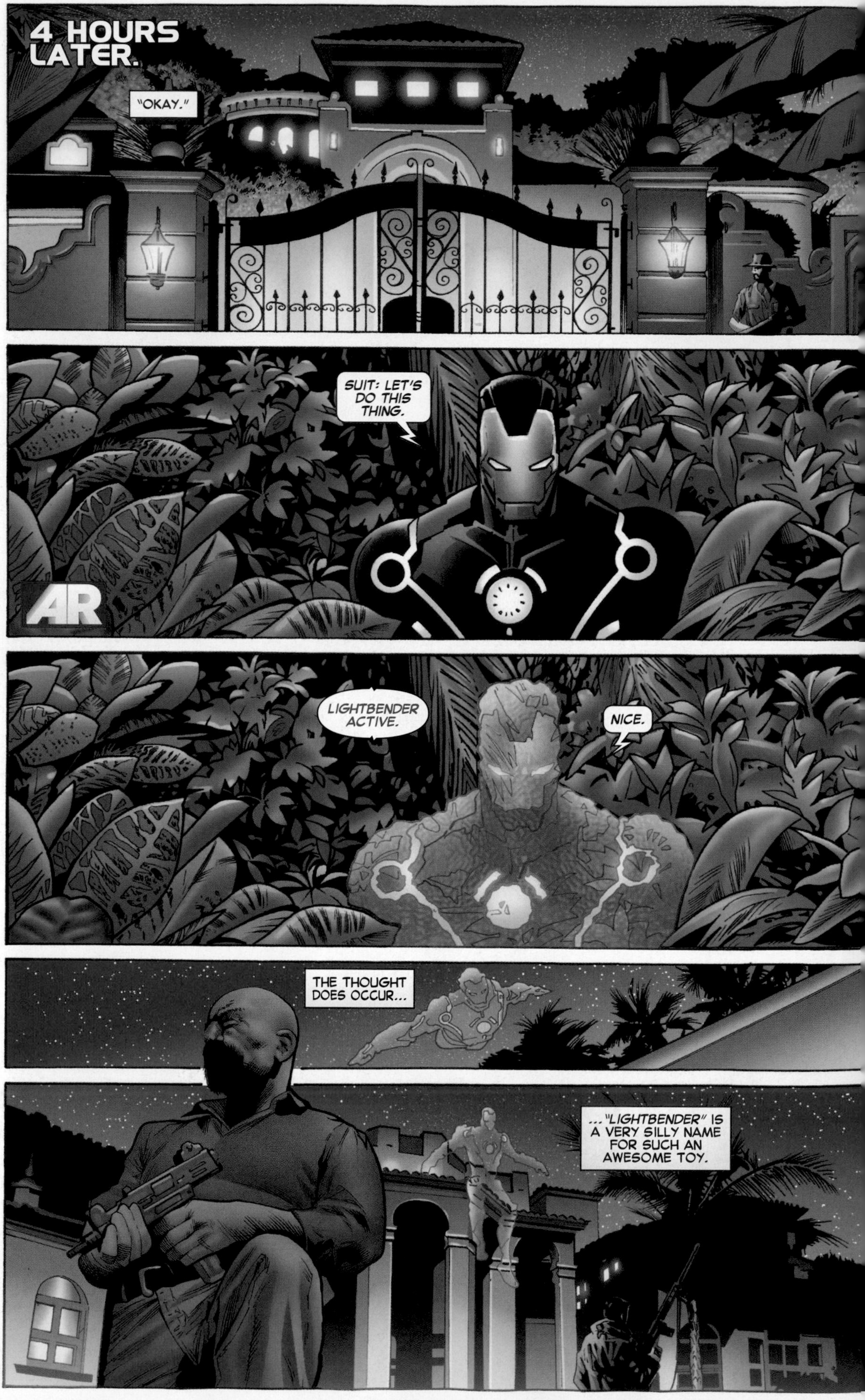
4 HOURS LATER.
"OKAY."
SUIT: LET'S DO THIS THING.
AR
LIGHTBENDER ACTIVE.
NICE.
THE THOUGHT DOES OCCUR...
..."LIGHTBENDER" IS A VERY SILLY NAME FOR SUCH AN AWESOME TOY.

OKAY.

DOCTOR DOOM IS D.J.-ING IN LATVERIA.

NO, THAT'S A SUPERSTAR DOOMBOT.

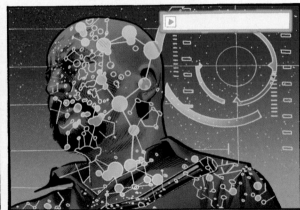

HOLOGRAM: ACTIVE.

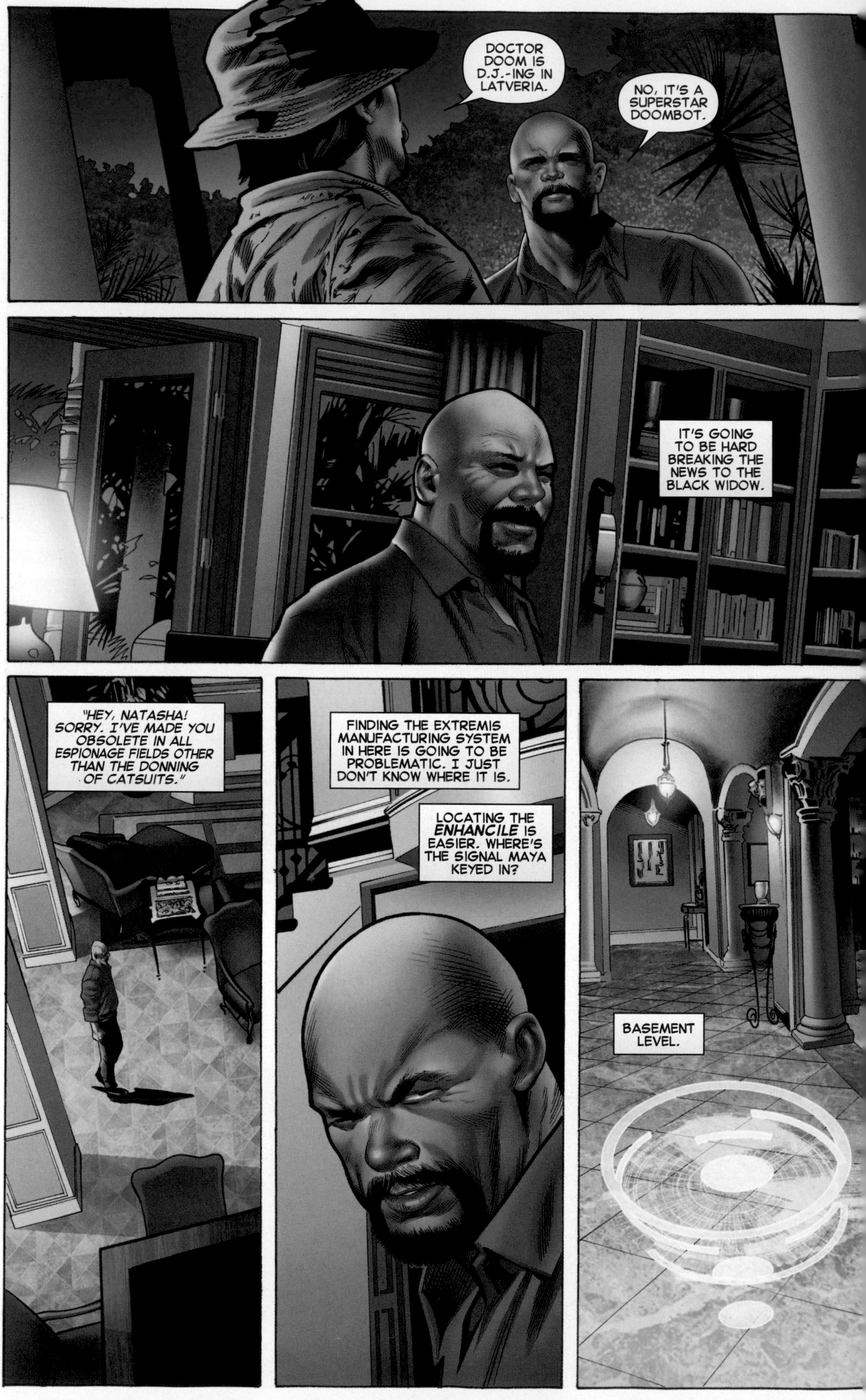
DOCTOR DOOM IS D.J.-ING IN LATVERIA.
NO, IT'S A SUPERSTAR DOOMBOT.
IT'S GOING TO BE HARD BREAKING THE NEWS TO THE BLACK WIDOW.
"HEY, NATASHA! SORRY. I'VE MADE YOU OBSOLETE IN ALL ESPIONAGE FIELDS OTHER THAN THE DONNING OF CATSUITS."
FINDING THE EXTREMIS MANUFACTURING SYSTEM IN HERE IS GOING TO BE PROBLEMATIC. I JUST DON'T KNOW WHERE IT IS.
LOCATING THE ENHANCILE IS EASIER. WHERE'S THE SIGNAL MAYA KEYED IN?
BASEMENT LEVEL.

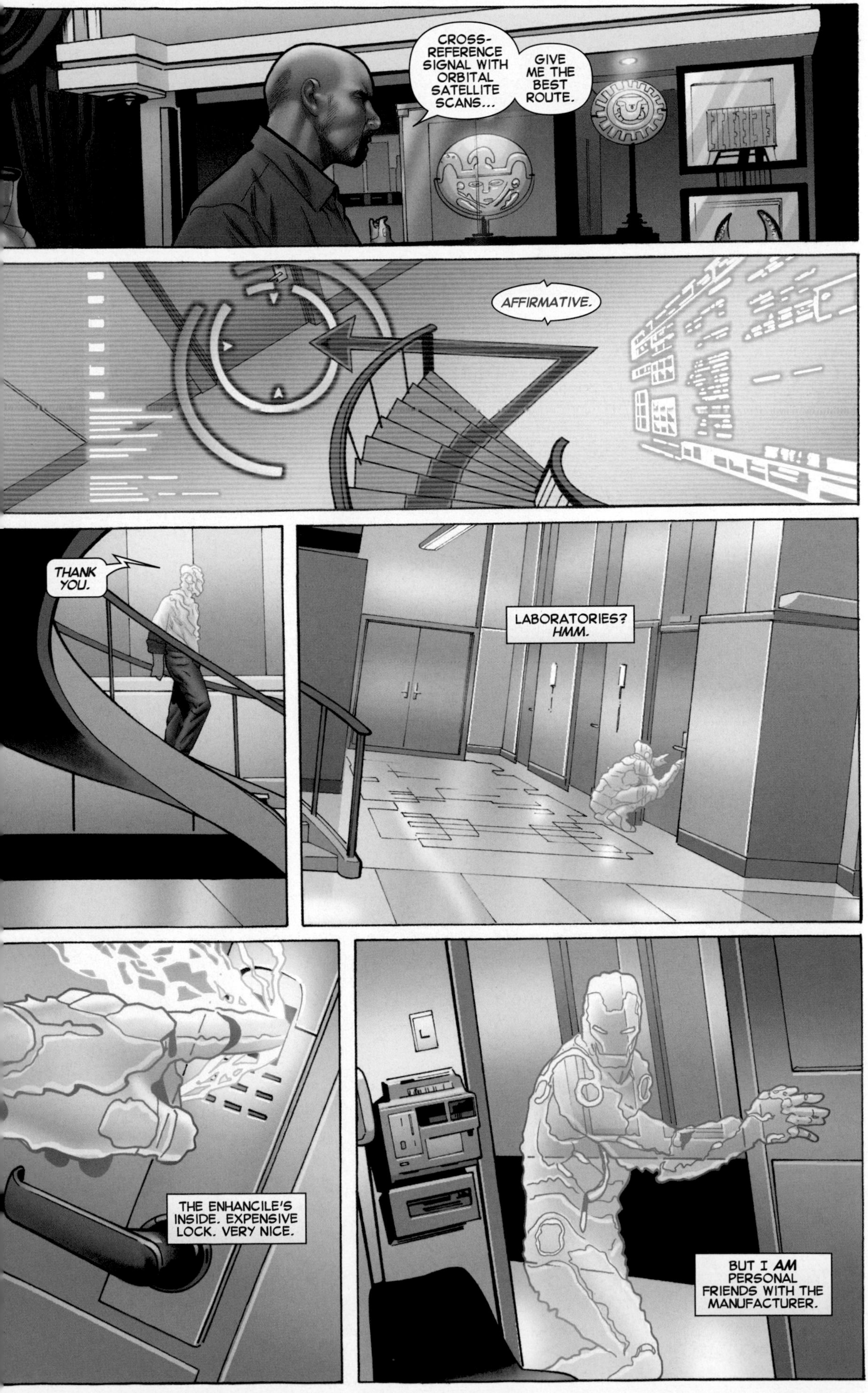
CROSS-REFERENCE SIGNAL WITH ORBITAL SATELLITE SCANS...
GIVE ME THE BEST ROUTE.
AFFIRMATIVE.
THANK YOU.
LABORATORIES? HMM.
THE ENHANCILE'S INSIDE. EXPENSIVE LOCK. VERY NICE.
BUT I AM PERSONAL FRIENDS WITH THE MANUFACTURER.

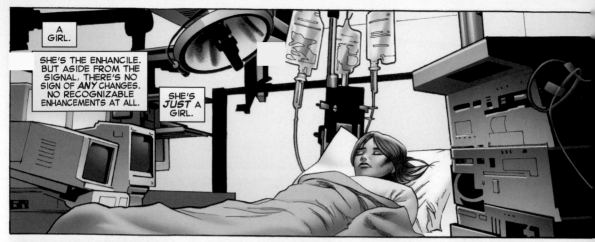

A GIRL.

SHE'S THE ENHANCILE. BUT ASIDE FROM THE SIGNAL, THERE'S NO SIGN OF *ANY* CHANGES. NO RECOGNIZABLE ENHANCEMENTS AT ALL.

SHE'S *JUST A GIRL.*

SHE'S A VICTIM. SHE HAS TO BE. THEY'RE RUNNING SOME KIND OF EXPERIMENT.

TIME TO TAKE A CHANCE...

I'M IRON MAN. I'M HERE TO SAVE YOU. DO YOU REMEMBER WHERE THEY PERFORMED THE OPERATION?

GUARDS!

SORRY, NATASHA.

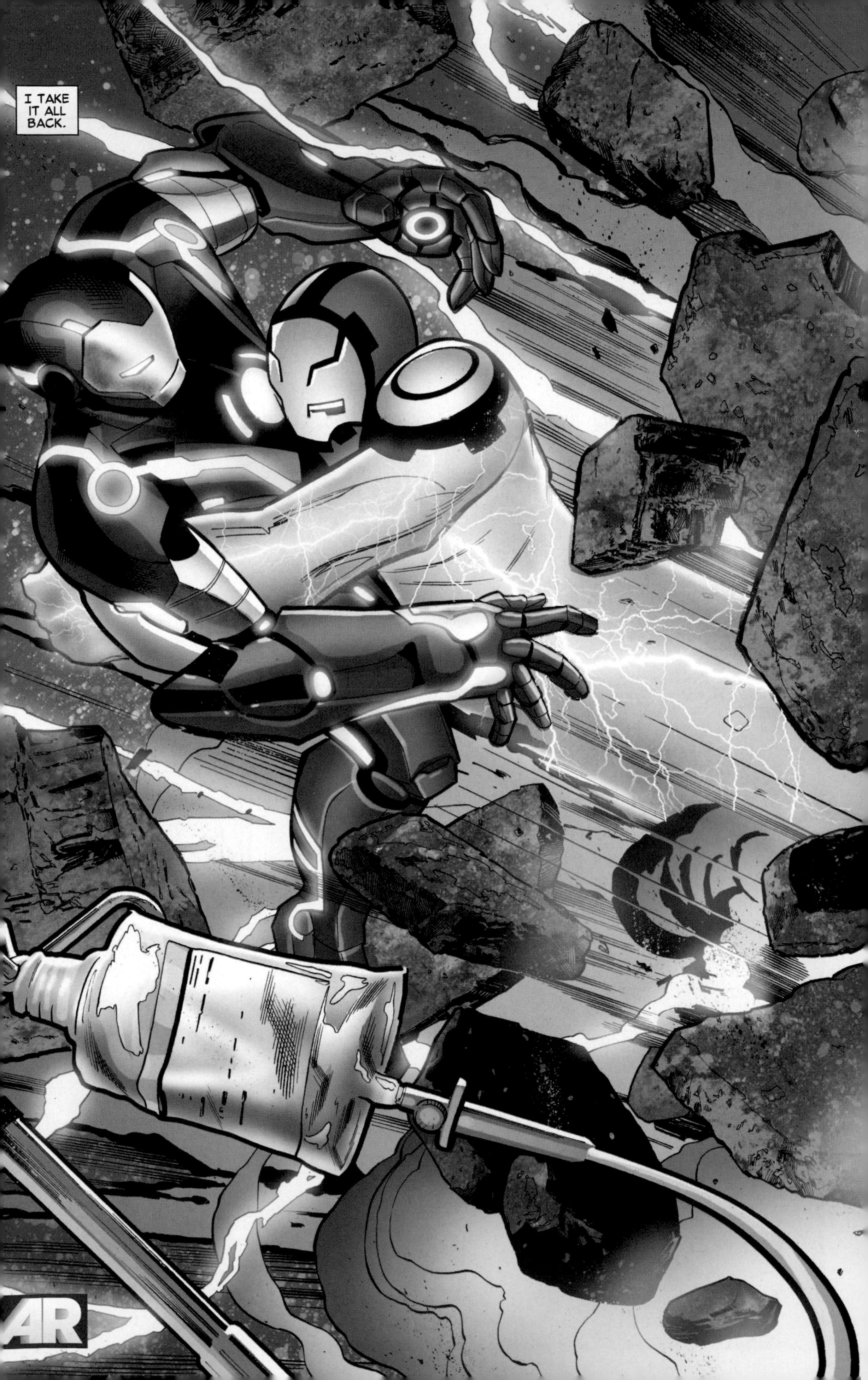
I TAKE IT ALL BACK.

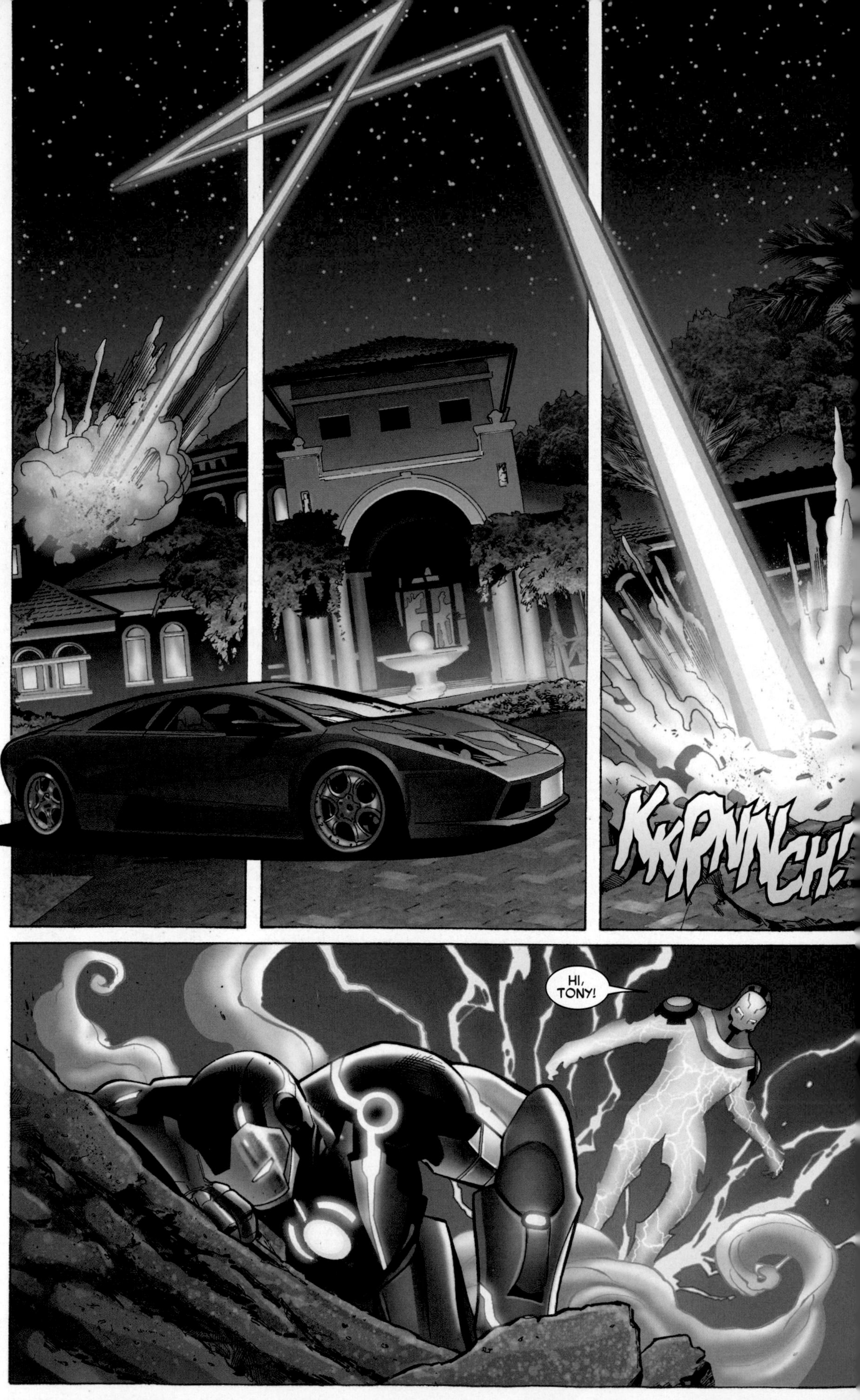
KKRNNNCH!
HI, TONY!

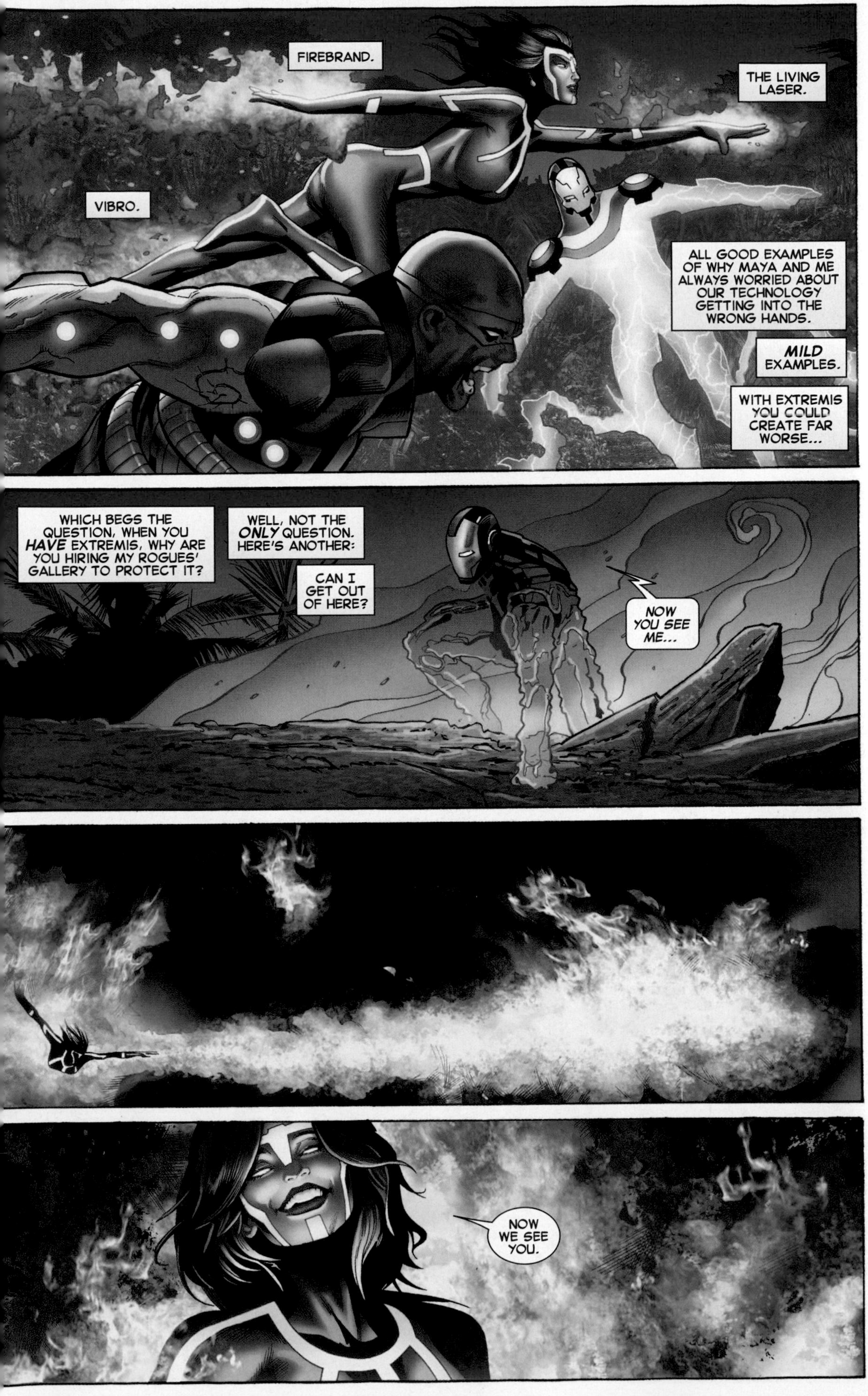
FIREBRAND.
THE LIVING LASER.
VIBRO.
ALL GOOD EXAMPLES OF WHY MAYA AND ME ALWAYS WORRIED ABOUT OUR TECHNOLOGY GETTING INTO THE WRONG HANDS.
MILD EXAMPLES.
WITH EXTREMIS YOU COULD CREATE FAR WORSE...
WHICH BEGS THE QUESTION, WHEN YOU HAVE EXTREMIS, WHY ARE YOU HIRING MY ROGUES' GALLERY TO PROTECT IT?
WELL, NOT THE ONLY QUESTION. HERE'S ANOTHER:
CAN I GET OUT OF HERE?
NOW YOU SEE ME...
NOW WE SEE YOU.

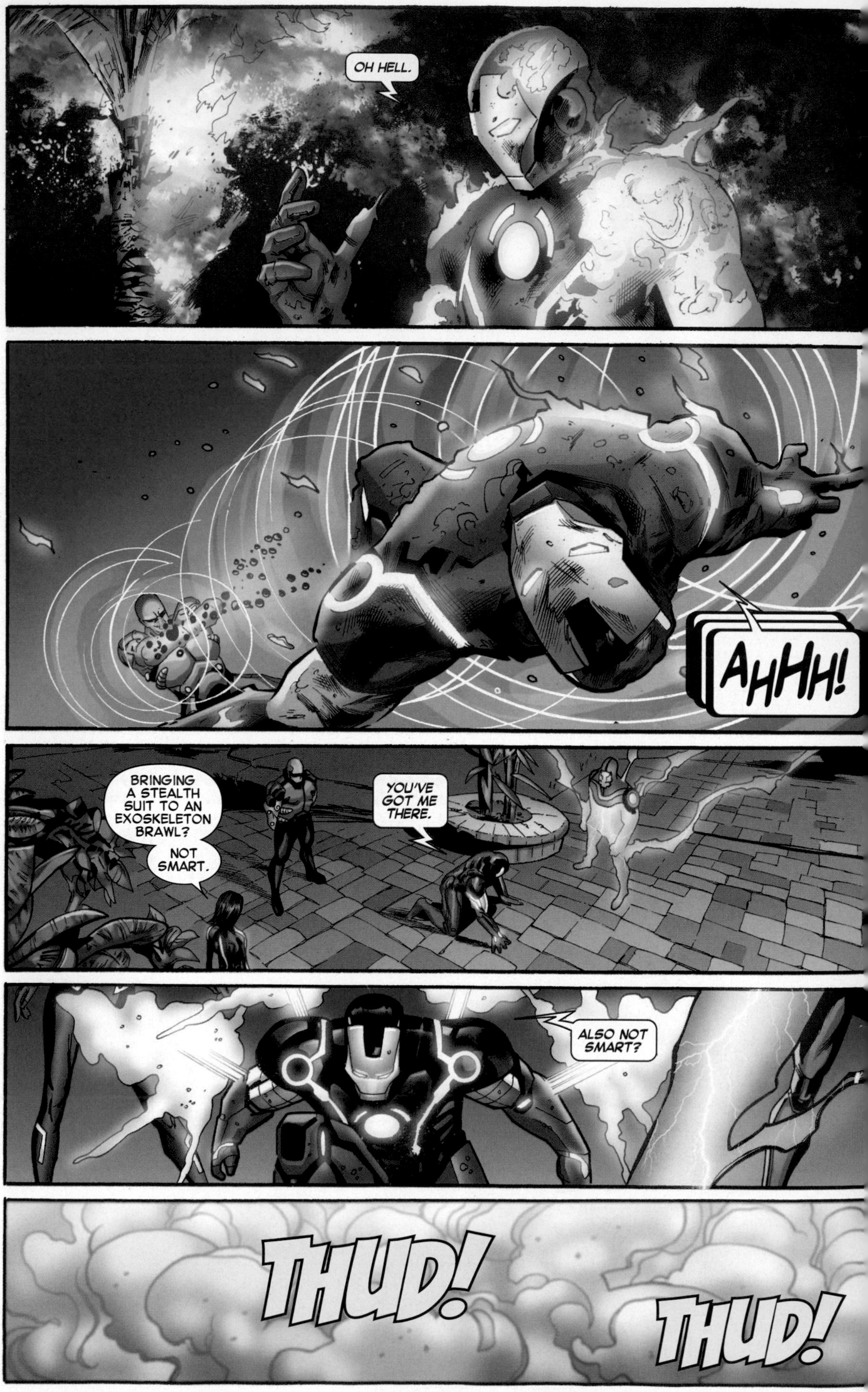
OH HELL.
AHHH!
BRINGING A STEALTH SUIT TO AN EXOSKELETON BRAWL?
NOT SMART.
YOU'VE GOT ME THERE.
ALSO NOT SMART?
THUD!
THUD!

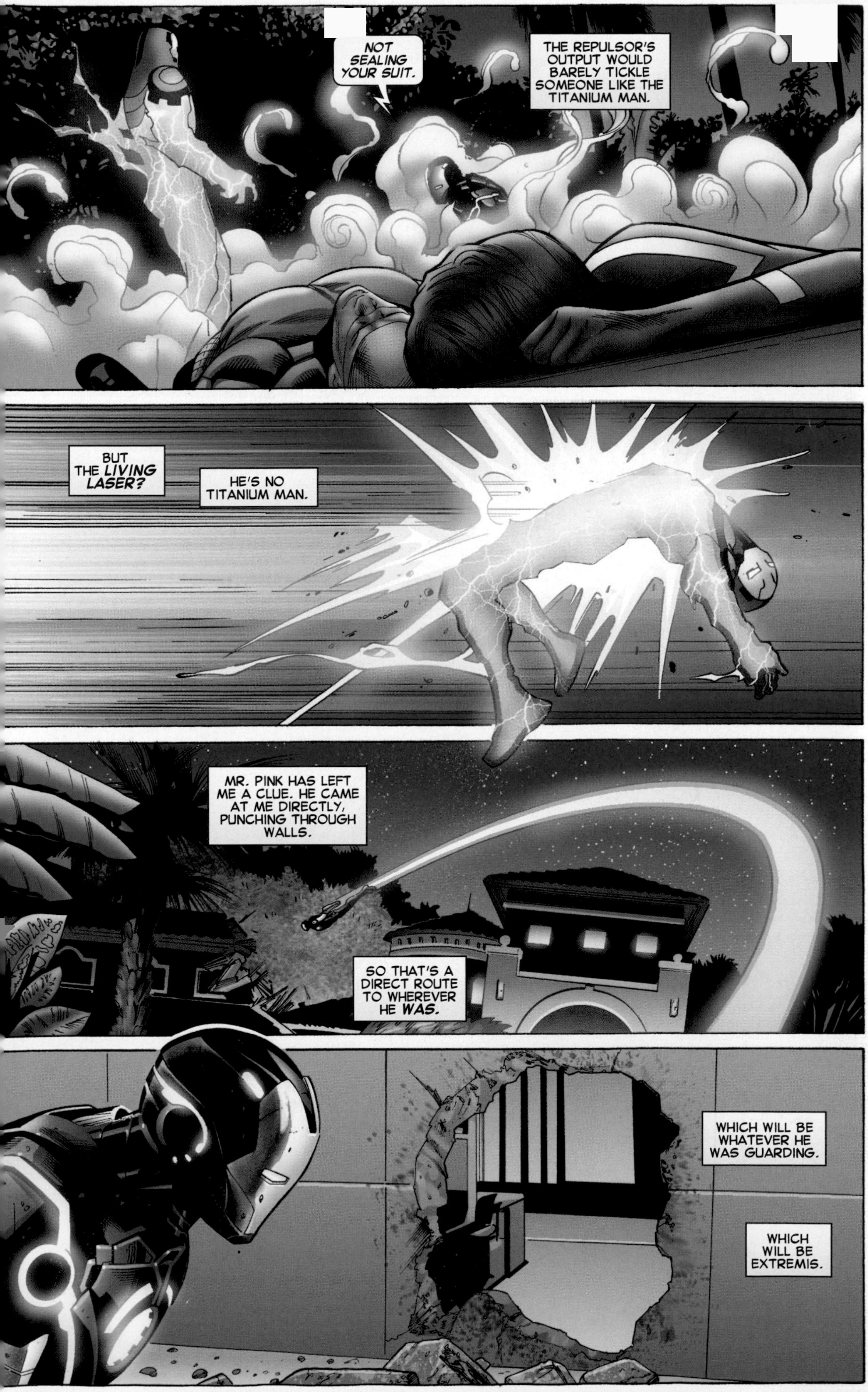
NOT SEALING YOUR SUIT.
THE REPULSOR'S OUTPUT WOULD BARELY TICKLE SOMEONE LIKE THE TITANIUM MAN.
BUT THE LIVING LASER?
HE'S NO TITANIUM MAN.
MR. PINK HAS LEFT ME A CLUE. HE CAME AT ME DIRECTLY, PUNCHING THROUGH WALLS.
SO THAT'S A DIRECT ROUTE TO WHEREVER HE WAS.
WHICH WILL BE WHATEVER HE WAS GUARDING.
WHICH WILL BE EXTREMIS.

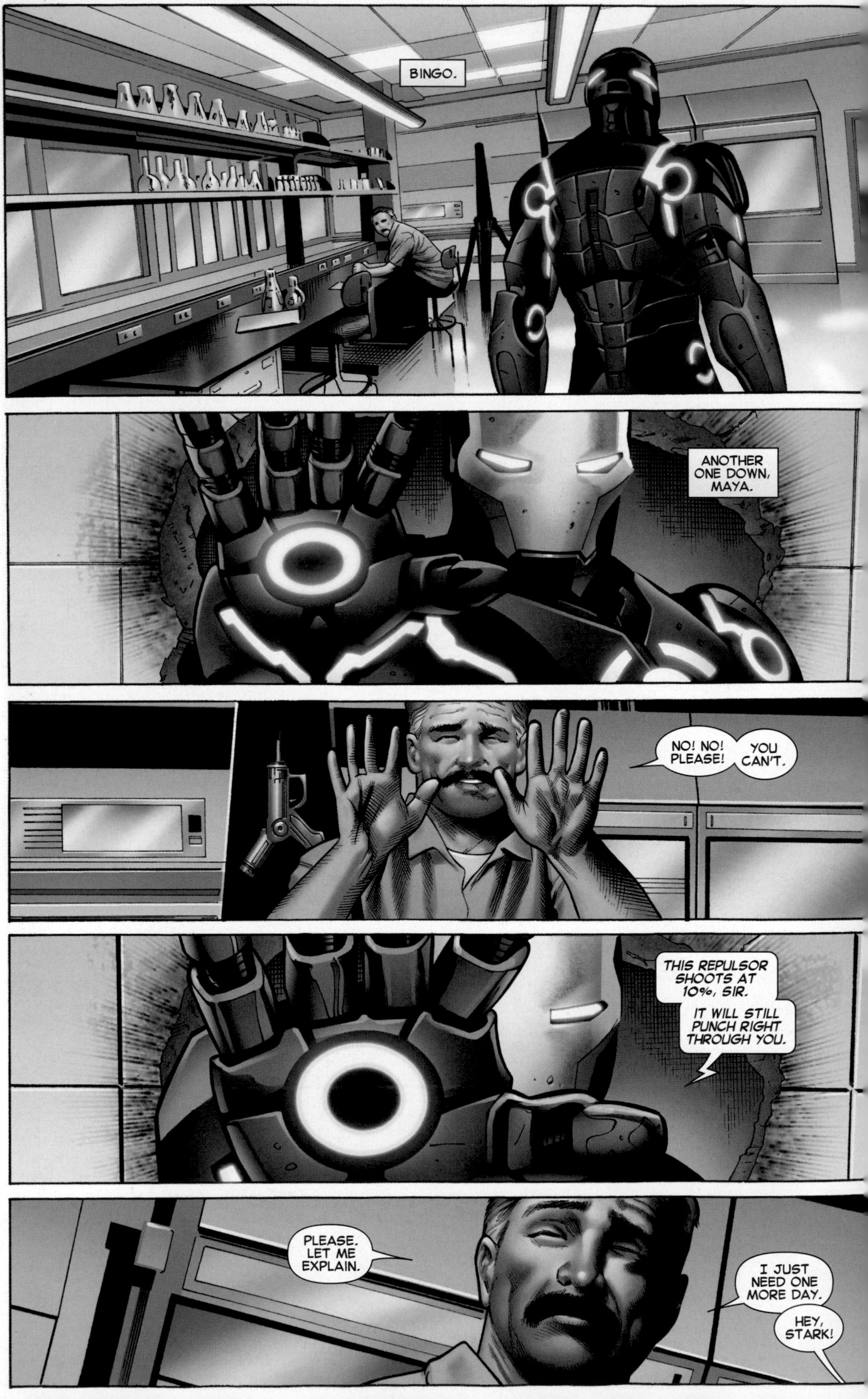
BINGO.
ANOTHER ONE DOWN, MAYA.
NO! NO! PLEASE!
YOU CAN'T.
THIS REPULSOR SHOOTS AT 10%, SIR.
IT WILL STILL PUNCH RIGHT THROUGH YOU.
PLEASE. LET ME EXPLAIN.
I JUST NEED ONE MORE DAY.
HEY, STARK!

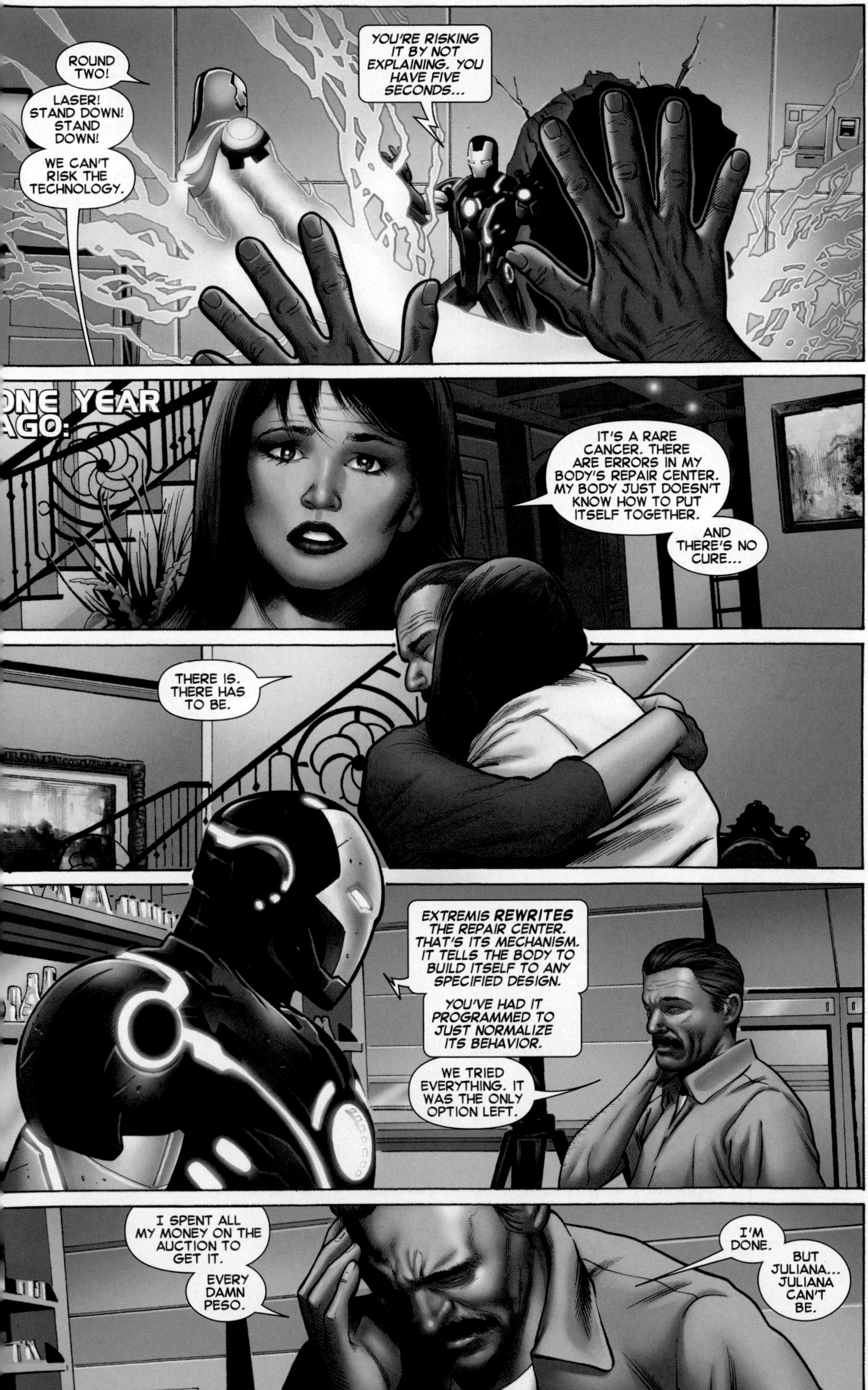
ROUND TWO!
LASER! STAND DOWN! STAND DOWN!
WE CAN'T RISK THE TECHNOLOGY.
YOU'RE RISKING IT BY NOT EXPLAINING. YOU HAVE FIVE SECONDS...
ONE YEAR AGO:
IT'S A RARE CANCER. THERE ARE ERRORS IN MY BODY'S REPAIR CENTER. MY BODY JUST DOESN'T KNOW HOW TO PUT ITSELF TOGETHER.
AND THERE'S NO CURE...
THERE IS. THERE HAS TO BE.
EXTREMIS REWRITES THE REPAIR CENTER. THAT'S ITS MECHANISM. IT TELLS THE BODY TO BUILD ITSELF TO ANY SPECIFIED DESIGN.
YOU'VE HAD IT PROGRAMMED TO JUST NORMALIZE ITS BEHAVIOR.
WE TRIED EVERYTHING. IT WAS THE ONLY OPTION LEFT.
I SPENT ALL MY MONEY ON THE AUCTION TO GET IT.
EVERY DAMN PESO.
I'M DONE.
BUT JULIANA... JULIANA CAN'T BE.

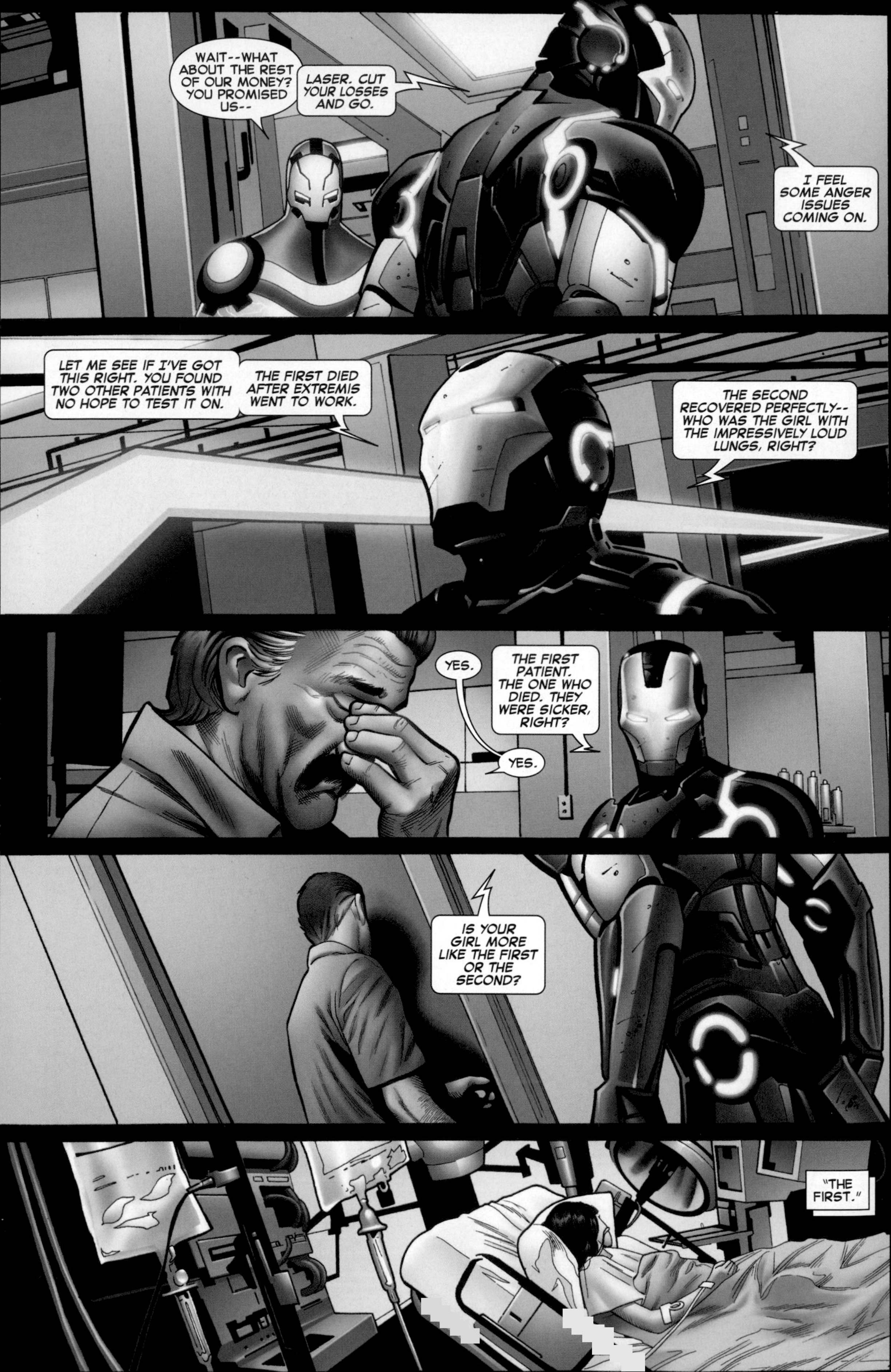
WAIT--WHAT ABOUT THE REST OF OUR MONEY? YOU PROMISED US--
LASER. CUT YOUR LOSSES AND GO.
I FEEL SOME ANGER ISSUES COMING ON.
LET ME SEE IF I'VE GOT THIS RIGHT. YOU FOUND TWO OTHER PATIENTS WITH NO HOPE TO TEST IT ON.
THE FIRST DIED AFTER EXTREMIS WENT TO WORK.
THE SECOND RECOVERED PERFECTLY-- WHO WAS THE GIRL WITH THE IMPRESSIVELY LOUD LUNGS, RIGHT?
YES.
THE FIRST PATIENT. THE ONE WHO DIED. THEY WERE SICKER, RIGHT?
YES.
IS YOUR GIRL MORE LIKE THE FIRST OR THE SECOND?
"THE FIRST."

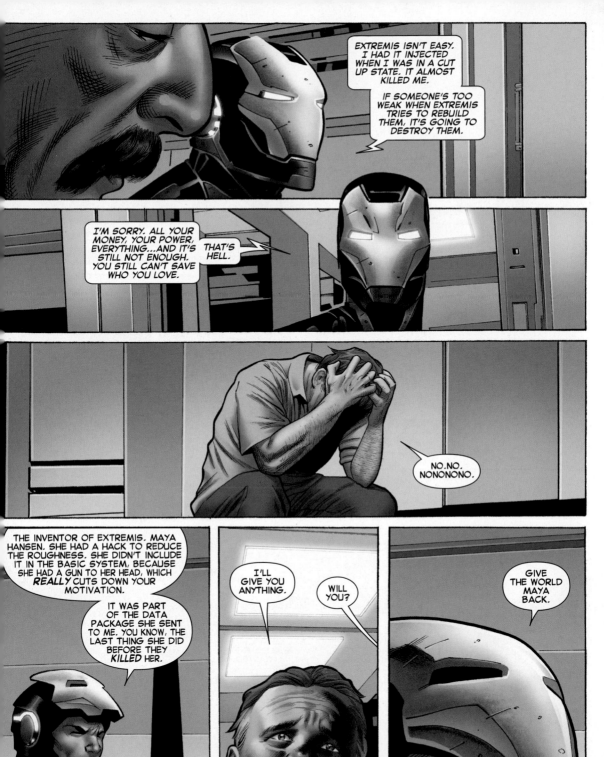

EXTREMIS ISN'T EASY. I HAD IT INJECTED WHEN I WAS IN A CUT UP STATE. IT ALMOST KILLED ME.

IF SOMEONE'S TOO WEAK WHEN EXTREMIS TRIES TO REBUILD THEM, IT'S GOING TO DESTROY THEM.

I'M SORRY. ALL YOUR MONEY, YOUR POWER, EVERYTHING...AND IT'S STILL NOT ENOUGH. YOU STILL CAN'T SAVE WHO YOU LOVE.

THAT'S HELL.

NO. NO. NONONONO.

THE INVENTOR OF EXTREMIS. MAYA HANSEN. SHE HAD A HACK TO REDUCE THE ROUGHNESS. SHE DIDN'T INCLUDE IT IN THE BASIC SYSTEM, BECAUSE SHE HAD A GUN TO HER HEAD, WHICH *REALLY* CUTS DOWN YOUR MOTIVATION.

IT WAS PART OF THE DATA PACKAGE SHE SENT TO ME. YOU KNOW, THE LAST THING SHE DID BEFORE THEY *KILLED* HER.

I'LL GIVE YOU ANYTHING.

WILL YOU?

GIVE THE WORLD MAYA BACK.

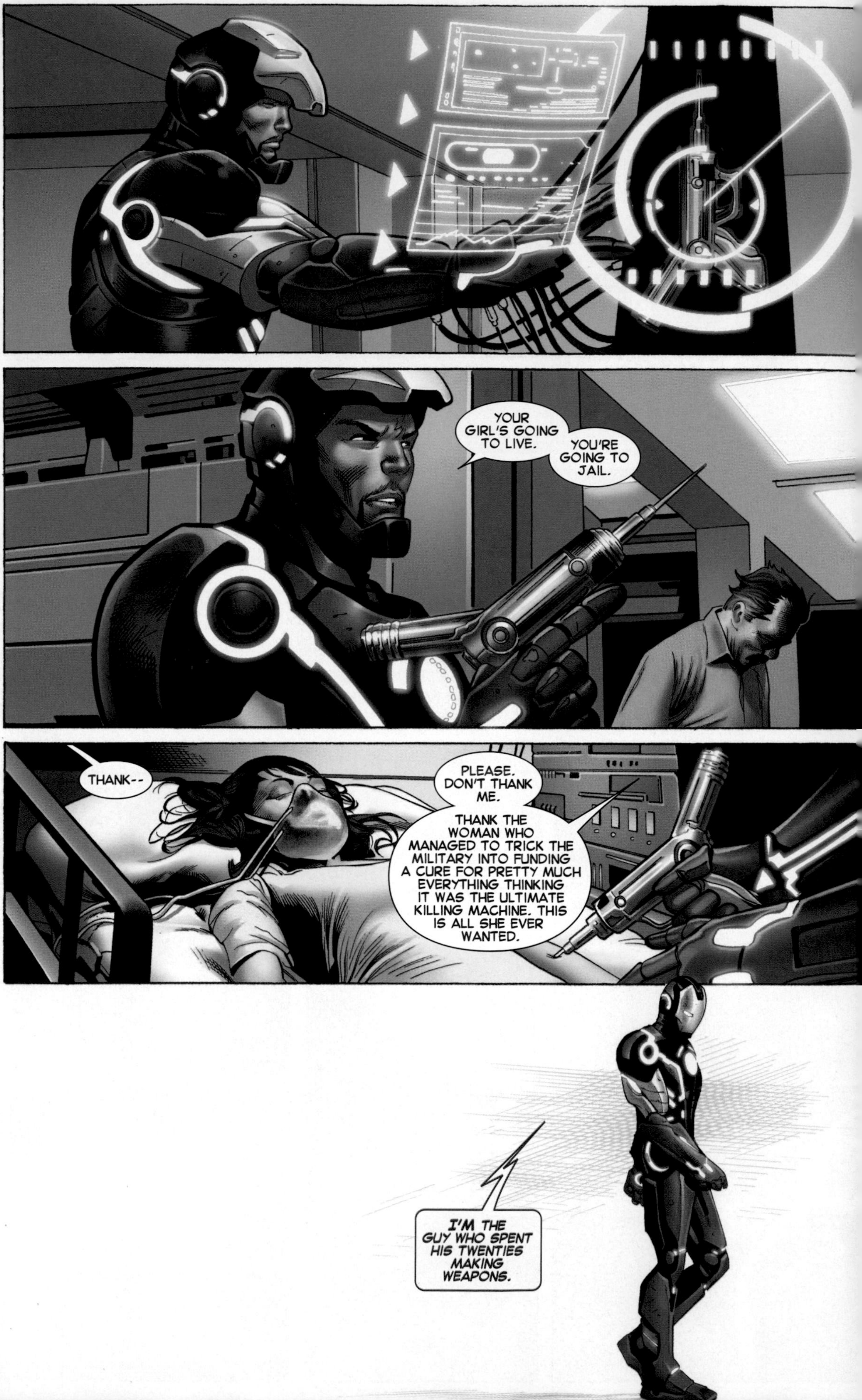
YOUR GIRL'S GOING TO LIVE.
YOU'RE GOING TO JAIL.
THANK--
PLEASE. DON'T THANK ME.
THANK THE WOMAN WHO MANAGED TO TRICK THE MILITARY INTO FUNDING A CURE FOR PRETTY MUCH EVERYTHING THINKING IT WAS THE ULTIMATE KILLING MACHINE. THIS IS ALL SHE EVER WANTED.
I'M THE GUY WHO SPENT HIS TWENTIES MAKING WEAPONS.

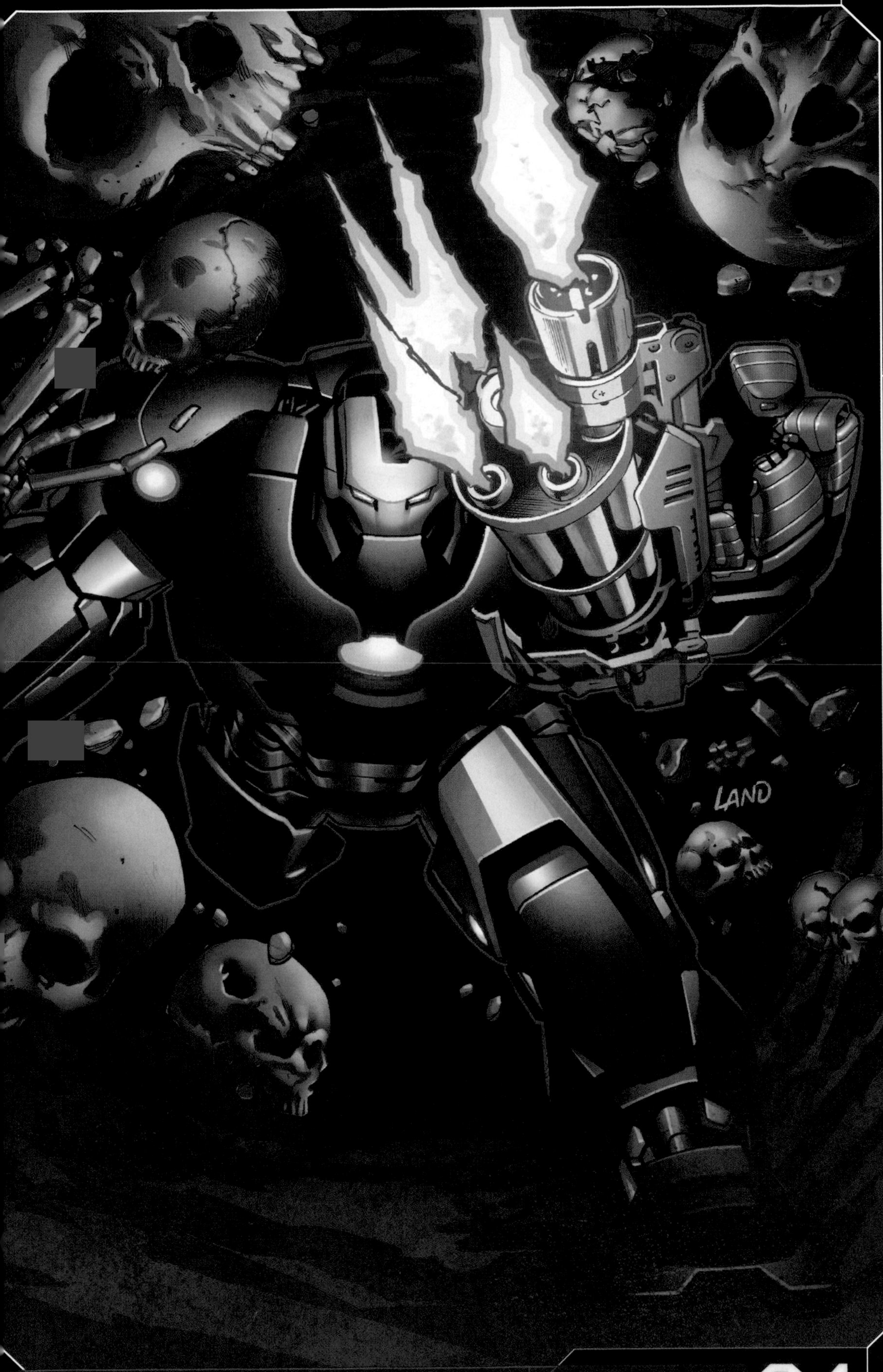
LAND

FEAR OF THE VOID 04

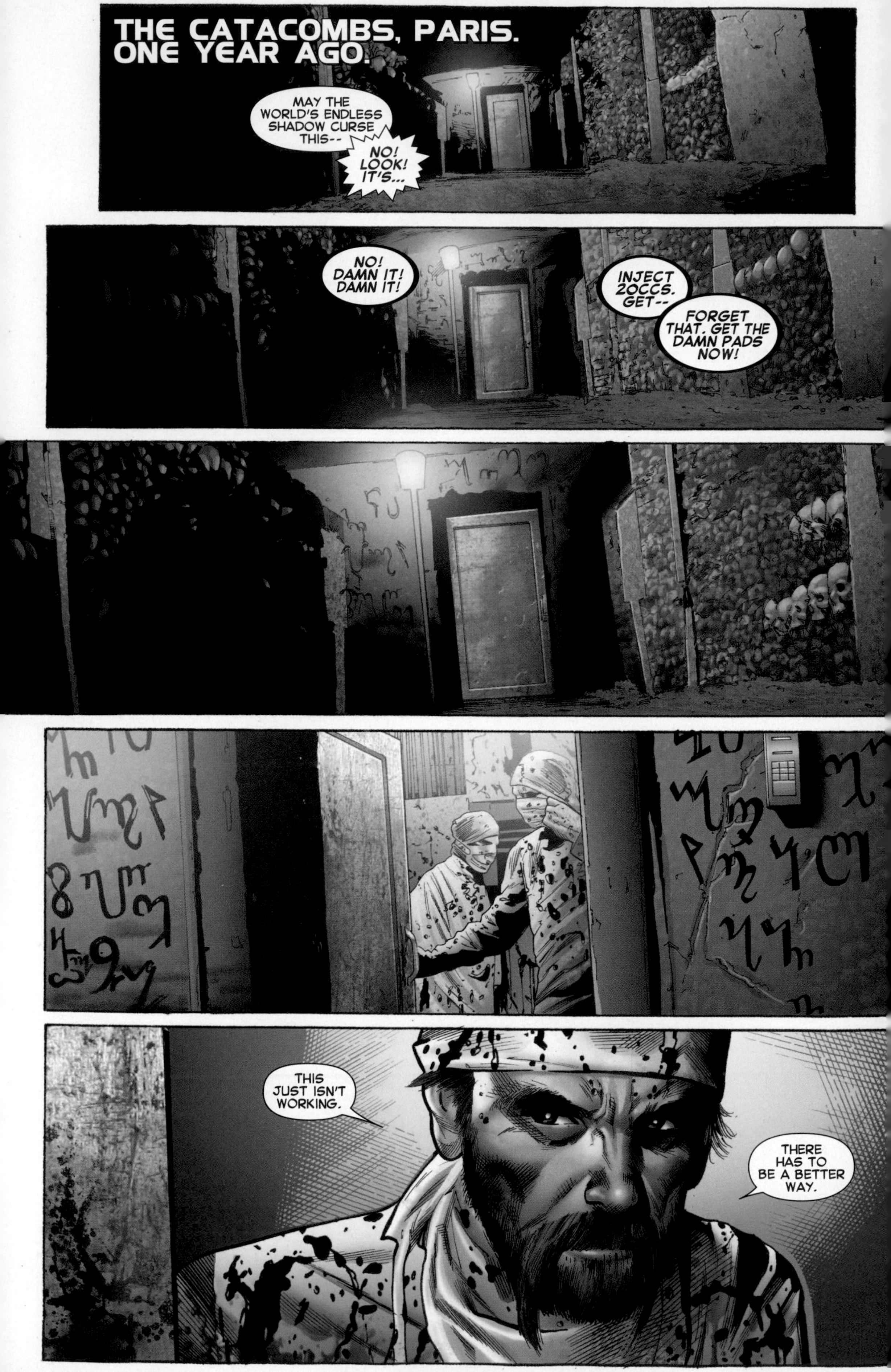
THE CATACOMBS, PARIS. ONE YEAR AGO.
MAY THE WORLD'S ENDLESS SHADOW CURSE THIS--
NO! LOOK! IT'S...
NO! DAMN IT! DAMN IT!
INJECT 20CCS. GET--
FORGET THAT. GET THE DAMN PADS NOW!
THIS JUST ISN'T WORKING.
THERE HAS TO BE A BETTER WAY.

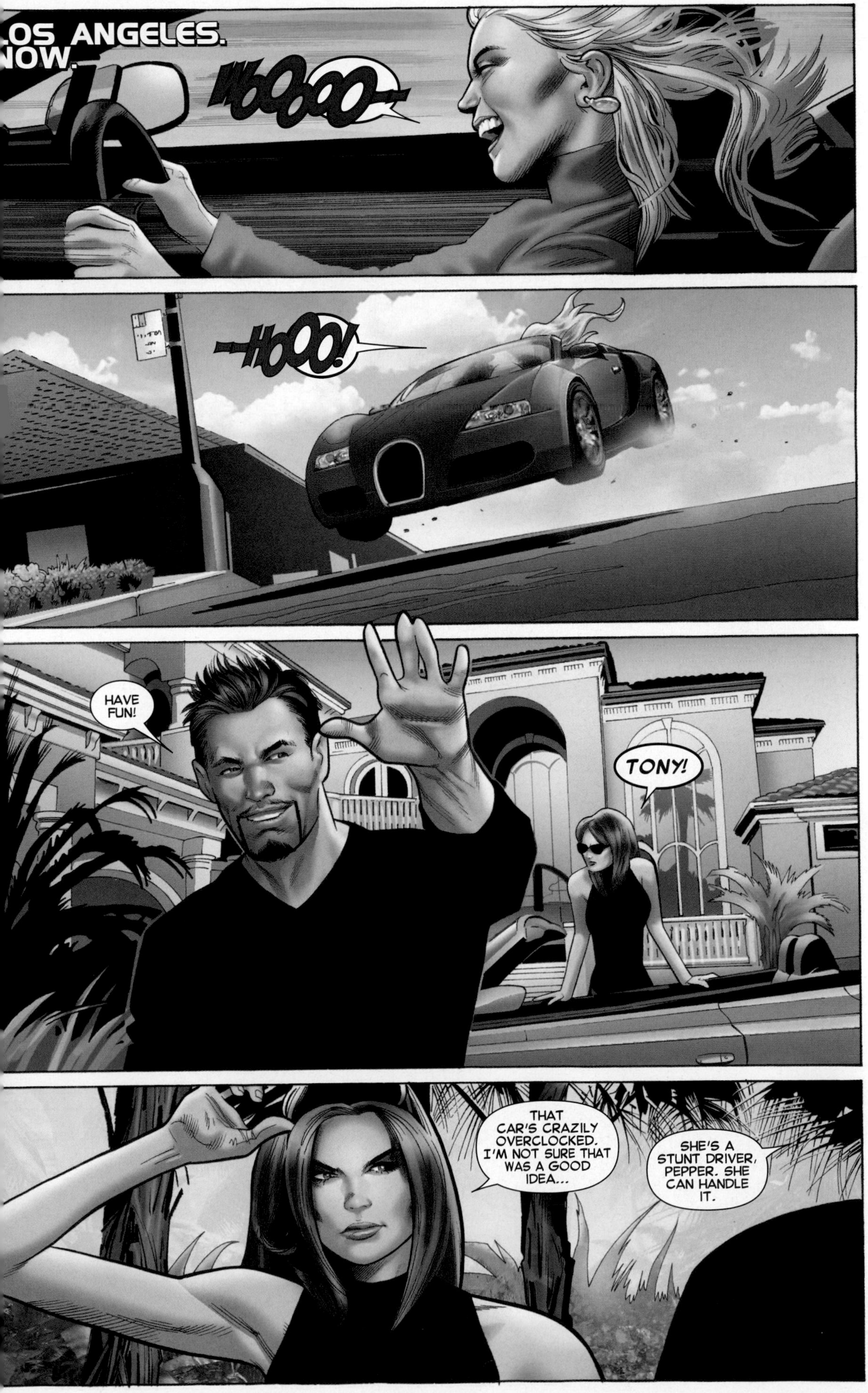
LOS ANGELES.
NOW.
WOOOOO--
--HOOO!
HAVE FUN!
TONY!
THAT CAR'S CRAZILY OVERCLOCKED. I'M NOT SURE THAT WAS A GOOD IDEA...
SHE'S A STUNT DRIVER, PEPPER. SHE CAN HANDLE IT.

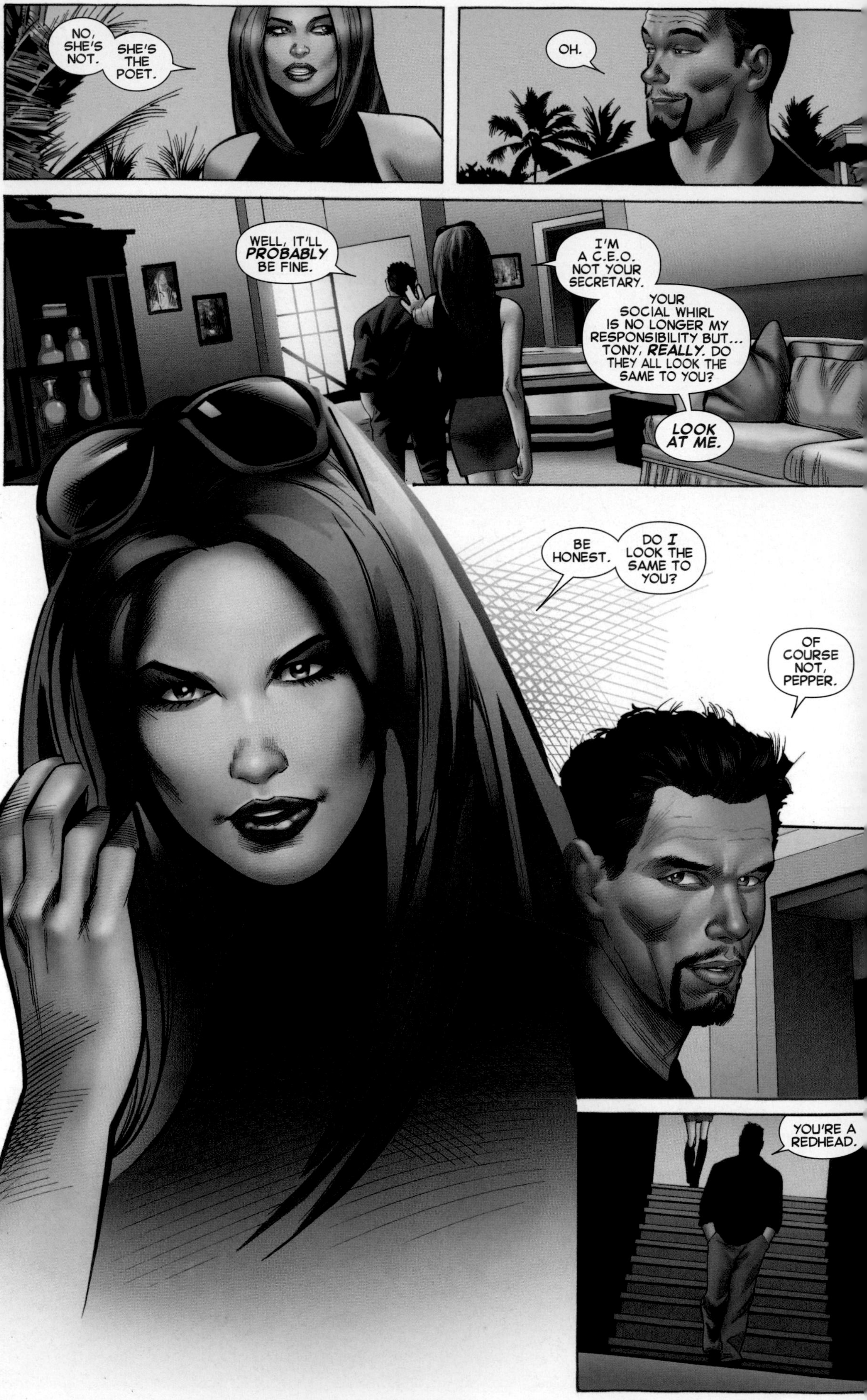
NO, SHE'S NOT.
SHE'S THE POET.
OH.
WELL, IT'LL PROBABLY BE FINE.
I'M A C.E.O. NOT YOUR SECRETARY.
YOUR SOCIAL WHIRL IS NO LONGER MY RESPONSIBILITY BUT... TONY, REALLY. DO THEY ALL LOOK THE SAME TO YOU?
LOOK AT ME.
BE HONEST.
DO I LOOK THE SAME TO YOU?
OF COURSE NOT, PEPPER.
YOU'RE A REDHEAD.

ONLY IN BEING A[N] APPOINTMENT [AR]E YOU NEVER A[N] [A]PPOINTMENT...

OKAY. THE [MI]SSING EXTREMIS [SI]TUATION. MADE [A]NY PROGRESS? AND [A]NY IDEA HOW MANY [P]EOPLE IT'S BEEN USED ON?

I MEAN, EXACTLY HOW MANY UNETHICALLY CREATED POST-HUMANS ARE WE TALKING ABOUT?

THE LAST TWO EXTREMIS KITS ARE PROBLEMATIC. WE'RE SEEING MULTIPLE ENHANCILES, BUT THANKFULLY THEY'RE STILL IN A LIMITED LOCALE...

SUIT! SHOW US THE TRACES.

DO I REALLY HAVE TO?

YES!

A.I. STILL NEEDS SOME WORK?

GETTING THERE.

THE PERSONALITY IS GOING THROUGH ITS AWKWARD TEENS, METAPHORICALLY SPEAKING.

IT'S HORMONAL AND SURLY.

ONE CLUSTER IS SIX ENHANCILES, BUT THE SIGNAL'S STRANGE. IT FADES IN AND OUT. ALMOST CERTAINLY MOBILE.

PARIS

FRANCE

THE OTHER ONE IS STATIONARY, IN THE PARIS CATACOMBS. THIRTEEN ENHANCILES. THEY HAVEN'T MOVED IN THE LAST TWO DAYS AT ALL.

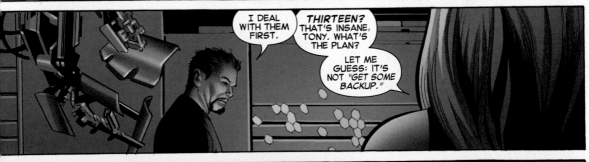

I DEAL WITH THEM FIRST.

THIRTEEN? THAT'S INSANE, TONY. WHAT'S THE PLAN?

LET ME GUESS: IT'S NOT "GET SOME BACKUP."

OF COURSE NOT. HEAVY OPPOSITION? CLOSE CONFINED AREA? NO ROOM TO MANEUVER?

IT'S GOING TO BE A STAND-UP FIGHT.

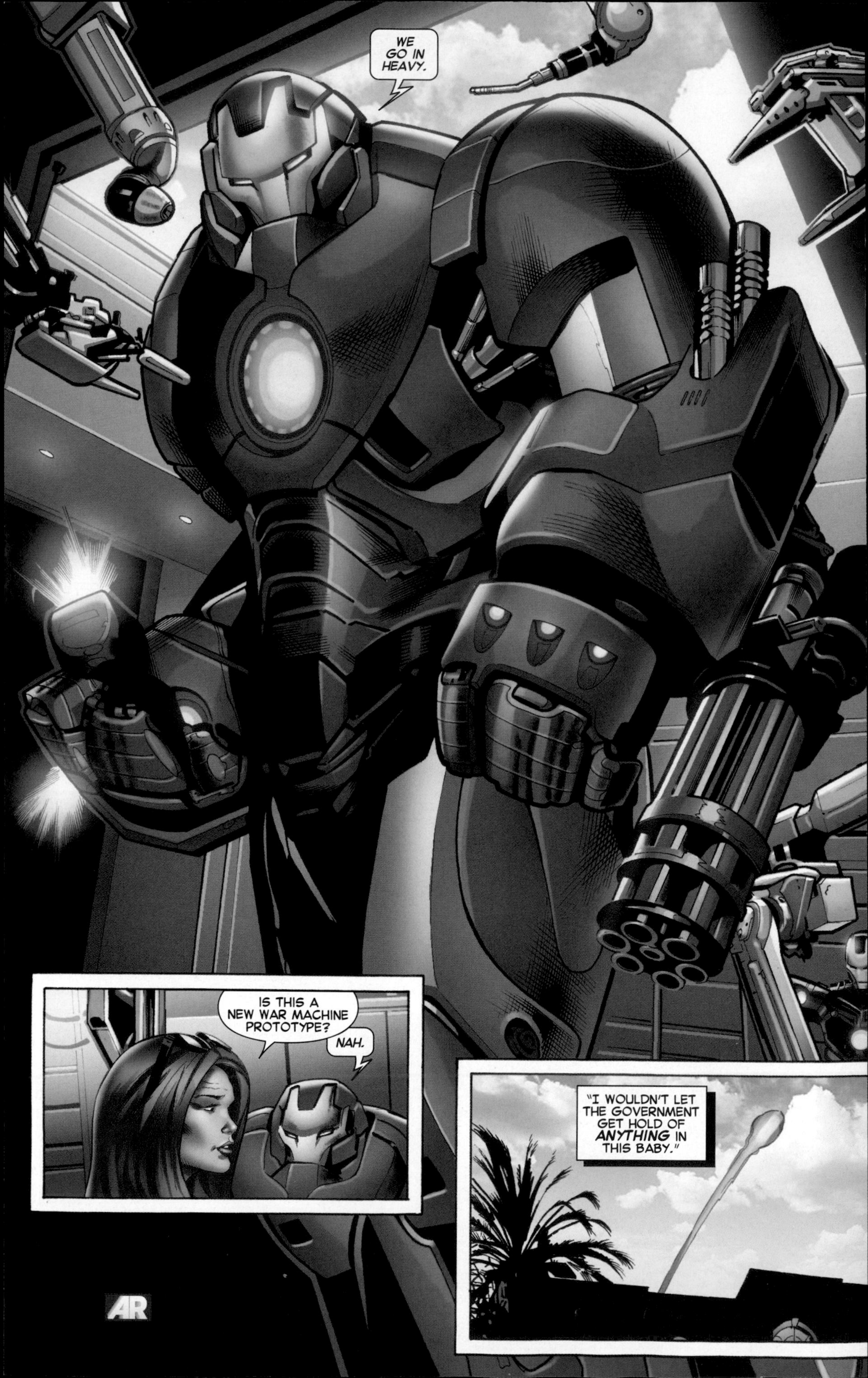
WE GO IN HEAVY.
IS THIS A NEW WAR MACHINE PROTOTYPE?
NAH.
"I WOULDN'T LET THE GOVERNMENT GET HOLD OF ANYTHING IN THIS BABY."
AR

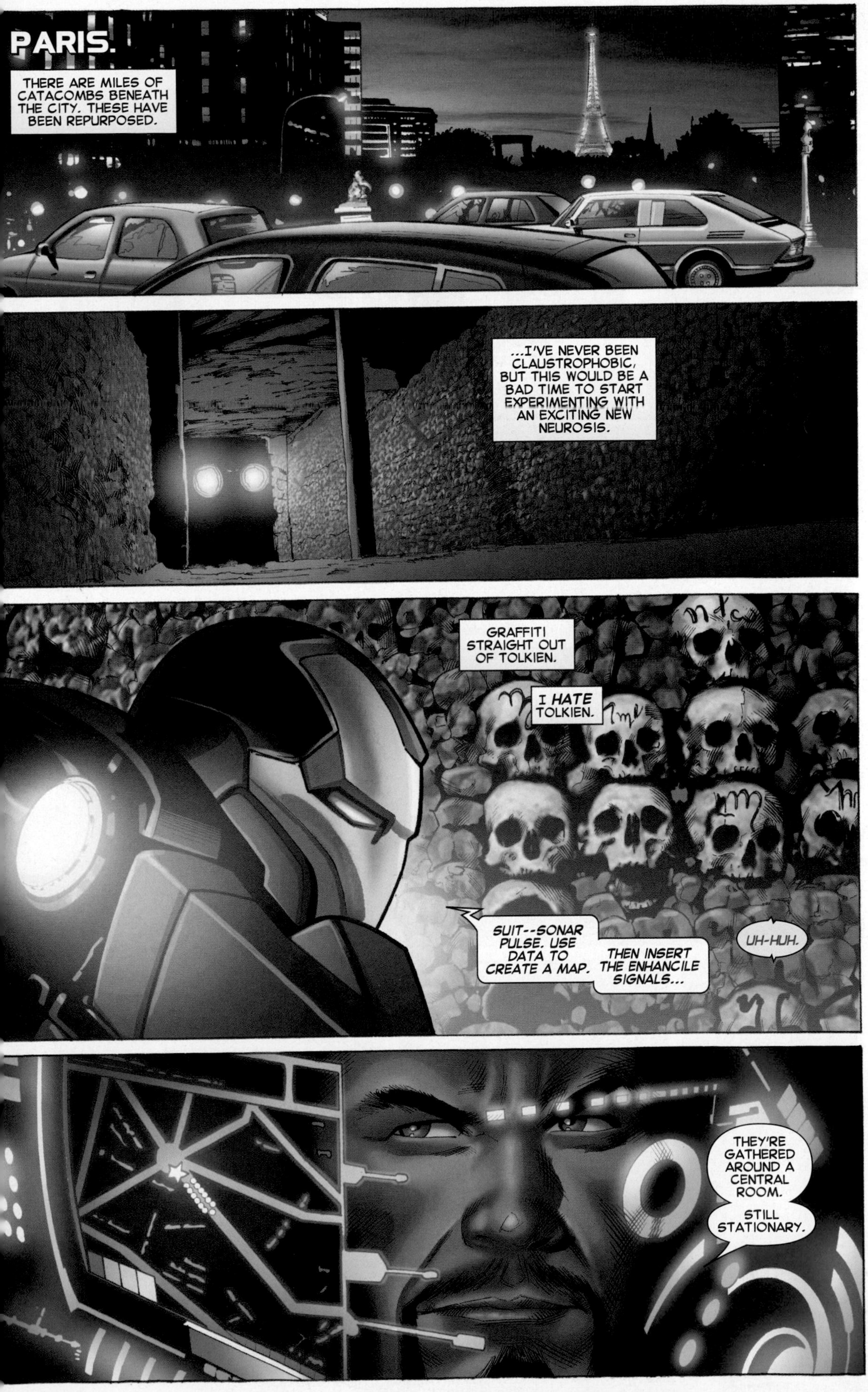
PARIS.
THERE ARE MILES OF CATACOMBS BENEATH THE CITY. THESE HAVE BEEN REPURPOSED.
...I'VE NEVER BEEN CLAUSTROPHOBIC, BUT THIS WOULD BE A BAD TIME TO START EXPERIMENTING WITH AN EXCITING NEW NEUROSIS.
GRAFFITI STRAIGHT OUT OF TOLKIEN.
I HATE TOLKIEN.
SUIT--SONAR PULSE. USE DATA TO CREATE A MAP.
THEN INSERT THE ENHANCILE SIGNALS...
UH-HUH.
THEY'RE GATHERED AROUND A CENTRAL ROOM.
STILL STATIONARY.

THIS LOOKS LIKE A SECURITY SYSTEM.

SUIT, LINK ME UP. GIVE ME A CAMERA IN THAT CORE AREA...

...WHATEVER.

THERE WE GO. SIXTY METERS...

THE MISSING EXTREMIS SYSTEM.

AND A... SCIENTIST? ARMED. AND SCARED.

ANY OTHER CAMERAS?

GIVE THEM TO ME.

YEAH.

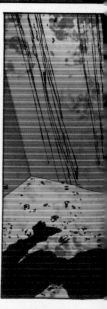

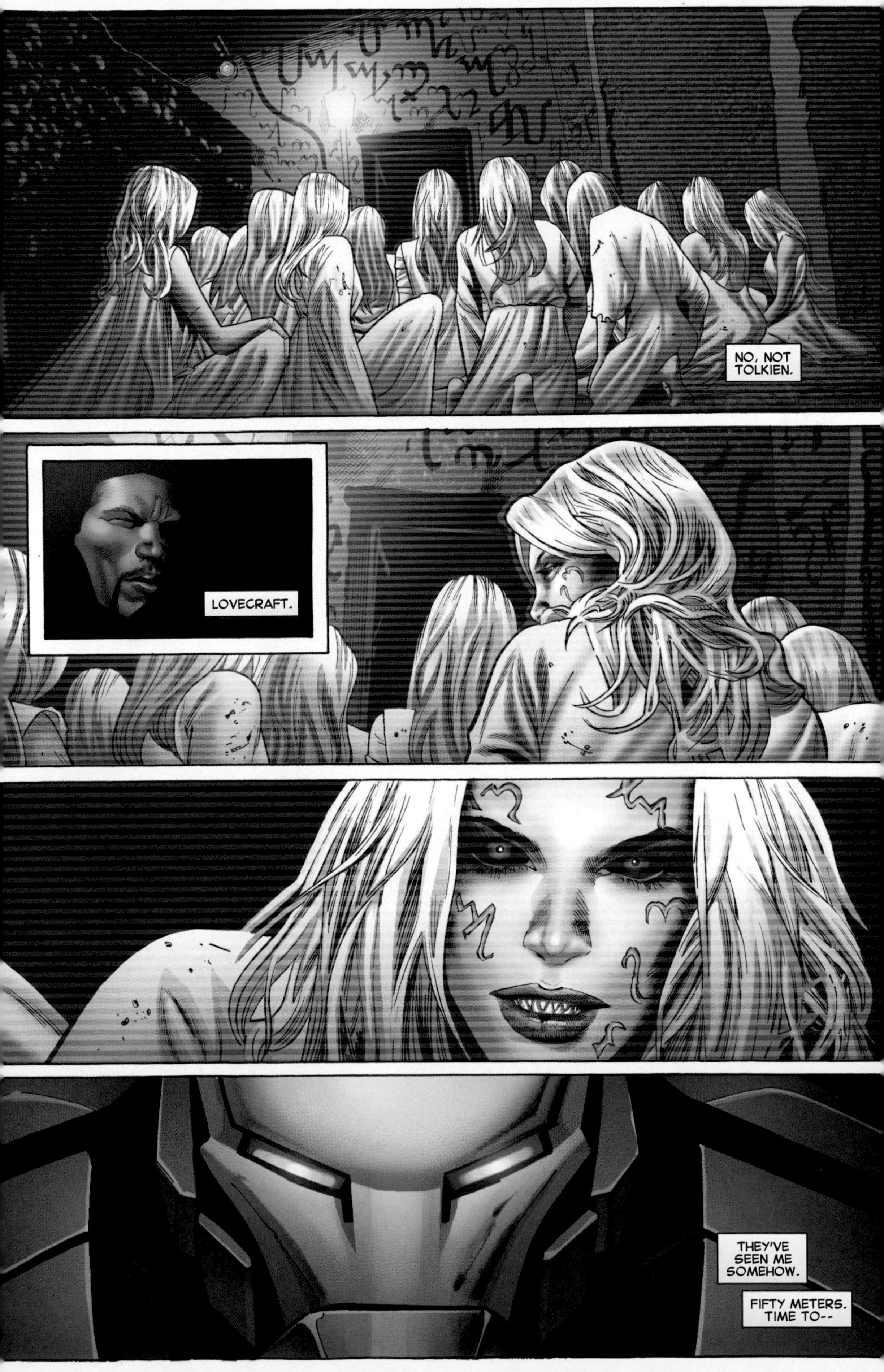
NO, NOT TOLKIEN.
LOVECRAFT.
THEY'VE SEEN ME SOMEHOW.
FIFTY METERS. TIME TO--

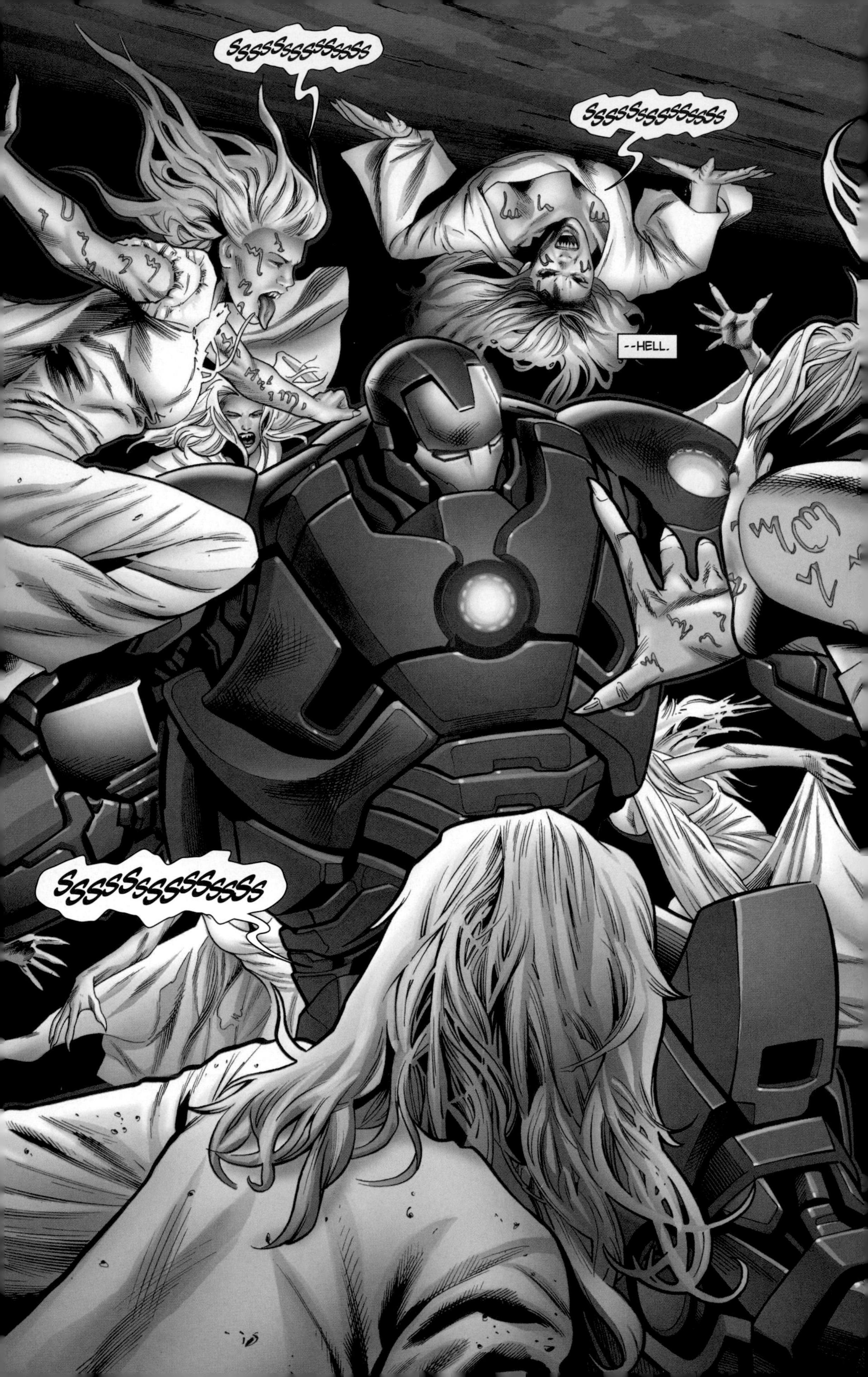
SsssSsssssssss
SsssSssssssssss
--HELL.
SsssSsssssssssss

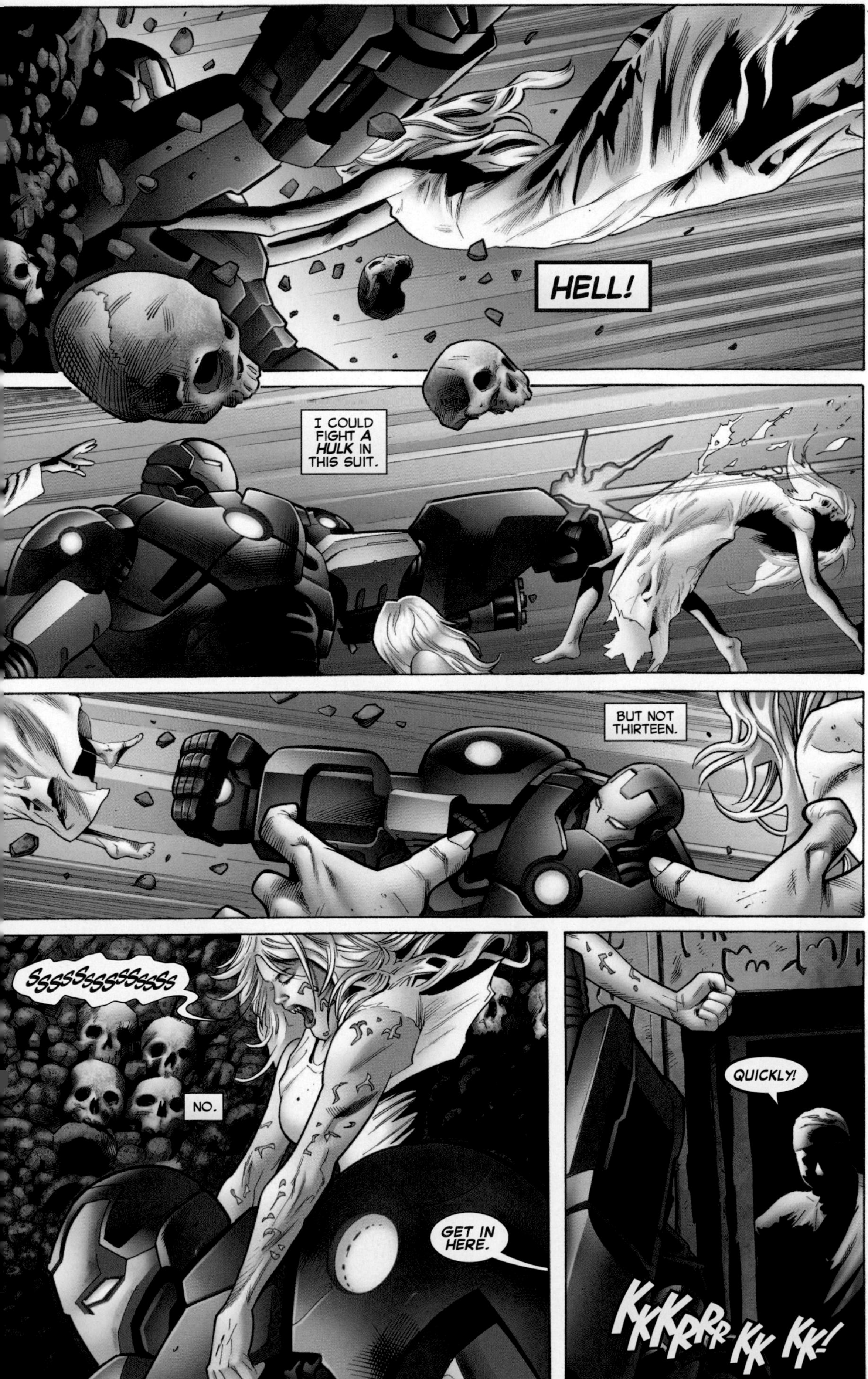
HELL!
I COULD FIGHT A HULK IN THIS SUIT.
BUT NOT THIRTEEN.
SsssSssssSsssSs
NO.
GET IN HERE.
QUICKLY!
KKKRRRR-KK KK!

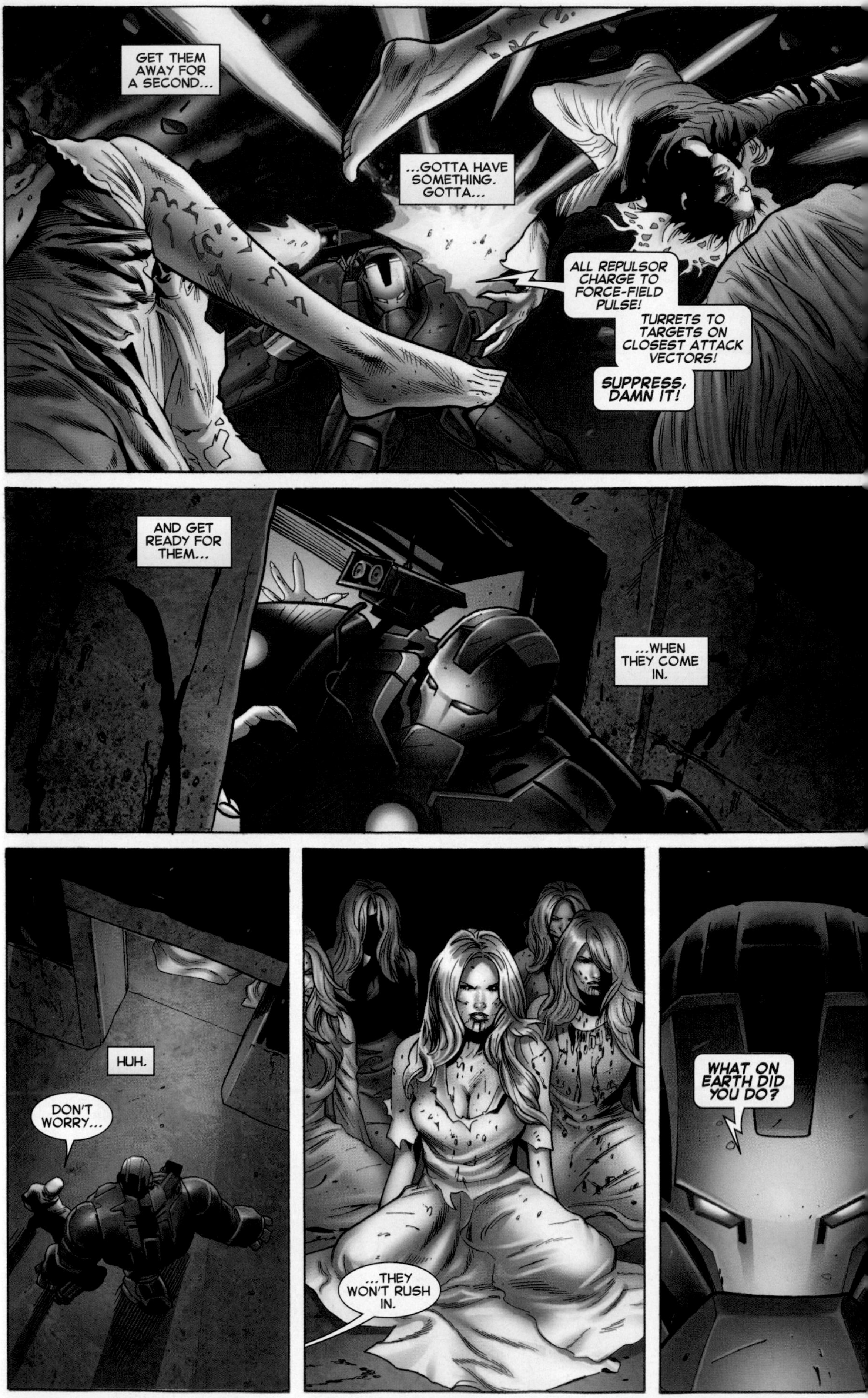
GET THEM AWAY FOR A SECOND...
...GOTTA HAVE SOMETHING. GOTTA...
ALL REPULSOR CHARGE TO FORCE-FIELD PULSE!
TURRETS TO TARGETS ON CLOSEST ATTACK VECTORS!
SUPPRESS, DAMN IT!
AND GET READY FOR THEM...
...WHEN THEY COME IN.
HUH.
DON'T WORRY...
...THEY WON'T RUSH IN.
WHAT ON EARTH DID YOU DO?

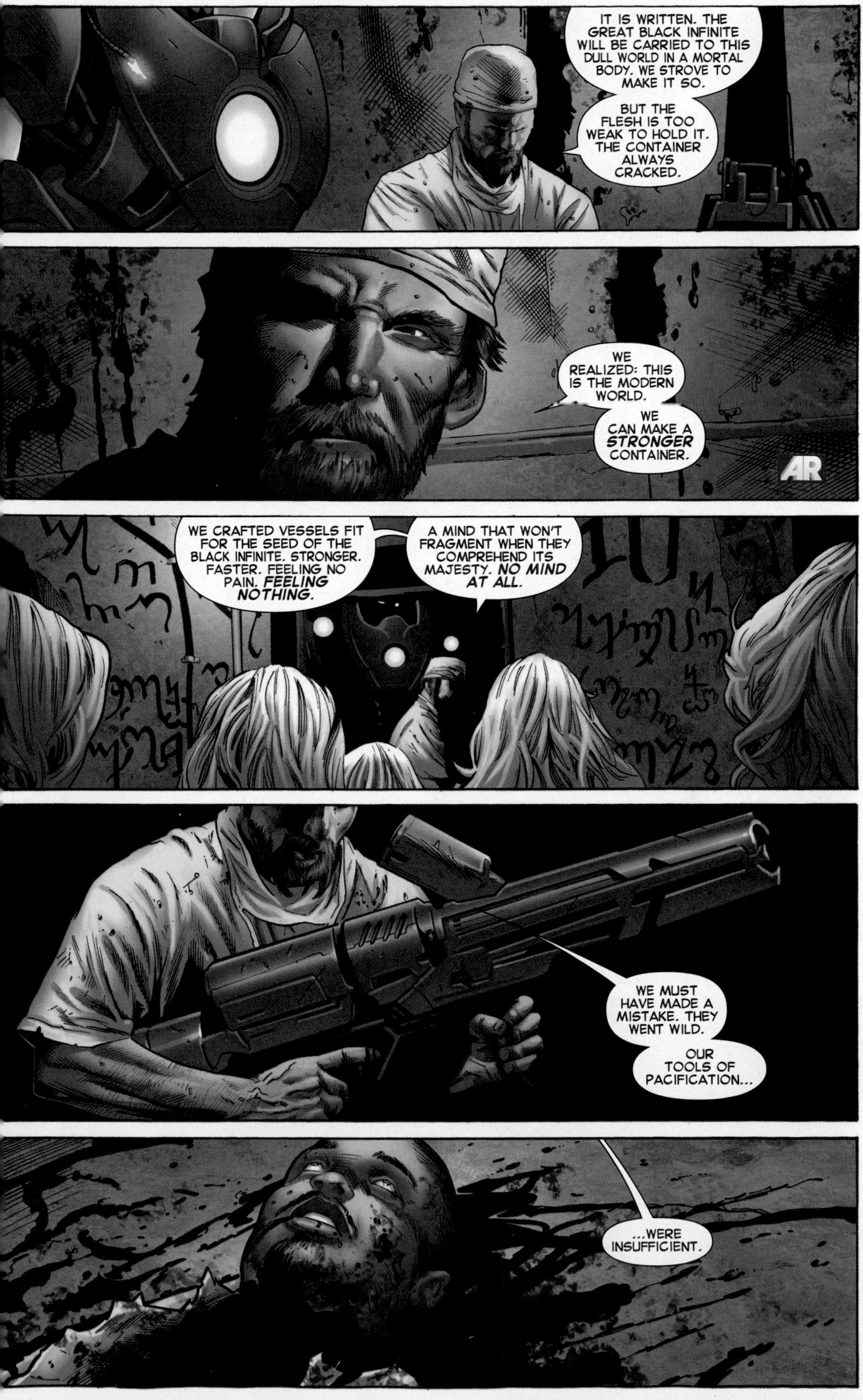
IT IS WRITTEN. THE GREAT BLACK INFINITE WILL BE CARRIED TO THIS DULL WORLD IN A MORTAL BODY. WE STROVE TO MAKE IT SO.
BUT THE FLESH IS TOO WEAK TO HOLD IT. THE CONTAINER ALWAYS CRACKED.
WE REALIZED: THIS IS THE MODERN WORLD.
WE CAN MAKE A STRONGER CONTAINER.
AR
WE CRAFTED VESSELS FIT FOR THE SEED OF THE BLACK INFINITE. STRONGER. FASTER. FEELING NO PAIN. FEELING NOTHING.
A MIND THAT WON'T FRAGMENT WHEN THEY COMPREHEND ITS MAJESTY. NO MIND AT ALL.
WE MUST HAVE MADE A MISTAKE. THEY WENT WILD.
OUR TOOLS OF PACIFICATION...
...WERE INSUFFICIENT.

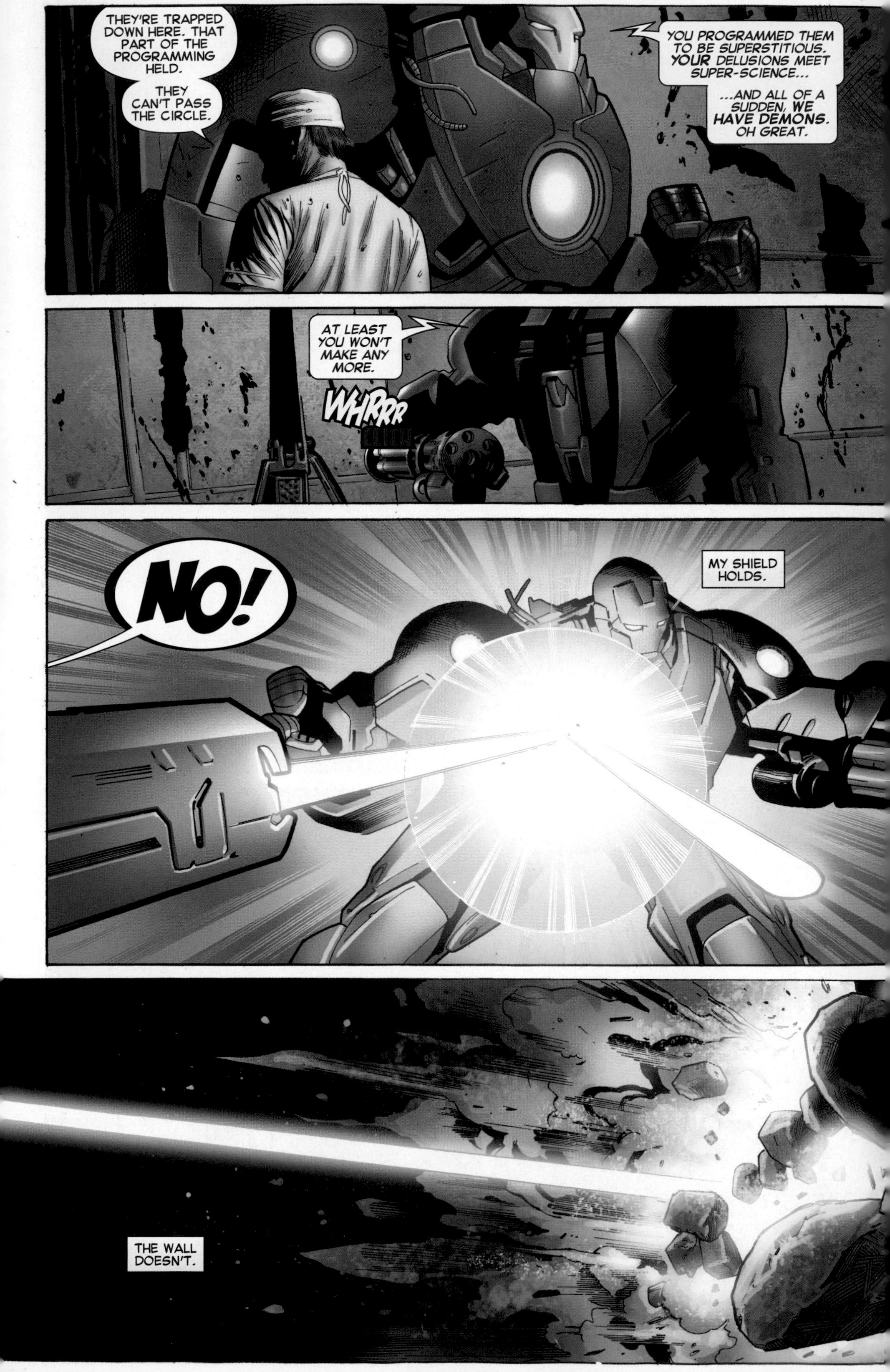
THEY'RE TRAPPED DOWN HERE. THAT PART OF THE PROGRAMMING HELD.
THEY CAN'T PASS THE CIRCLE.
YOU PROGRAMMED THEM TO BE SUPERSTITIOUS. YOUR DELUSIONS MEET SUPER-SCIENCE...
...AND ALL OF A SUDDEN, WE HAVE DEMONS. OH GREAT.
AT LEAST YOU WON'T MAKE ANY MORE.
WHRRR
NO!
MY SHIELD HOLDS.
THE WALL DOESN'T.

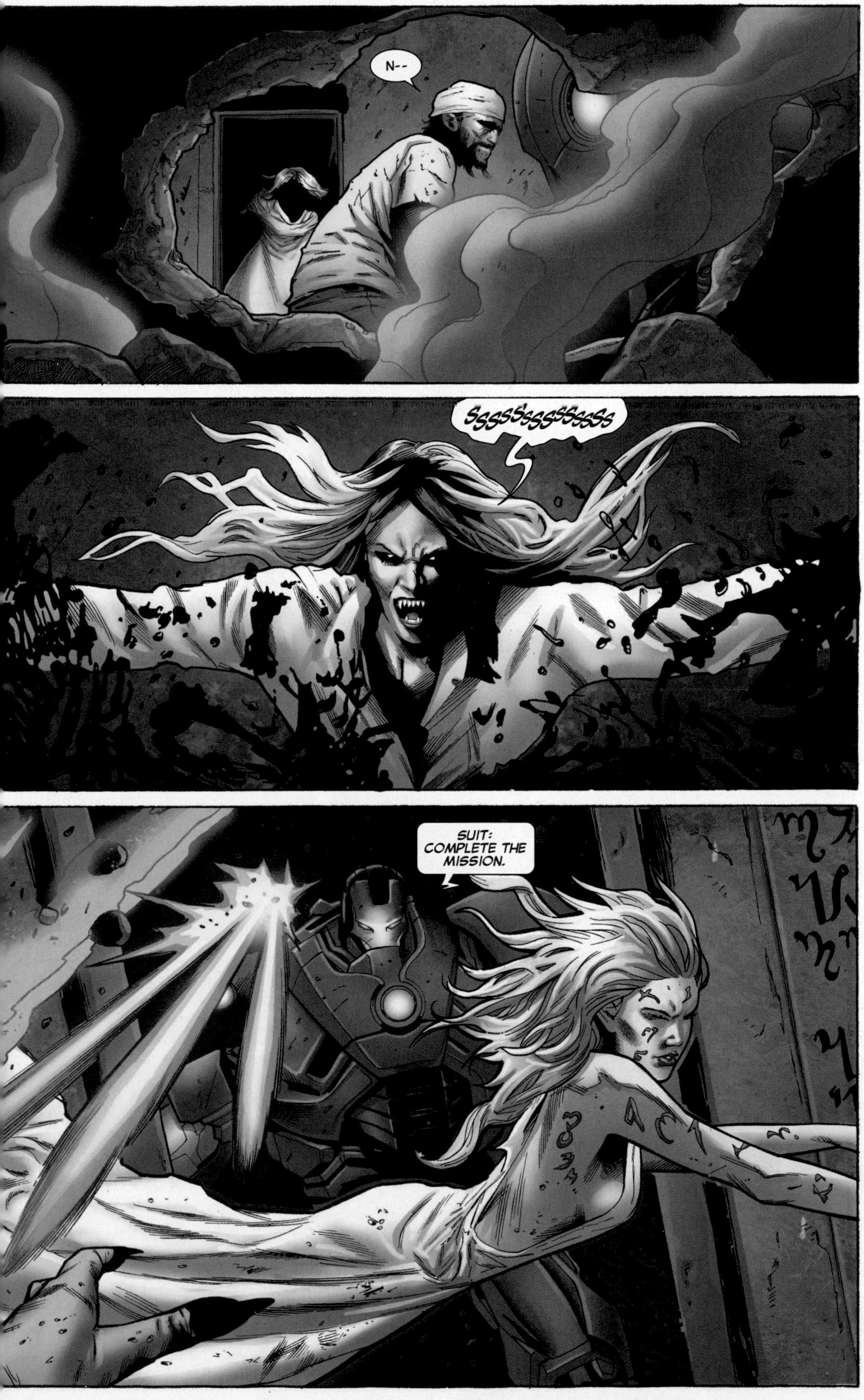
N--
SSSSSSSSSSSSSS
SUIT: COMPLETE THE MISSION.

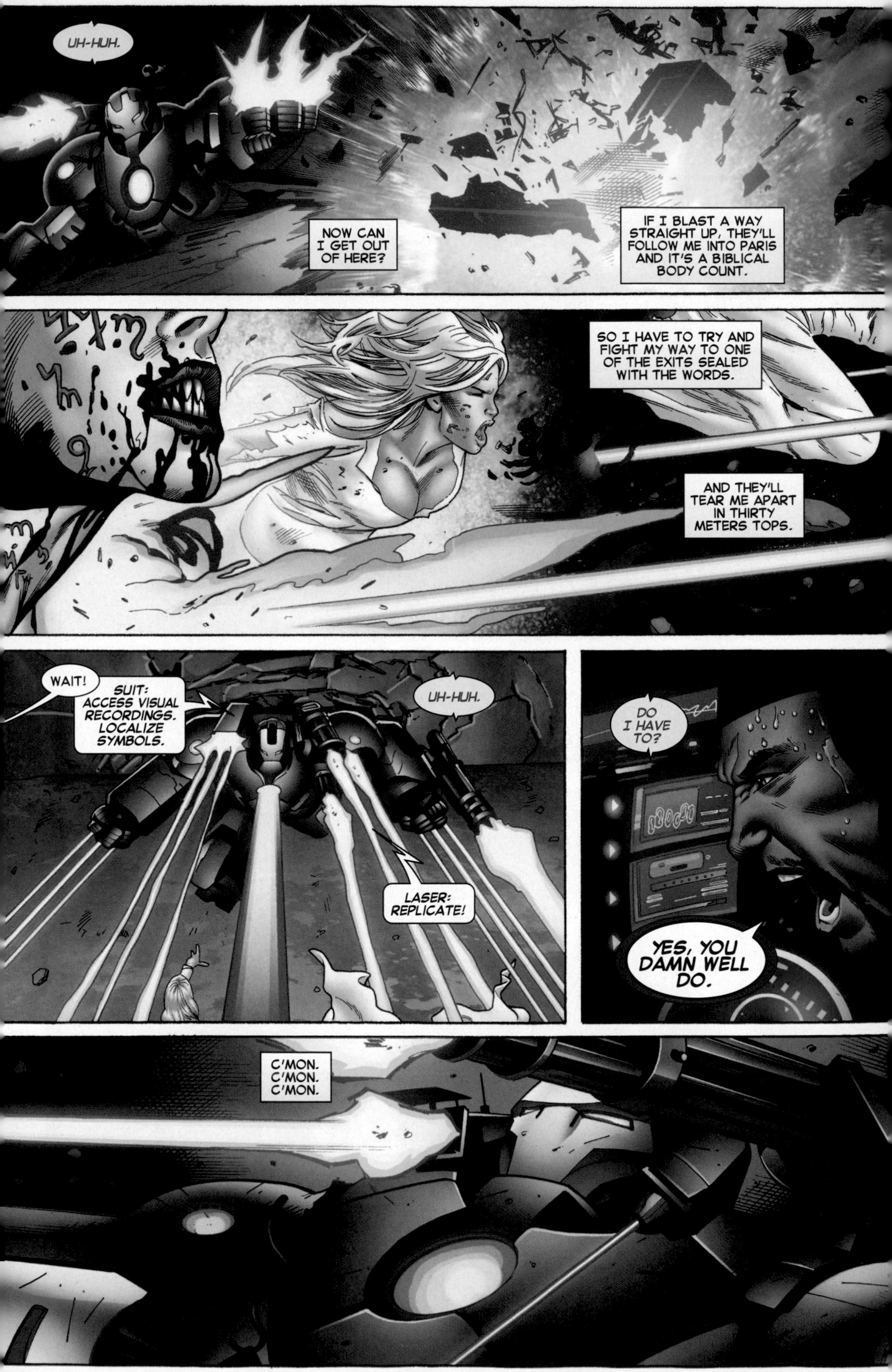
UH-HUH.
NOW CAN I GET OUT OF HERE?
IF I BLAST A WAY STRAIGHT UP, THEY'LL FOLLOW ME INTO PARIS AND IT'S A BIBLICAL BODY COUNT.
SO I HAVE TO TRY AND FIGHT MY WAY TO ONE OF THE EXITS SEALED WITH THE WORDS.
AND THEY'LL TEAR ME APART IN THIRTY METERS TOPS.
WAIT!
SUIT: ACCESS VISUAL RECORDINGS. LOCALIZE SYMBOLS.
UH-HUH.
LASER: REPLICATE!
DO I HAVE TO?
YES, YOU DAMN WELL DO.
C'MON. C'MON. C'MON.

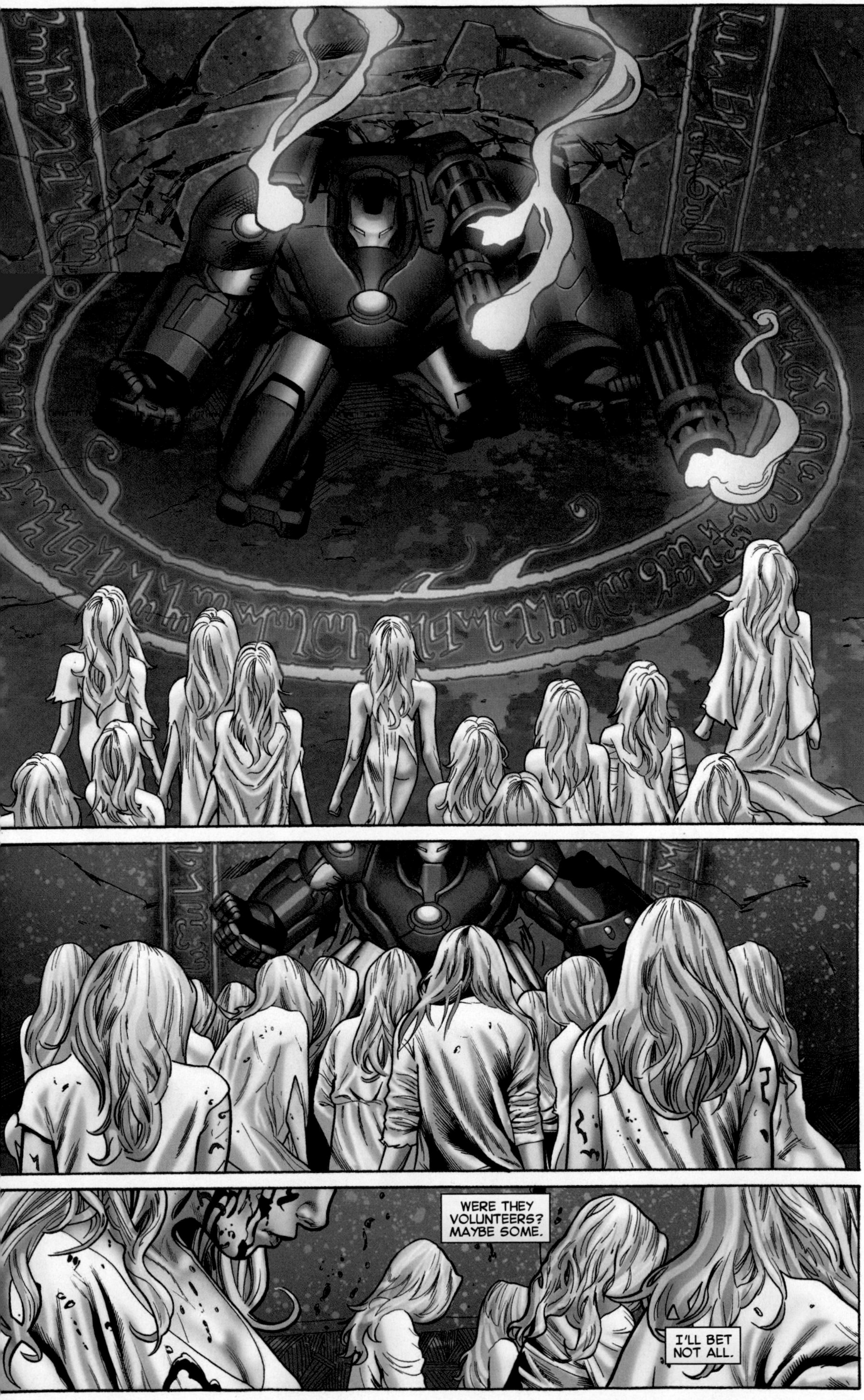
WERE THEY VOLUNTEERS? MAYBE SOME.
I'LL BET NOT ALL.

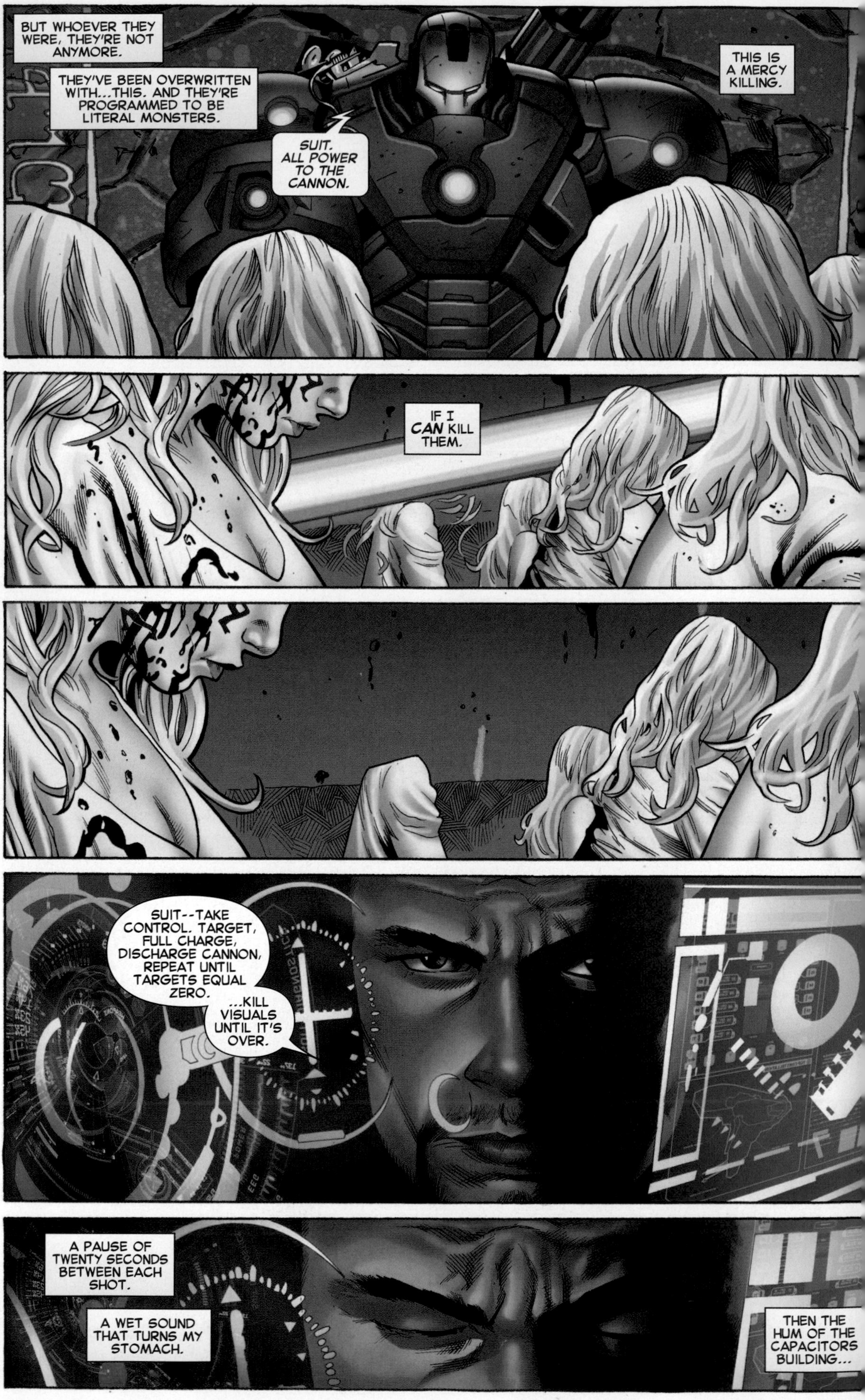
BUT WHOEVER THEY WERE, THEY'RE NOT ANYMORE.
THEY'VE BEEN OVERWRITTEN WITH...THIS. AND THEY'RE PROGRAMMED TO BE LITERAL MONSTERS.
SUIT. ALL POWER TO THE CANNON.
THIS IS A MERCY KILLING.
IF I CAN KILL THEM.
SUIT--TAKE CONTROL. TARGET, FULL CHARGE, DISCHARGE CANNON, REPEAT UNTIL TARGETS EQUAL ZERO.
...KILL VISUALS UNTIL IT'S OVER.
A PAUSE OF TWENTY SECONDS BETWEEN EACH SHOT.
A WET SOUND THAT TURNS MY STOMACH.
THEN THE HUM OF THE CAPACITORS BUILDING...

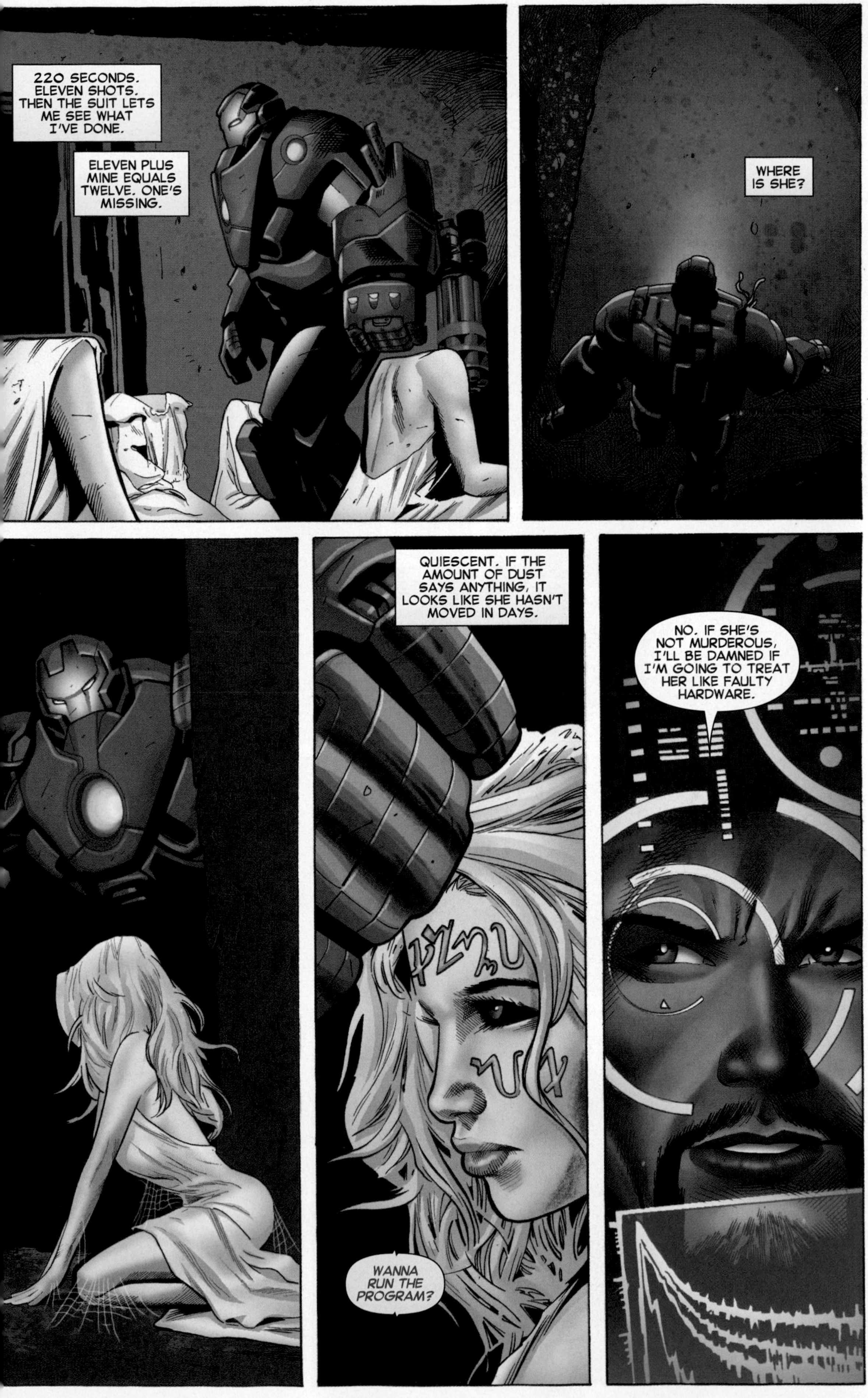
220 SECONDS. ELEVEN SHOTS. THEN THE SUIT LETS ME SEE WHAT I'VE DONE.
ELEVEN PLUS MINE EQUALS TWELVE. ONE'S MISSING.
WHERE IS SHE?
QUIESCENT. IF THE AMOUNT OF DUST SAYS ANYTHING, IT LOOKS LIKE SHE HASN'T MOVED IN DAYS.
WANNA RUN THE PROGRAM?
NO. IF SHE'S NOT MURDEROUS, I'LL BE DAMNED IF I'M GOING TO TREAT HER LIKE FAULTY HARDWARE.

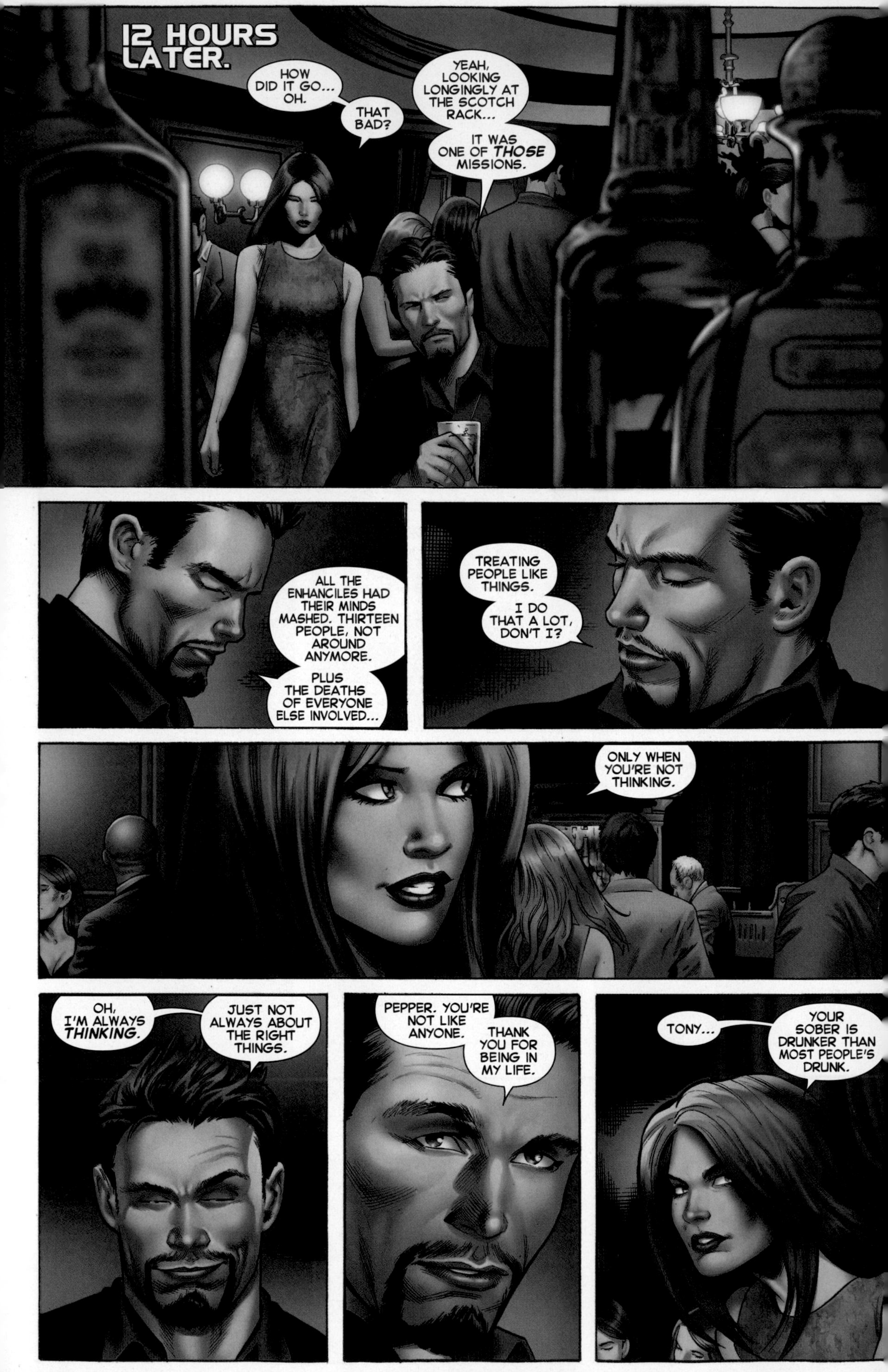
12 HOURS LATER.
HOW DID IT GO... OH.
THAT BAD?
YEAH, LOOKING LONGINGLY AT THE SCOTCH RACK...
IT WAS ONE OF *THOSE* MISSIONS.
ALL THE ENHANCILES HAD THEIR MINDS MASHED. THIRTEEN PEOPLE, NOT AROUND ANYMORE.
PLUS THE DEATHS OF EVERYONE ELSE INVOLVED...
TREATING PEOPLE LIKE THINGS.
I DO THAT A LOT, DON'T I?
ONLY WHEN YOU'RE NOT THINKING.
OH, I'M ALWAYS *THINKING*.
JUST NOT ALWAYS ABOUT THE RIGHT THINGS.
PEPPER. YOU'RE NOT LIKE ANYONE.
THANK YOU FOR BEING IN MY LIFE.
TONY...
YOUR SOBER IS DRUNKER THAN MOST PEOPLE'S DRUNK.

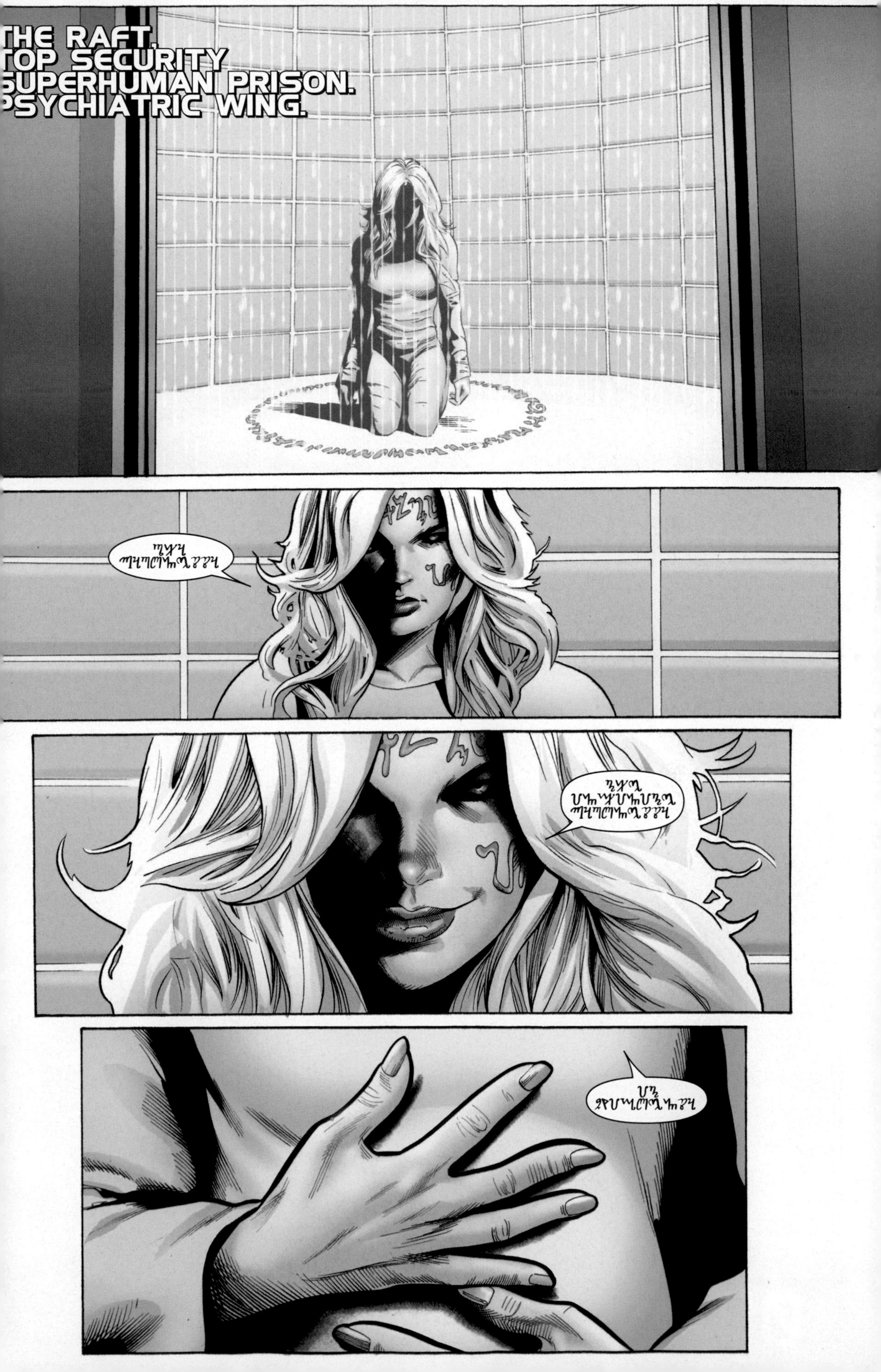
THE RAFT.
TOP SECURITY
SUPERHUMAN PRISON.
PSYCHIATRIC WING.

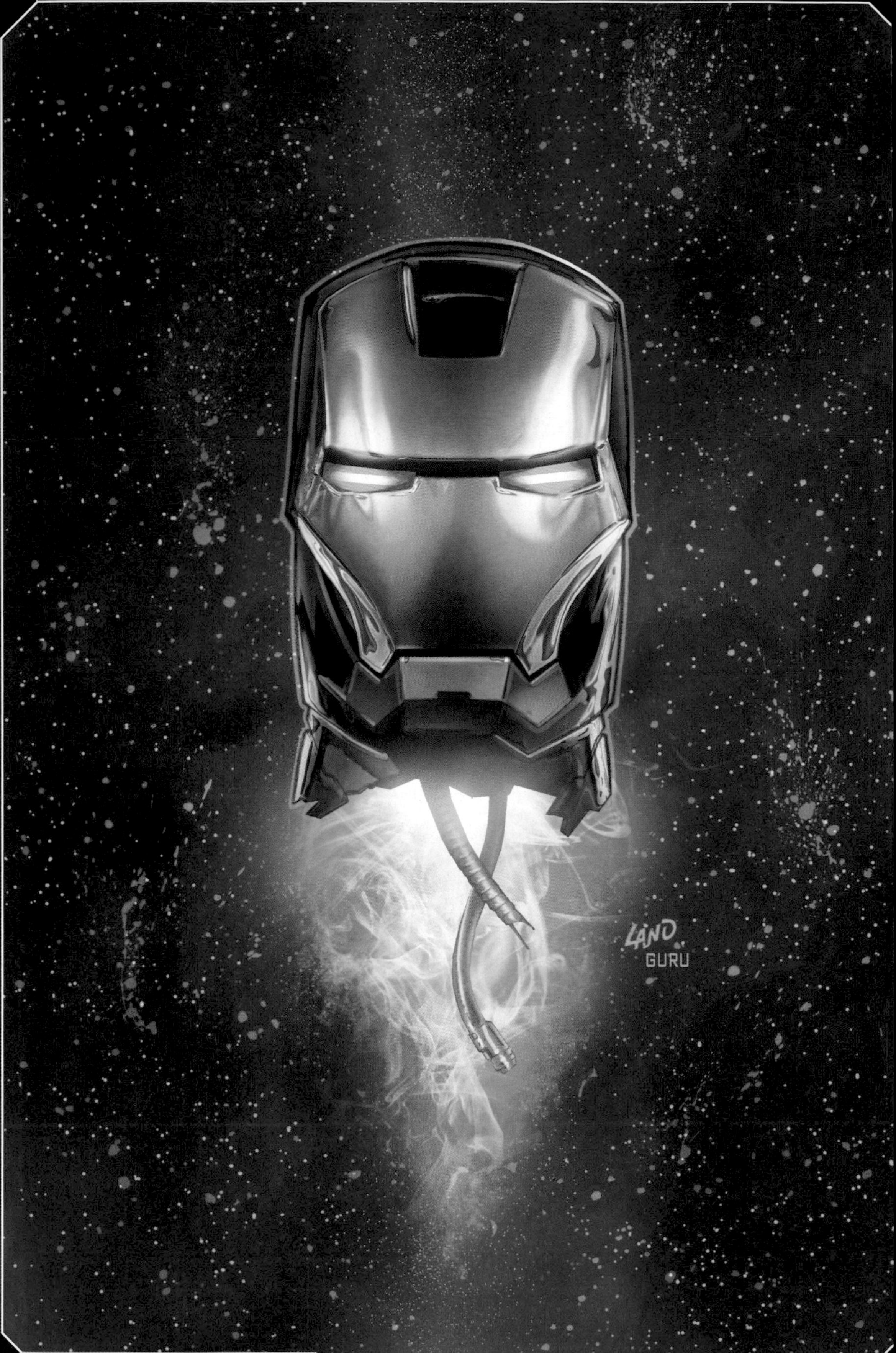
LAND
GURU

05 MEN OF THE WORLD

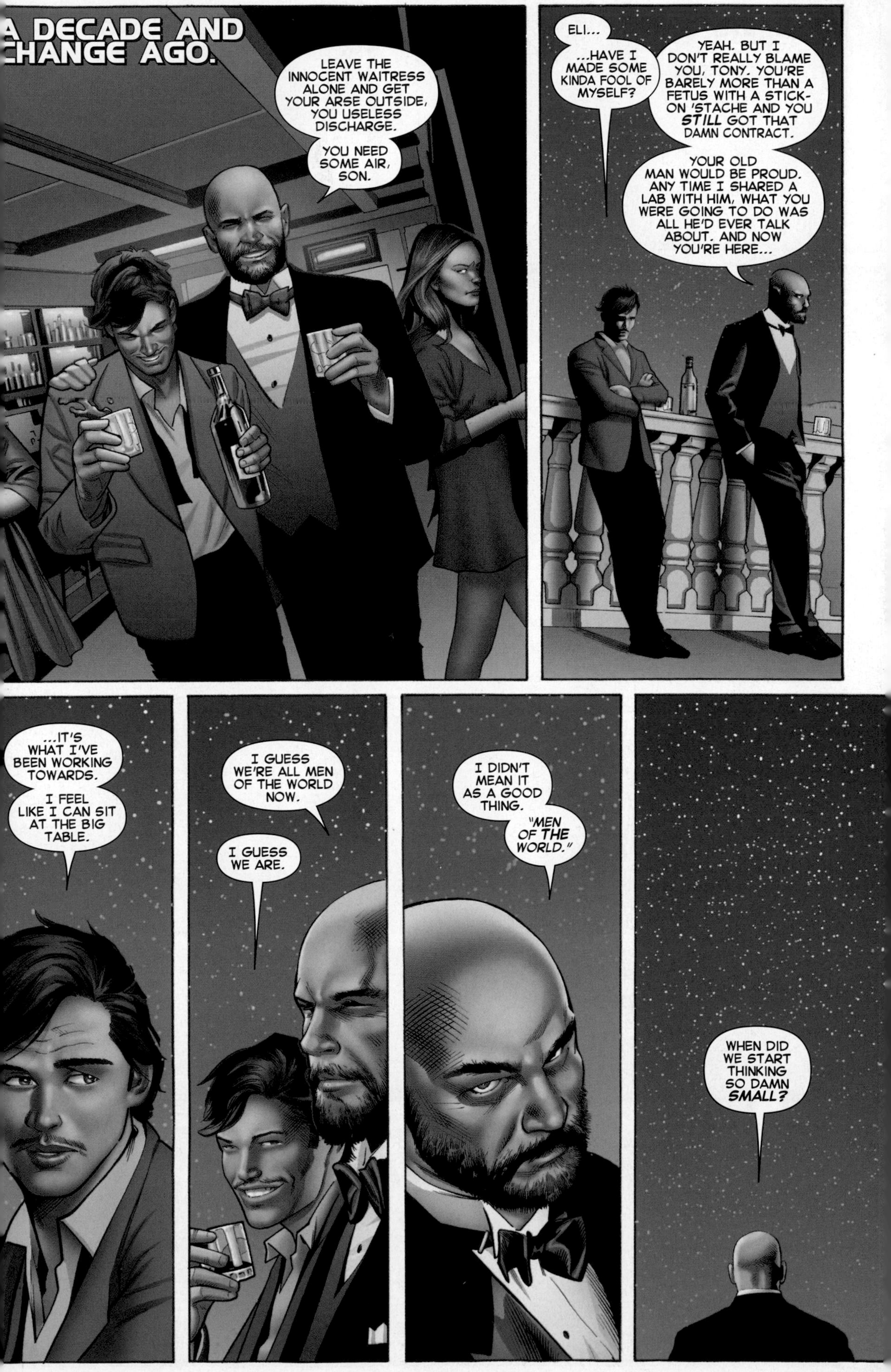
A DECADE AND CHANGE AGO.
LEAVE THE INNOCENT WAITRESS ALONE AND GET YOUR ARSE OUTSIDE, YOU USELESS DISCHARGE.
YOU NEED SOME AIR, SON.
ELI...
...HAVE I MADE SOME KINDA FOOL OF MYSELF?
YEAH. BUT I DON'T REALLY BLAME YOU, TONY. YOU'RE BARELY MORE THAN A FETUS WITH A STICK-ON 'STACHE AND YOU STILL GOT THAT DAMN CONTRACT.
YOUR OLD MAN WOULD BE PROUD. ANY TIME I SHARED A LAB WITH HIM, WHAT YOU WERE GOING TO DO WAS ALL HE'D EVER TALK ABOUT. AND NOW YOU'RE HERE...
...IT'S WHAT I'VE BEEN WORKING TOWARDS.
I FEEL LIKE I CAN SIT AT THE BIG TABLE.
I GUESS WE'RE ALL MEN OF THE WORLD NOW.
I GUESS WE ARE.
I DIDN'T MEAN IT AS A GOOD THING.
"MEN OF THE WORLD."
WHEN DID WE START THINKING SO DAMN SMALL?

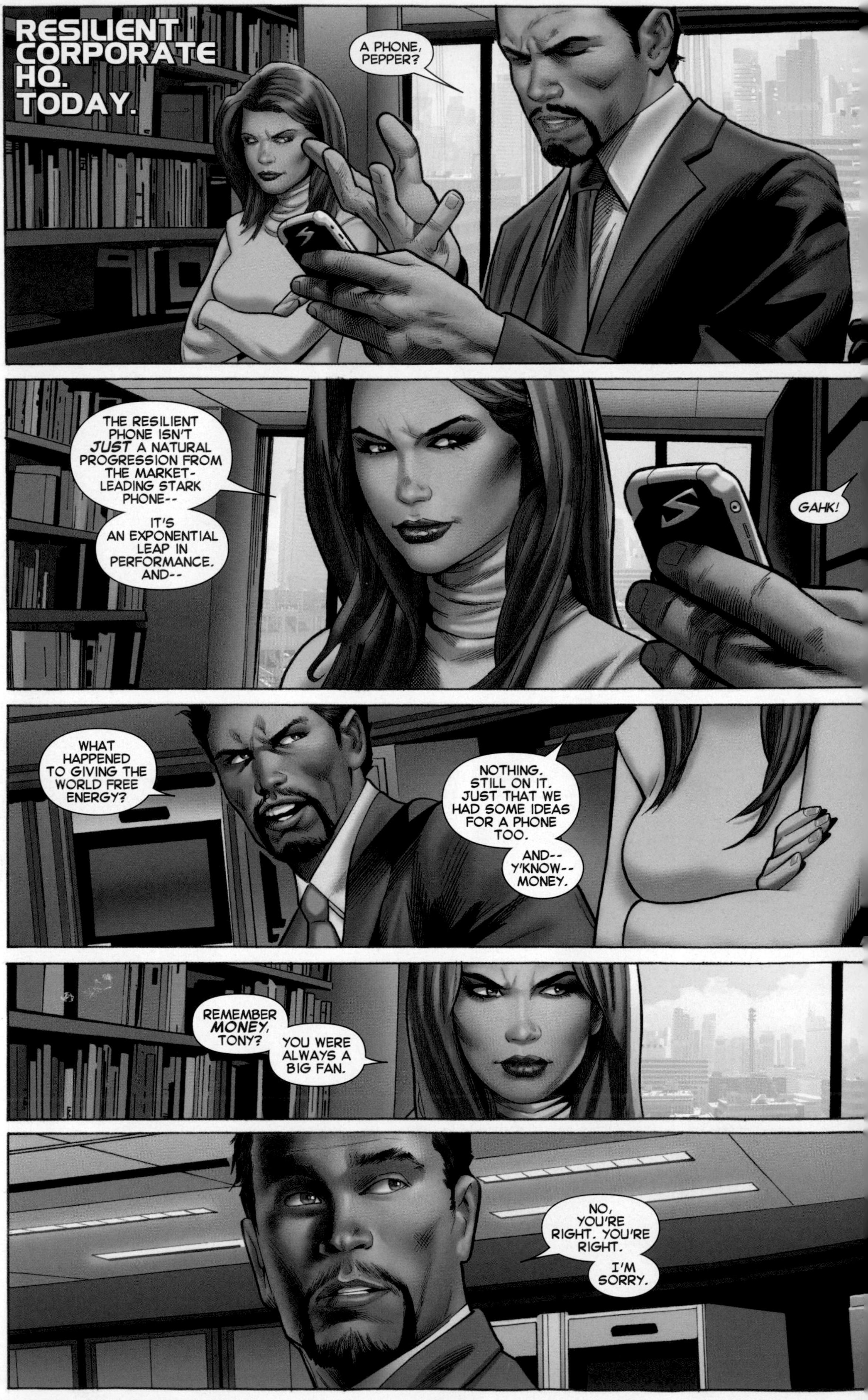
RESILIENT CORPORATE HQ. TODAY.
A PHONE, PEPPER?
THE RESILIENT PHONE ISN'T JUST A NATURAL PROGRESSION FROM THE MARKET-LEADING STARK PHONE--
IT'S AN EXPONENTIAL LEAP IN PERFORMANCE. AND--
GAHK!
WHAT HAPPENED TO GIVING THE WORLD FREE ENERGY?
NOTHING. STILL ON IT. JUST THAT WE HAD SOME IDEAS FOR A PHONE TOO.
AND-- Y'KNOW-- MONEY.
REMEMBER MONEY, TONY?
YOU WERE ALWAYS A BIG FAN.
NO, YOU'RE RIGHT. YOU'RE RIGHT.
I'M SORRY.

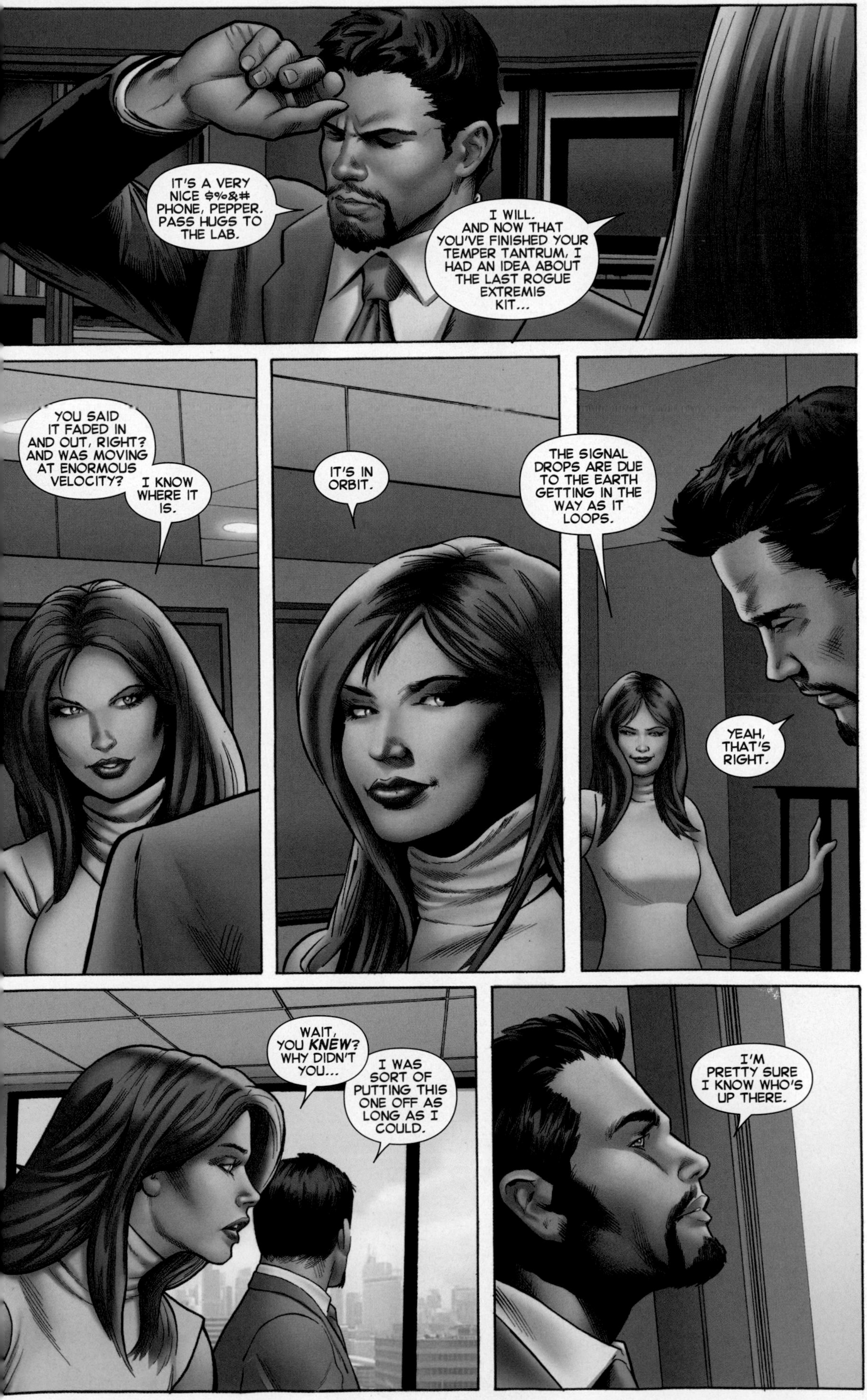
IT'S A VERY NICE $%&# PHONE, PEPPER. PASS HUGS TO THE LAB.
I WILL. AND NOW THAT YOU'VE FINISHED YOUR TEMPER TANTRUM, I HAD AN IDEA ABOUT THE LAST ROGUE EXTREMIS KIT...
YOU SAID IT FADED IN AND OUT, RIGHT? AND WAS MOVING AT ENORMOUS VELOCITY?
I KNOW WHERE IT IS.
IT'S IN ORBIT.
THE SIGNAL DROPS ARE DUE TO THE EARTH GETTING IN THE WAY AS IT LOOPS.
YEAH, THAT'S RIGHT.
WAIT, YOU *KNEW*? WHY DIDN'T YOU...
I WAS SORT OF PUTTING THIS ONE OFF AS LONG AS I COULD.
I'M PRETTY SURE I KNOW WHO'S UP THERE.

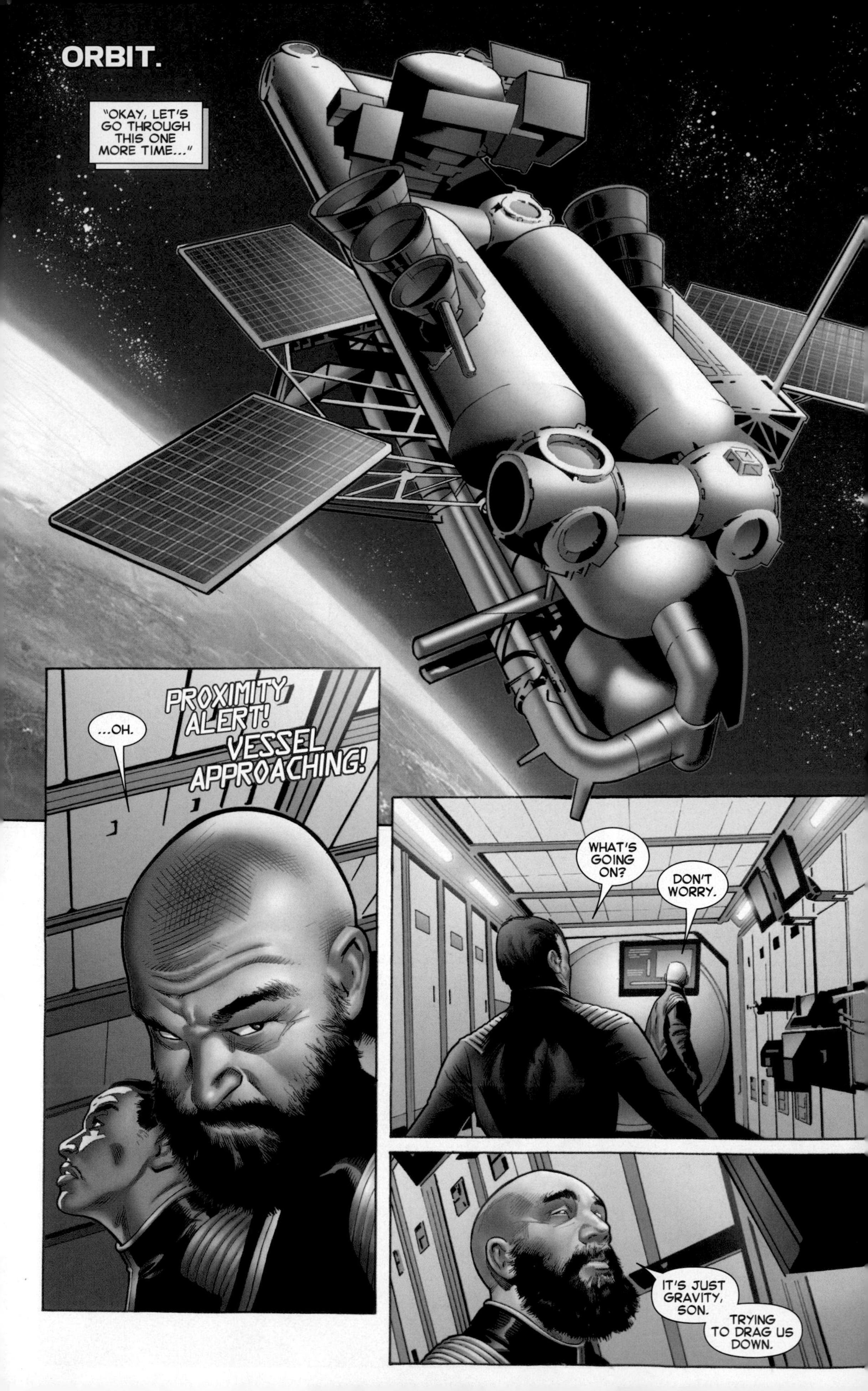
ORBIT.
"OKAY, LET'S GO THROUGH THIS ONE MORE TIME..."
PROXIMITY ALERT! VESSEL APPROACHING!
...OH.
WHAT'S GOING ON?
DON'T WORRY.
IT'S JUST GRAVITY, SON.
TRYING TO DRAG US DOWN.

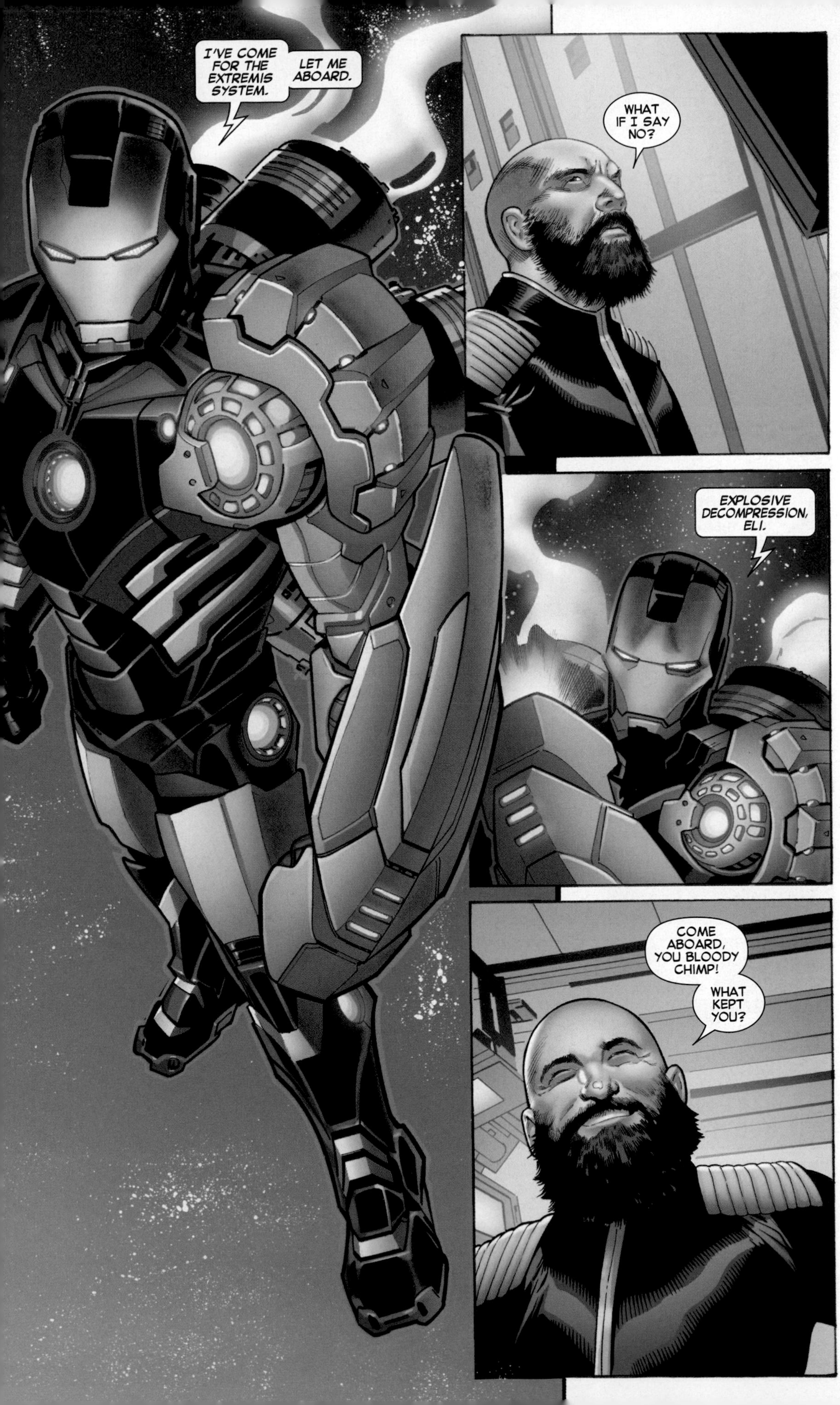
I'VE COME FOR THE EXTREMIS SYSTEM.
LET ME ABOARD.
WHAT IF I SAY NO?
EXPLOSIVE DECOMPRESSION, ELI.
COME ABOARD, YOU BLOODY CHIMP!
WHAT KEPT YOU?

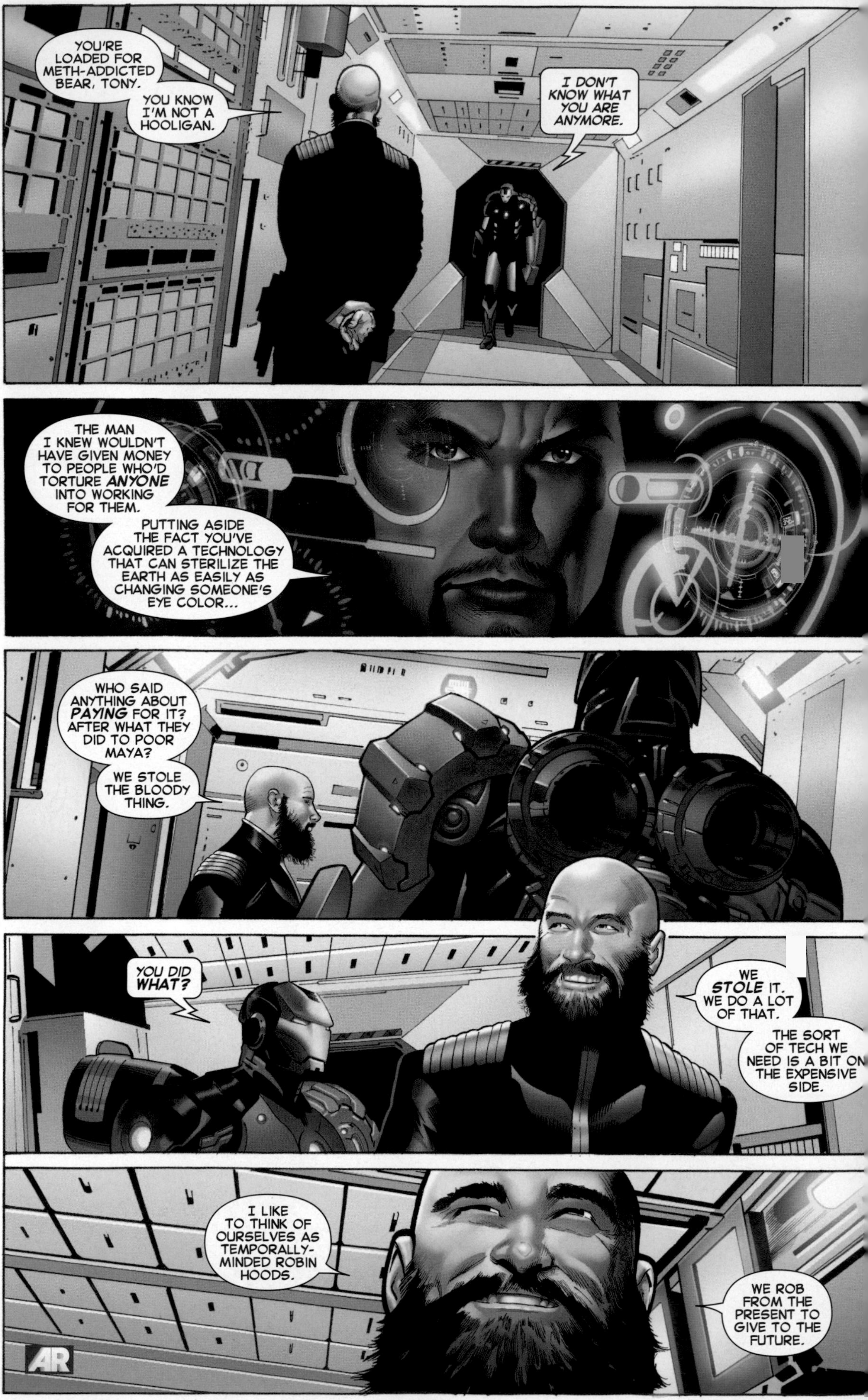
YOU'RE LOADED FOR METH-ADDICTED BEAR, TONY.
YOU KNOW I'M NOT A HOOLIGAN.
I DON'T KNOW WHAT YOU ARE ANYMORE.
THE MAN I KNEW WOULDN'T HAVE GIVEN MONEY TO PEOPLE WHO'D TORTURE ANYONE INTO WORKING FOR THEM.
PUTTING ASIDE THE FACT YOU'VE ACQUIRED A TECHNOLOGY THAT CAN STERILIZE THE EARTH AS EASILY AS CHANGING SOMEONE'S EYE COLOR...
WHO SAID ANYTHING ABOUT PAYING FOR IT? AFTER WHAT THEY DID TO POOR MAYA?
WE STOLE THE BLOODY THING.
YOU DID WHAT?
WE STOLE IT. WE DO A LOT OF THAT.
THE SORT OF TECH WE NEED IS A BIT ON THE EXPENSIVE SIDE.
I LIKE TO THINK OF OURSELVES AS TEMPORALLY-MINDED ROBIN HOODS.
WE ROB FROM THE PRESENT TO GIVE TO THE FUTURE.

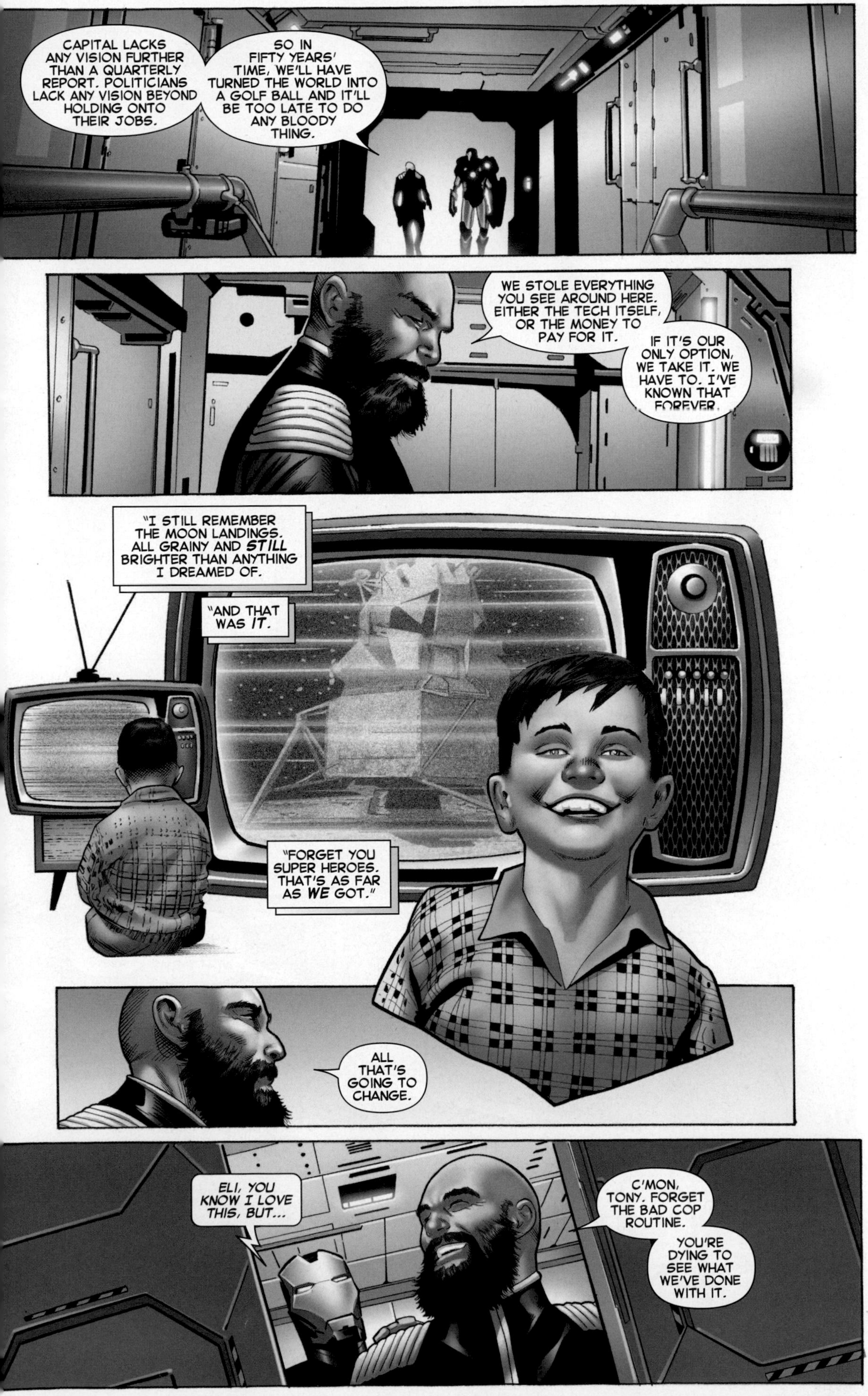
CAPITAL LACKS ANY VISION FURTHER THAN A QUARTERLY REPORT. POLITICIANS LACK ANY VISION BEYOND HOLDING ONTO THEIR JOBS.
SO IN FIFTY YEARS' TIME, WE'LL HAVE TURNED THE WORLD INTO A GOLF BALL AND IT'LL BE TOO LATE TO DO ANY BLOODY THING.
WE STOLE EVERYTHING YOU SEE AROUND HERE. EITHER THE TECH ITSELF, OR THE MONEY TO PAY FOR IT.
IF IT'S OUR ONLY OPTION, WE TAKE IT. WE HAVE TO. I'VE KNOWN THAT FOREVER.
"I STILL REMEMBER THE MOON LANDINGS. ALL GRAINY AND STILL BRIGHTER THAN ANYTHING I DREAMED OF.
"AND THAT WAS IT.
"FORGET YOU SUPER HEROES. THAT'S AS FAR AS WE GOT."
ALL THAT'S GOING TO CHANGE.
ELI, YOU KNOW I LOVE THIS, BUT...
C'MON, TONY. FORGET THE BAD COP ROUTINE.
YOU'RE DYING TO SEE WHAT WE'VE DONE WITH IT.

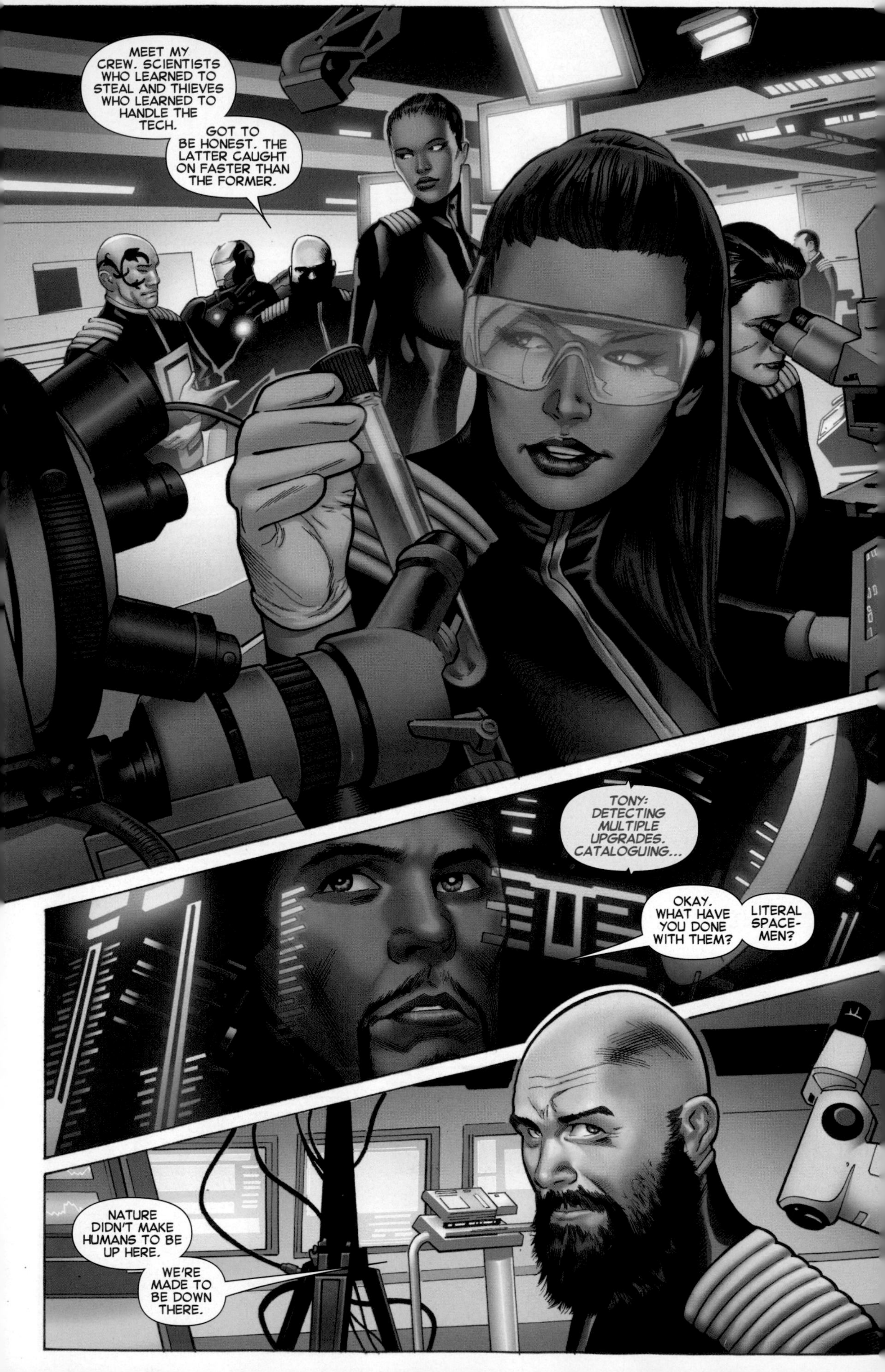
MEET MY CREW. SCIENTISTS WHO LEARNED TO STEAL AND THIEVES WHO LEARNED TO HANDLE THE TECH.
GOT TO BE HONEST. THE LATTER CAUGHT ON FASTER THAN THE FORMER.
TONY: DETECTING MULTIPLE UPGRADES. CATALOGUING...
OKAY. WHAT HAVE YOU DONE WITH THEM?
LITERAL SPACE-MEN?
NATURE DIDN'T MAKE HUMANS TO BE UP HERE.
WE'RE MADE TO BE DOWN THERE.

FORGET THE BIG THINGS LIKE RADIATION AND THE VACUUM.

WE STAY UP HERE? WE LOSE MUSCLE MASS. LOSE SKELETAL DENSITY. IN A FEW MONTHS, YOUR EYES ARE SQUISHED AND YOU'RE NOT SEEING PROPER.

WE GOT RID OF ALL THAT. RADIOACTIVE SHIELDING LACED SUBDERMALLY. UPPED STRUCTURAL INTEGRITY. REACTIVE MYOGLOBIN GENESIS. OSTEO-ENHANCEMENT. LOTS OF EXCITING NONSENSE TECH BUZZWORDS!

EVEN A PINCH OF VACUUM SURVIVABILITY.

WE WERE MADE FOR EARTH. BUT NOW, THANKS TO EXTREMIS, WE GET TO DECIDE WHAT WE WANT TO BE.

WE GET TO BE *GROWN-UPS.*

YOU'RE ALL UPGRADED NOW, SO...WHY DO YOU NEED THE KIT?

THE STANDARD DOSE IS HANDY, BUT IT'S MAINLY A BASAL STATE WE CAN TWIST WITH THE OTHER EXTREMIS MODS WE'RE WORKING ON.

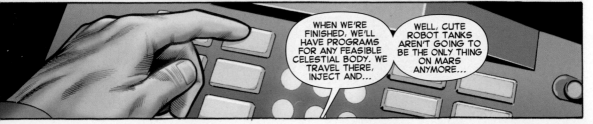

WHEN WE'RE FINISHED, WE'LL HAVE PROGRAMS FOR ANY FEASIBLE CELESTIAL BODY. WE TRAVEL THERE, INJECT AND...

WELL, CUTE ROBOT TANKS AREN'T GOING TO BE THE ONLY THING ON MARS ANYMORE...

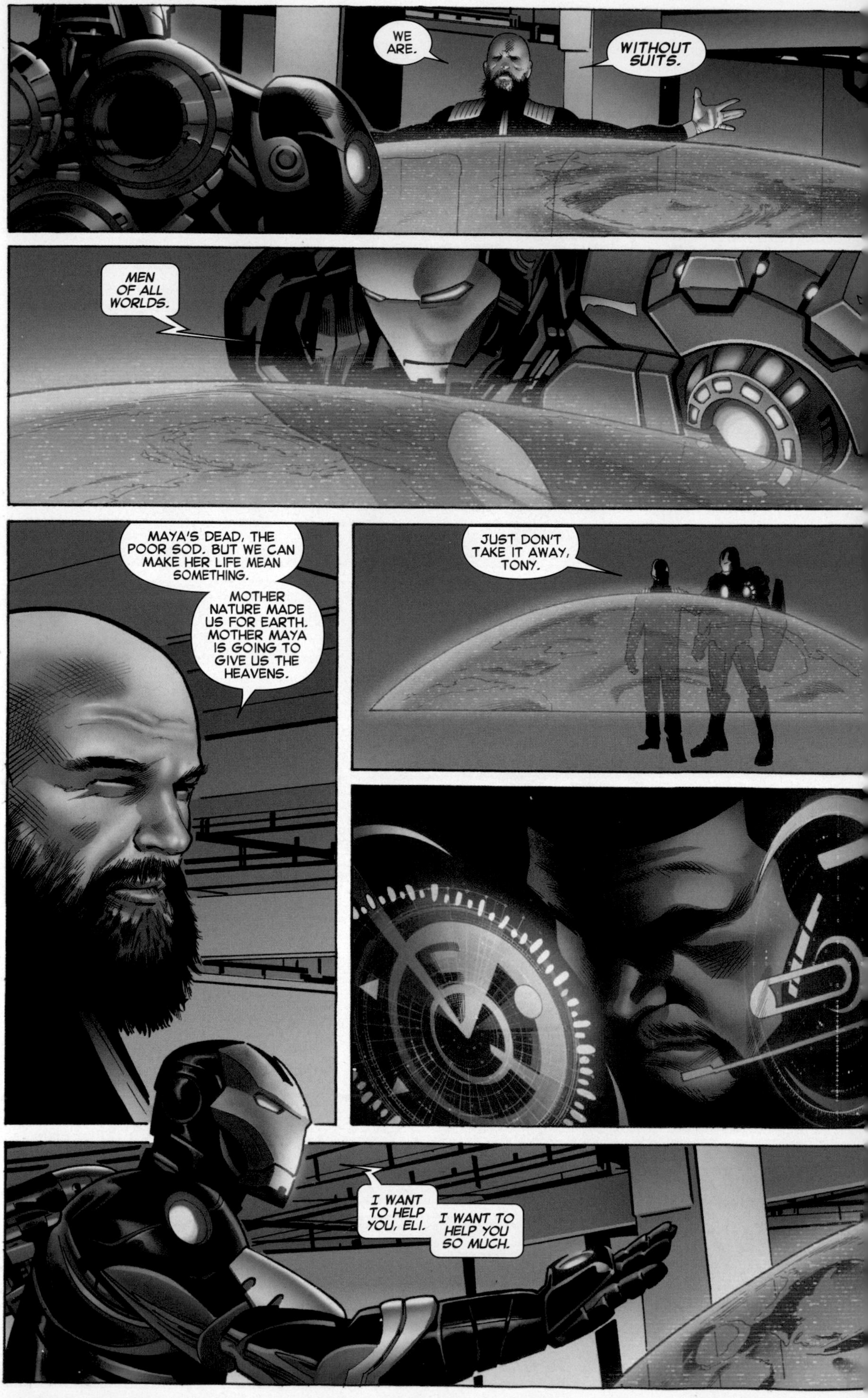

WE ARE.
WITHOUT SUITS.
MEN OF ALL WORLDS.
MAYA'S DEAD, THE POOR SOD. BUT WE CAN MAKE HER LIFE MEAN SOMETHING.
MOTHER NATURE MADE US FOR EARTH. MOTHER MAYA IS GOING TO GIVE US THE HEAVENS.
JUST DON'T TAKE IT AWAY, TONY.
I WANT TO HELP YOU, ELI.
I WANT TO HELP YOU SO MUCH.

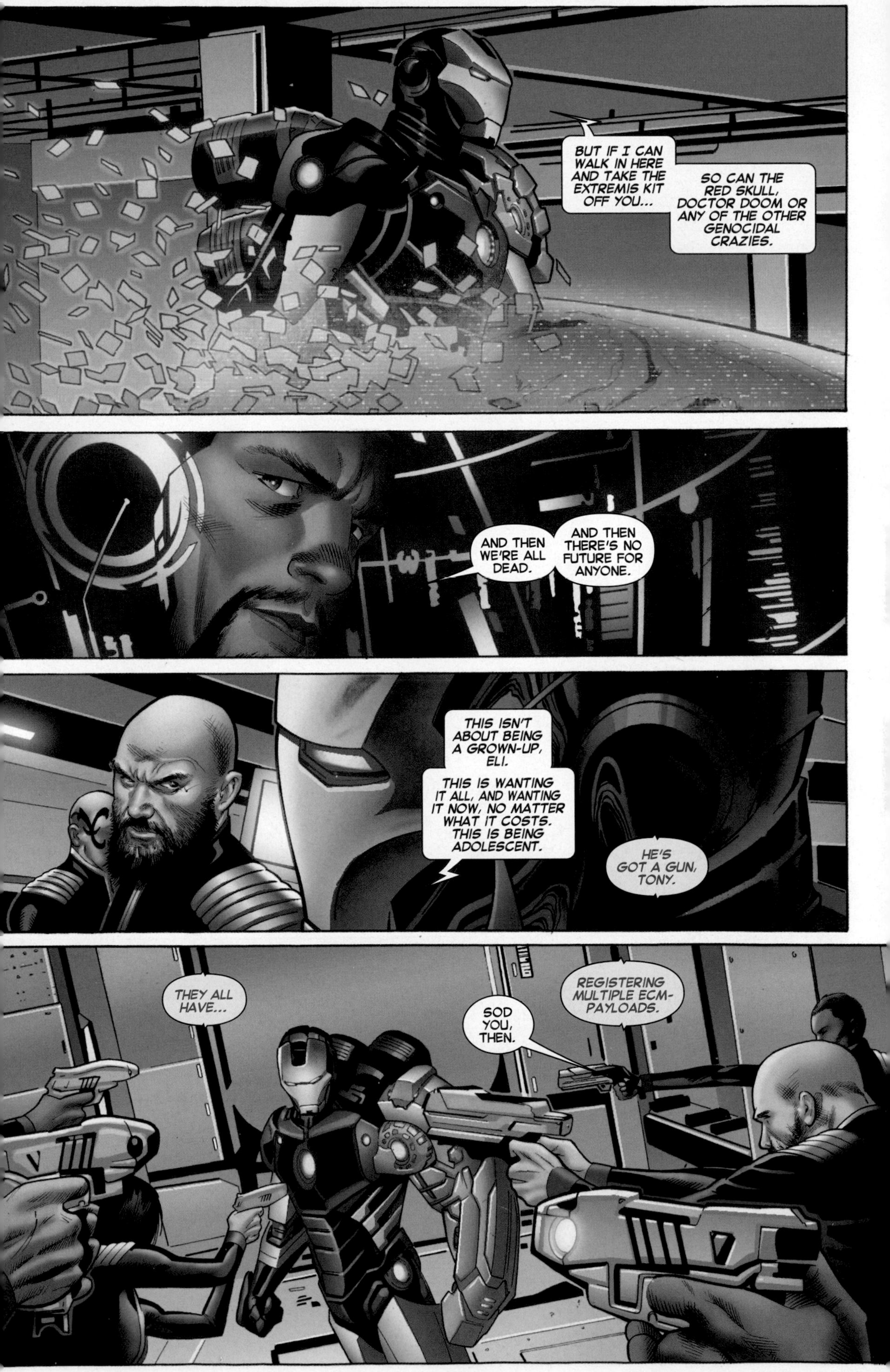
BUT IF I CAN WALK IN HERE AND TAKE THE EXTREMIS KIT OFF YOU...
SO CAN THE RED SKULL, DOCTOR DOOM OR ANY OF THE OTHER GENOCIDAL CRAZIES.
AND THEN WE'RE ALL DEAD.
AND THEN THERE'S NO FUTURE FOR ANYONE.
THIS ISN'T ABOUT BEING A GROWN-UP, ELI.
THIS IS WANTING IT ALL, AND WANTING IT NOW, NO MATTER WHAT IT COSTS. THIS IS BEING ADOLESCENT.
HE'S GOT A GUN, TONY.
THEY ALL HAVE...
SOD YOU, THEN.
REGISTERING MULTIPLE ECM-PAYLOADS.

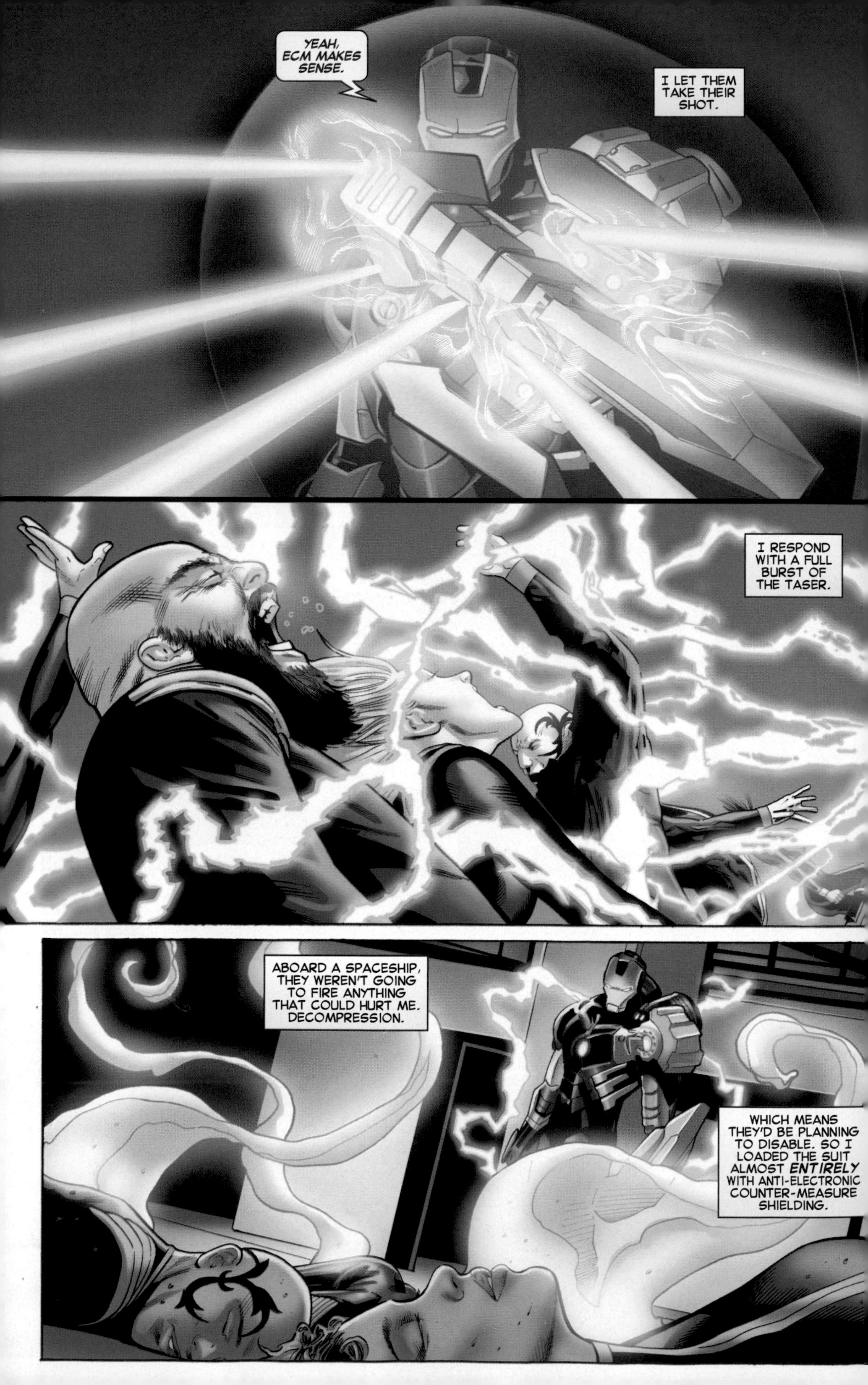
YEAH, ECM MAKES SENSE.
I LET THEM TAKE THEIR SHOT.
I RESPOND WITH A FULL BURST OF THE TASER.
ABOARD A SPACESHIP, THEY WEREN'T GOING TO FIRE ANYTHING THAT COULD HURT ME. DECOMPRESSION.
WHICH MEANS THEY'D BE PLANNING TO DISABLE. SO I LOADED THE SUIT ALMOST ENTIRELY WITH ANTI-ELECTRONIC COUNTER-MEASURE SHIELDING.

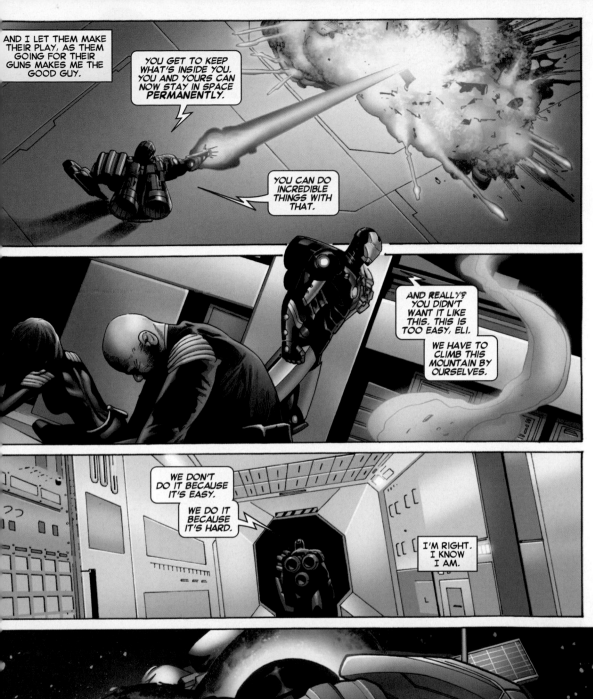

AND I LET THEM MAKE THEIR PLAY, AS THEM GOING FOR THEIR GUNS MAKES ME THE GOOD GUY.

YOU GET TO KEEP WHAT'S INSIDE YOU. YOU AND YOURS CAN NOW STAY IN SPACE PERMANENTLY.

YOU CAN DO INCREDIBLE THINGS WITH THAT.

AND REALLY? YOU DIDN'T WANT IT LIKE THIS. THIS IS TOO EASY, ELI.

WE HAVE TO CLIMB THIS MOUNTAIN BY OURSELVES.

WE DON'T DO IT BECAUSE IT'S EASY.

WE DO IT BECAUSE IT'S HARD.

I'M RIGHT. I KNOW I AM.

STILL NOT FEELING LIKE THE GOOD GUY.

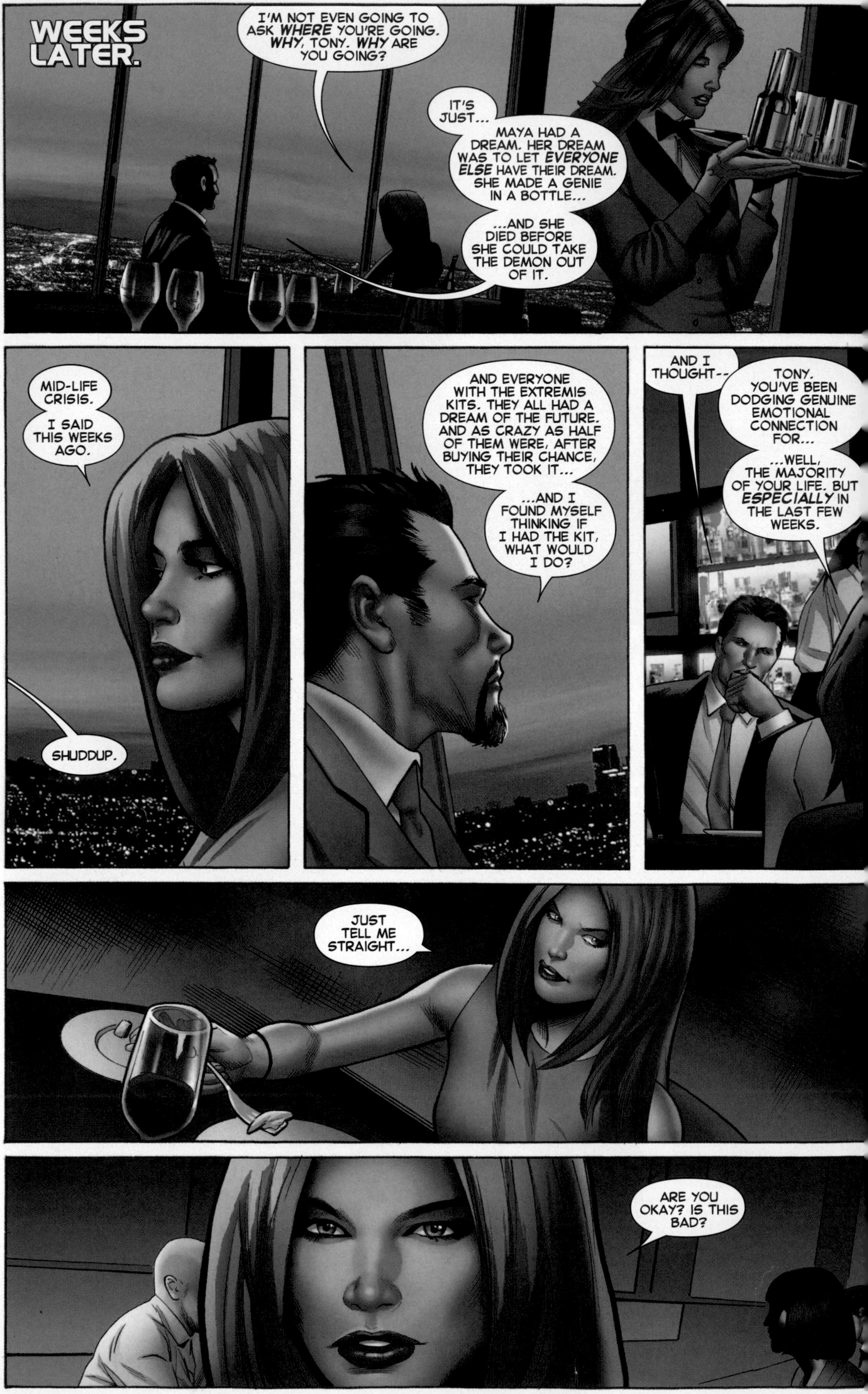
WEEKS LATER.
I'M NOT EVEN GOING TO ASK WHERE YOU'RE GOING. WHY, TONY. WHY ARE YOU GOING?
IT'S JUST...
MAYA HAD A DREAM. HER DREAM WAS TO LET EVERYONE ELSE HAVE THEIR DREAM. SHE MADE A GENIE IN A BOTTLE...
...AND SHE DIED BEFORE SHE COULD TAKE THE DEMON OUT OF IT.
MID-LIFE CRISIS.
I SAID THIS WEEKS AGO.
SHUDDUP.
AND EVERYONE WITH THE EXTREMIS KITS. THEY ALL HAD A DREAM OF THE FUTURE. AND AS CRAZY AS HALF OF THEM WERE, AFTER BUYING THEIR CHANCE, THEY TOOK IT...
...AND I FOUND MYSELF THINKING IF I HAD THE KIT, WHAT WOULD I DO?
AND I THOUGHT--
TONY. YOU'VE BEEN DODGING GENUINE EMOTIONAL CONNECTION FOR...
...WELL, THE MAJORITY OF YOUR LIFE. BUT ESPECIALLY IN THE LAST FEW WEEKS.
JUST TELL ME STRAIGHT...
ARE YOU OKAY? IS THIS BAD?

NO, THE OPPOSITE. IT'S GOOD.

IT'S ALL GOOD.

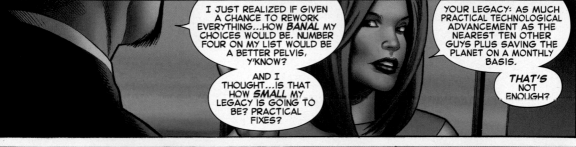

I JUST REALIZED IF GIVEN A CHANCE TO REWORK EVERYTHING...HOW *BANAL* MY CHOICES WOULD BE. NUMBER FOUR ON MY LIST WOULD BE A BETTER PELVIS, Y'KNOW?

AND I THOUGHT...IS THAT HOW *SMALL* MY LEGACY IS GOING TO BE? PRACTICAL FIXES?

YOUR LEGACY: AS MUCH PRACTICAL TECHNOLOGICAL ADVANCEMENT AS THE NEAREST TEN OTHER GUYS PLUS SAVING THE PLANET ON A MONTHLY BASIS.

THAT'S NOT ENOUGH?

IF IT'S LESS THAN I *COULD* DO, YEAH, IT'S NOT ENOUGH.

I NEED TO BE *INSPIRED.* I NEED TO THINK *BIGGER.* SO I NEED TO FIND A WAY TO BE *INSPIRED* IN A *BIGGER* WAY. AND THAT'S WHY I HAVE TO GO...

EVEN WHEN YOU'RE HAVING YOUR MOMENT OF HUMILITY, YOU'RE THE BIGGEST EGOMANIAC ON EARTH.

WELL, THIS IS A SOLUTION TO HALF OF THAT TOO...

TONY. GET THE HELL OUT OF HERE.

AND COME HOME SAFE.

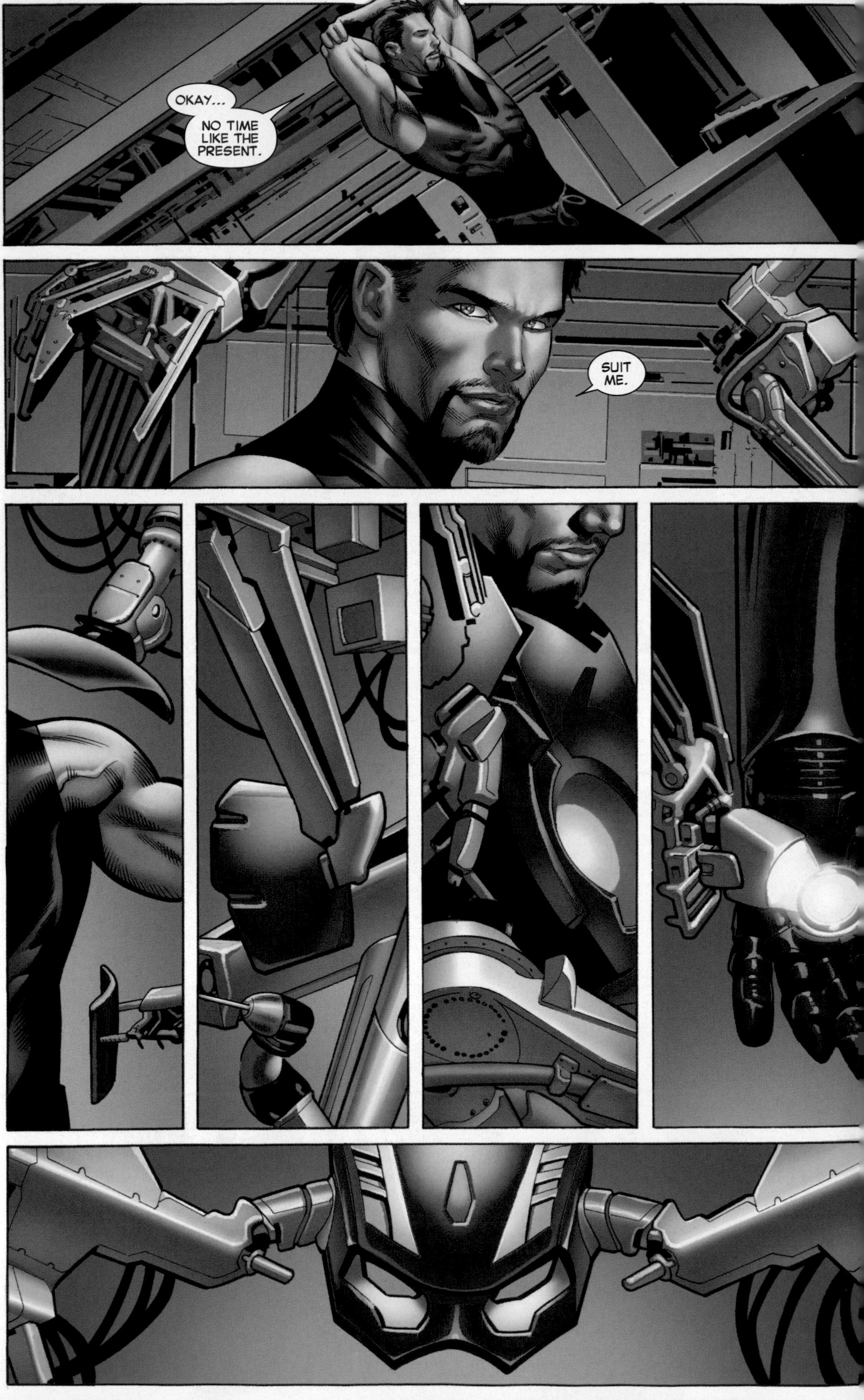
OKAY...
NO TIME LIKE THE PRESENT.
SUIT ME.

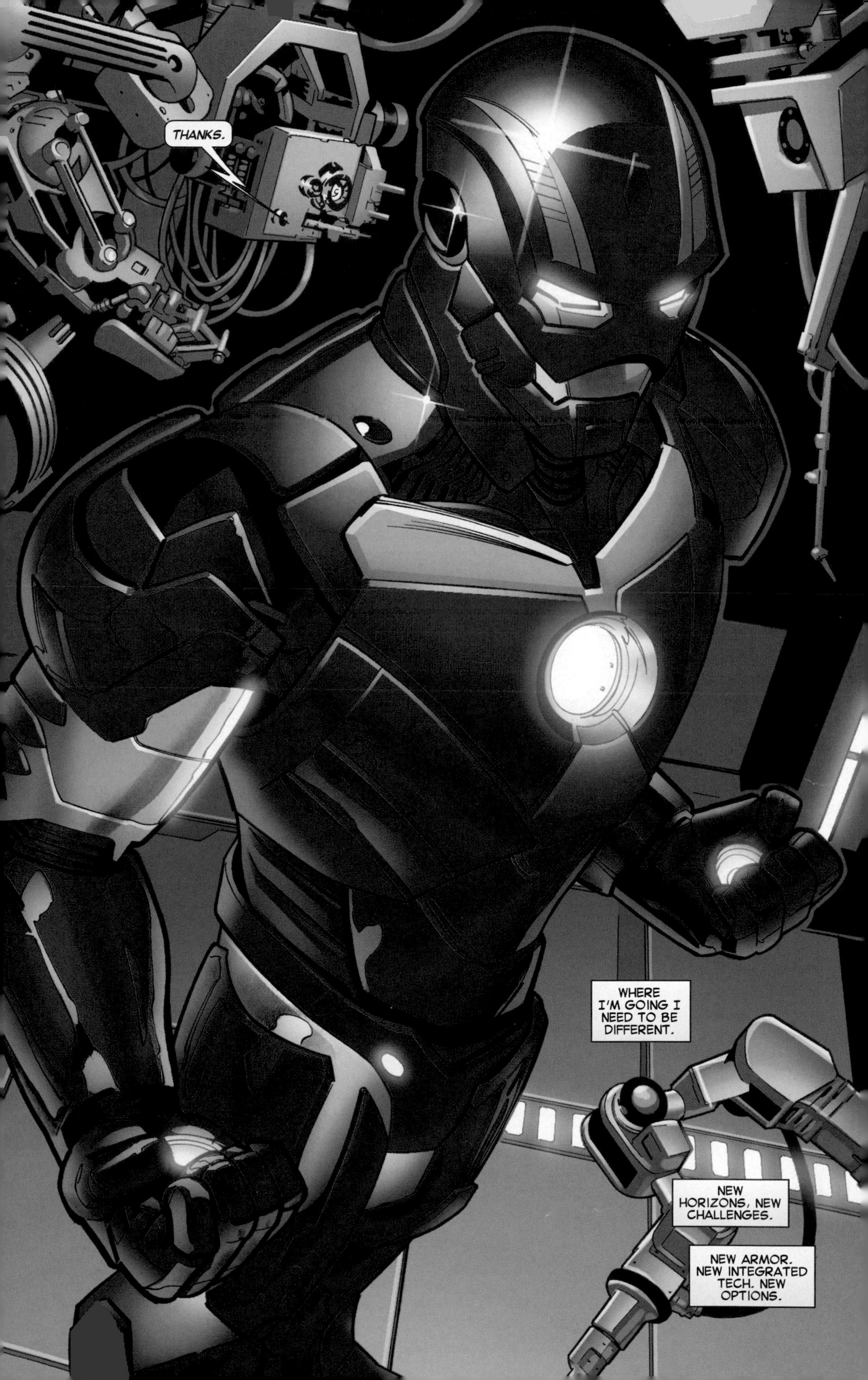
THANKS.
WHERE I'M GOING I NEED TO BE DIFFERENT.
NEW HORIZONS, NEW CHALLENGES.
NEW ARMOR. NEW INTEGRATED TECH. NEW OPTIONS.

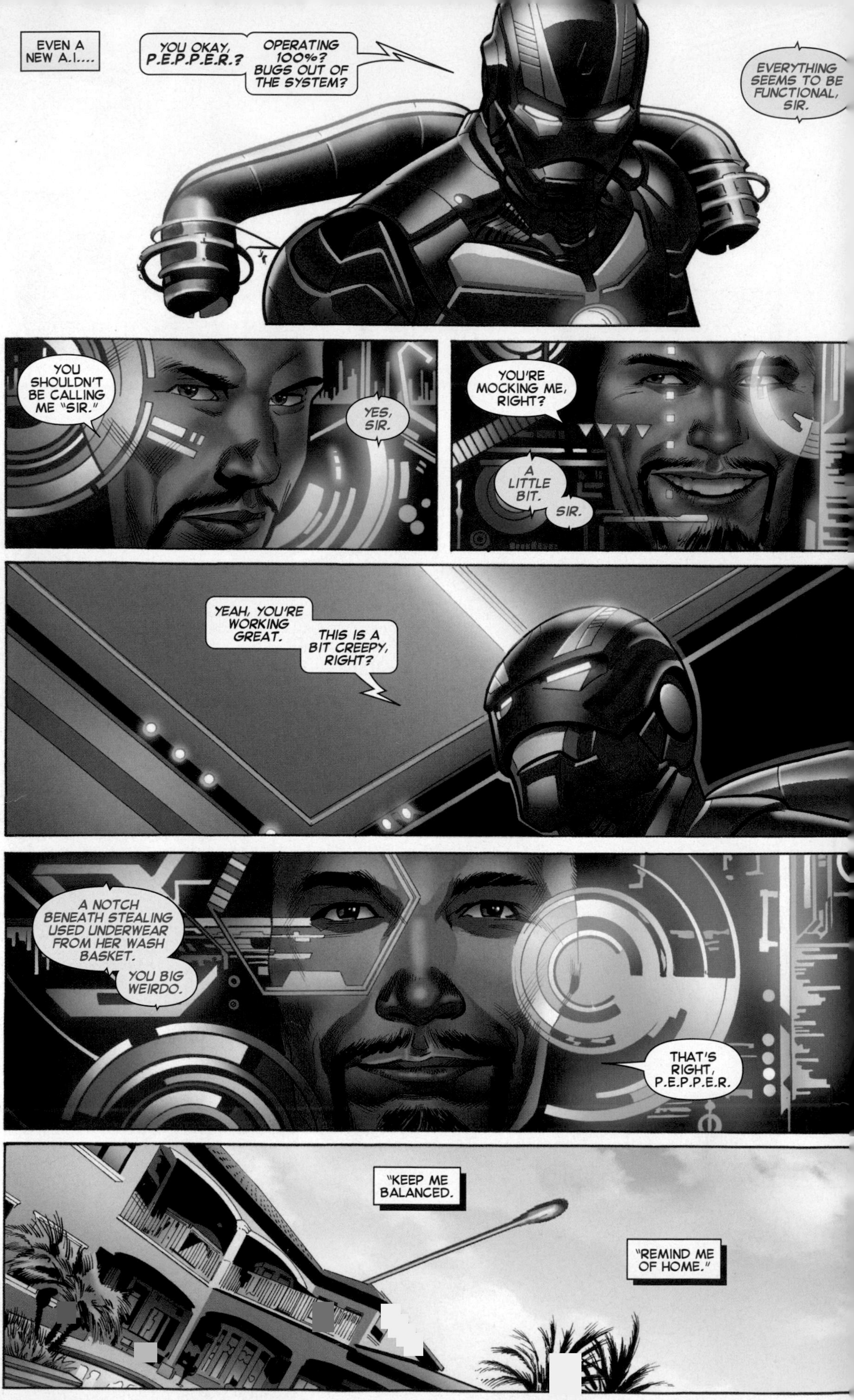
EVEN A NEW A.I....
YOU OKAY, P.E.P.P.E.R.?
OPERATING 100%? BUGS OUT OF THE SYSTEM?
EVERYTHING SEEMS TO BE FUNCTIONAL, SIR.
YOU SHOULDN'T BE CALLING ME "SIR."
YES, SIR.
YOU'RE MOCKING ME, RIGHT?
A LITTLE BIT.
SIR.
YEAH, YOU'RE WORKING GREAT.
THIS IS A BIT CREEPY, RIGHT?
A NOTCH BENEATH STEALING USED UNDERWEAR FROM HER WASH BASKET.
YOU BIG WEIRDO.
THAT'S RIGHT, P.E.P.P.E.R.
"KEEP ME BALANCED.
"REMIND ME OF HOME."

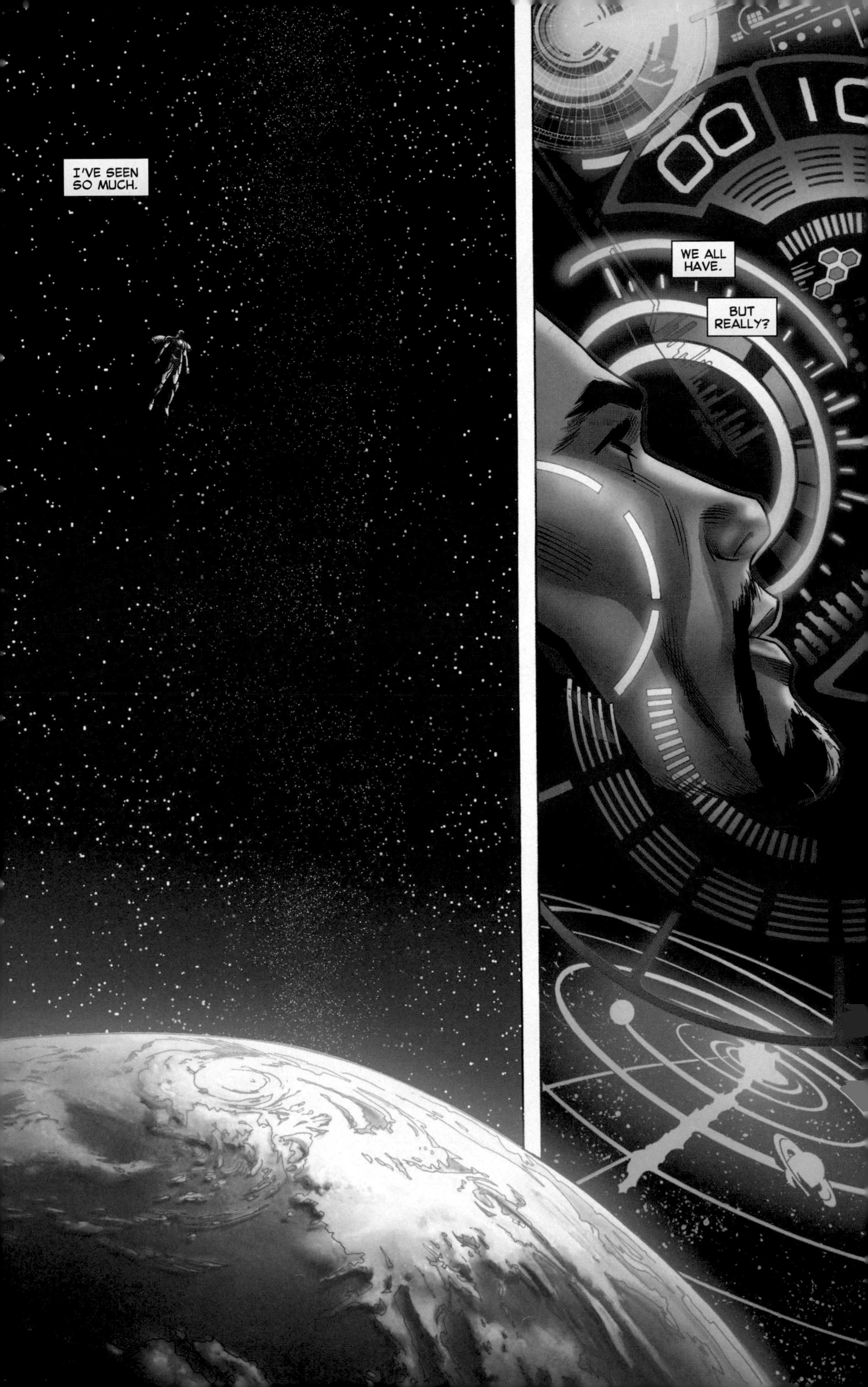
I'VE SEEN SO MUCH.
WE ALL HAVE.
BUT REALLY?

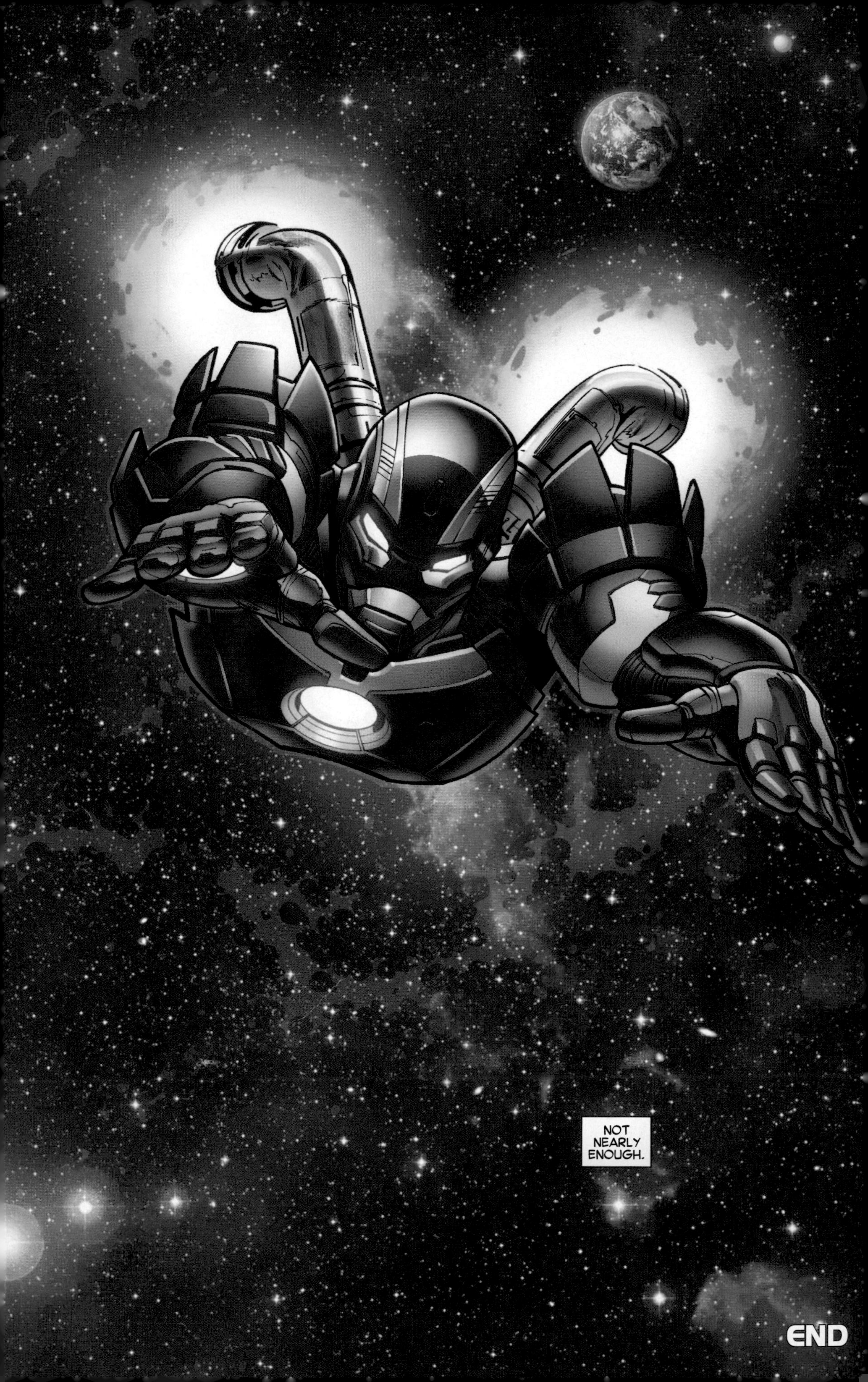
NOT NEARLY ENOUGH.
END

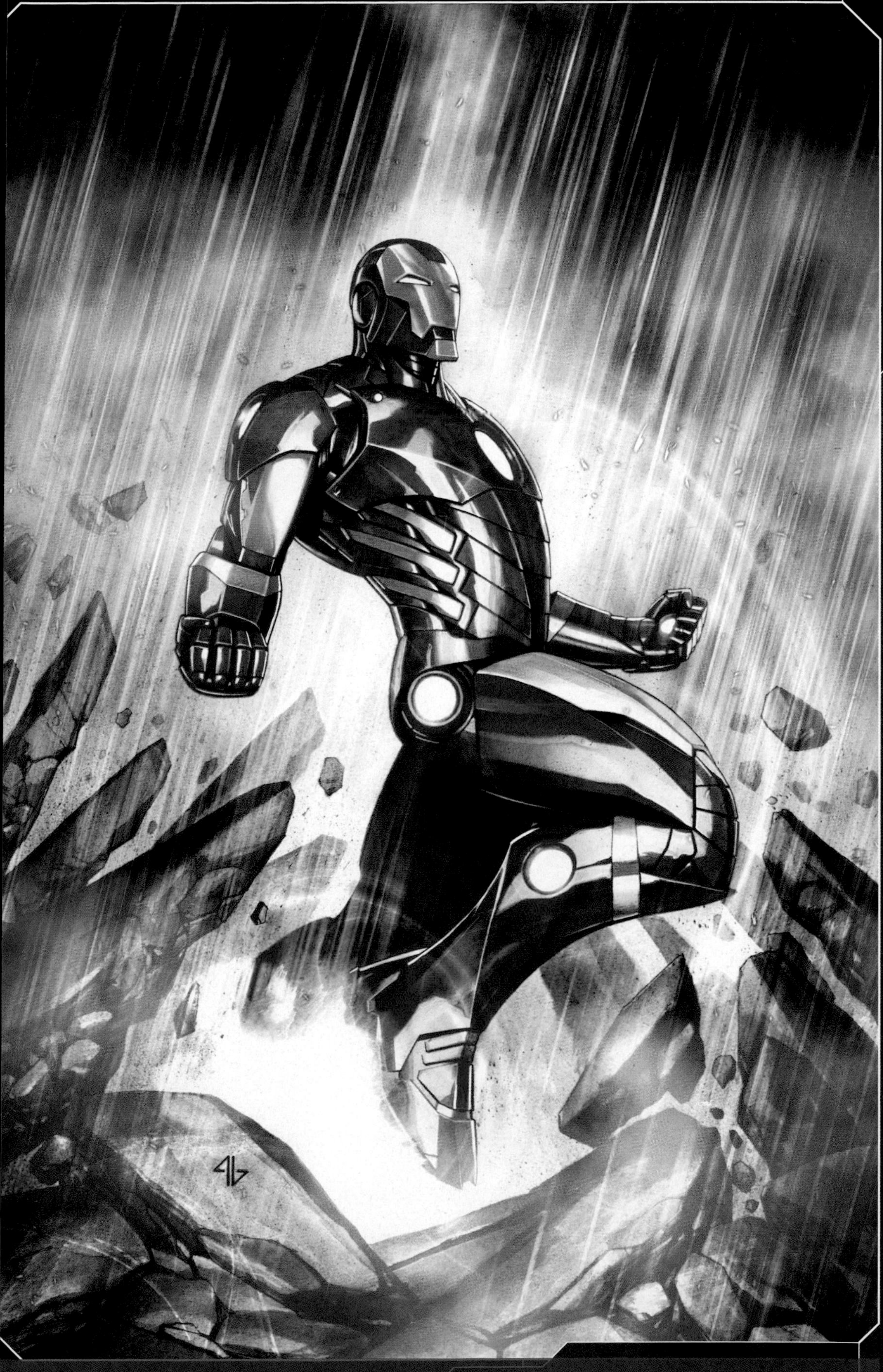

#1 VARIANT BY ADI GRANOV

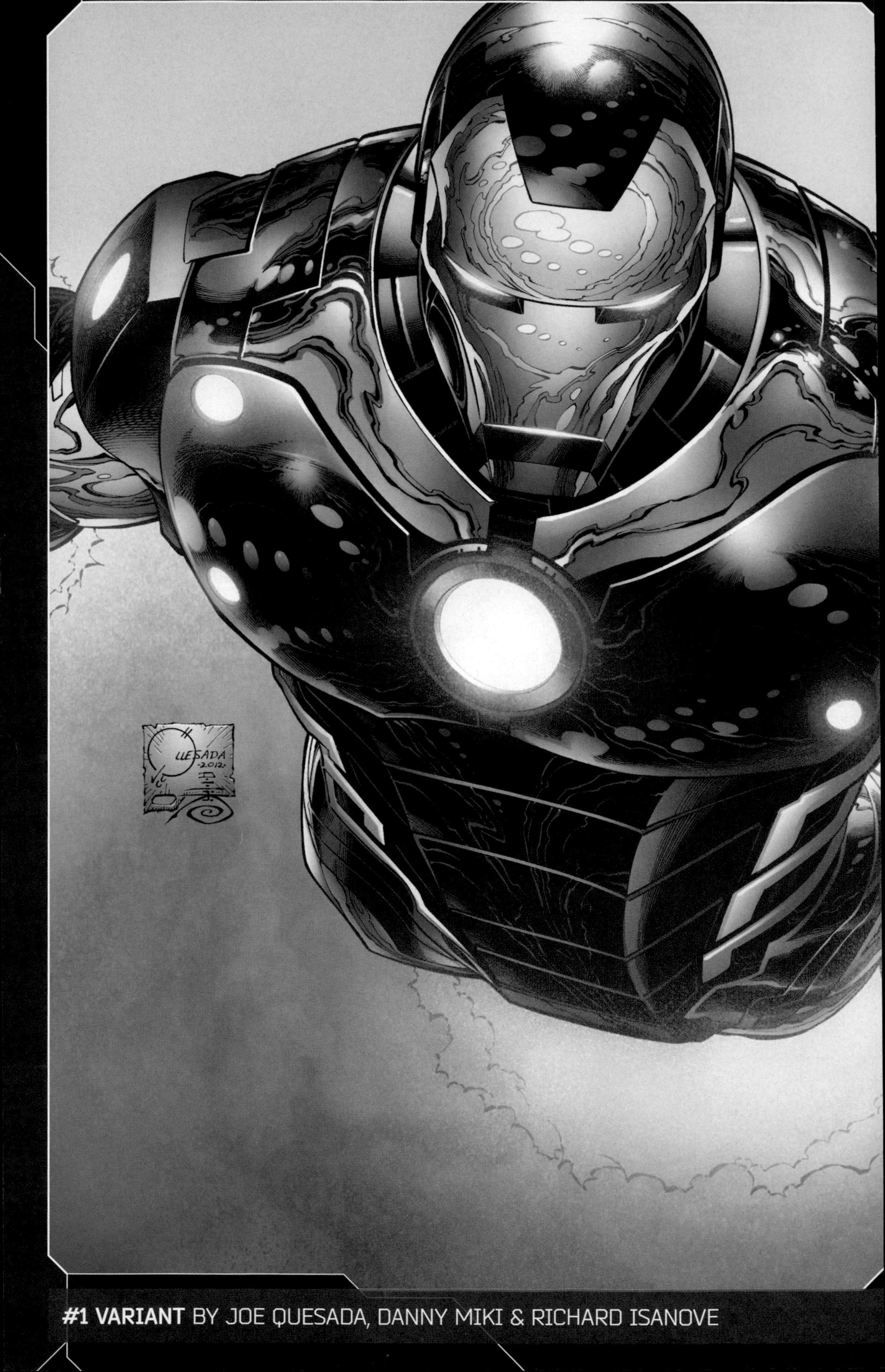

#1 VARIANT BY JOE QUESADA, DANNY MIKI & RICHARD ISANOVE

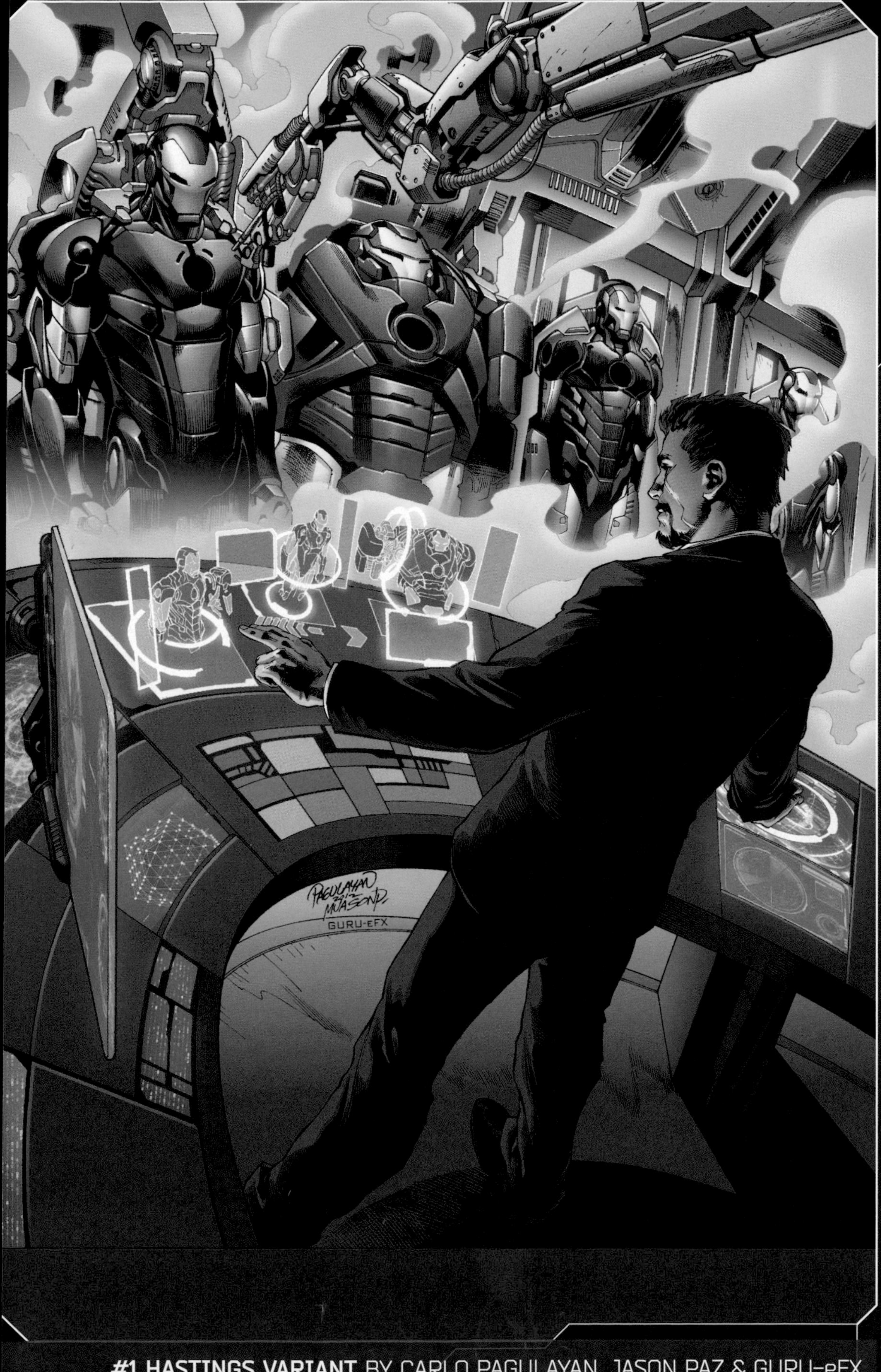
GURU-eFX

#1 HASTINGS VARIANT BY CARLO PAGULAYAN, JASON PAZ & GURU-eFX

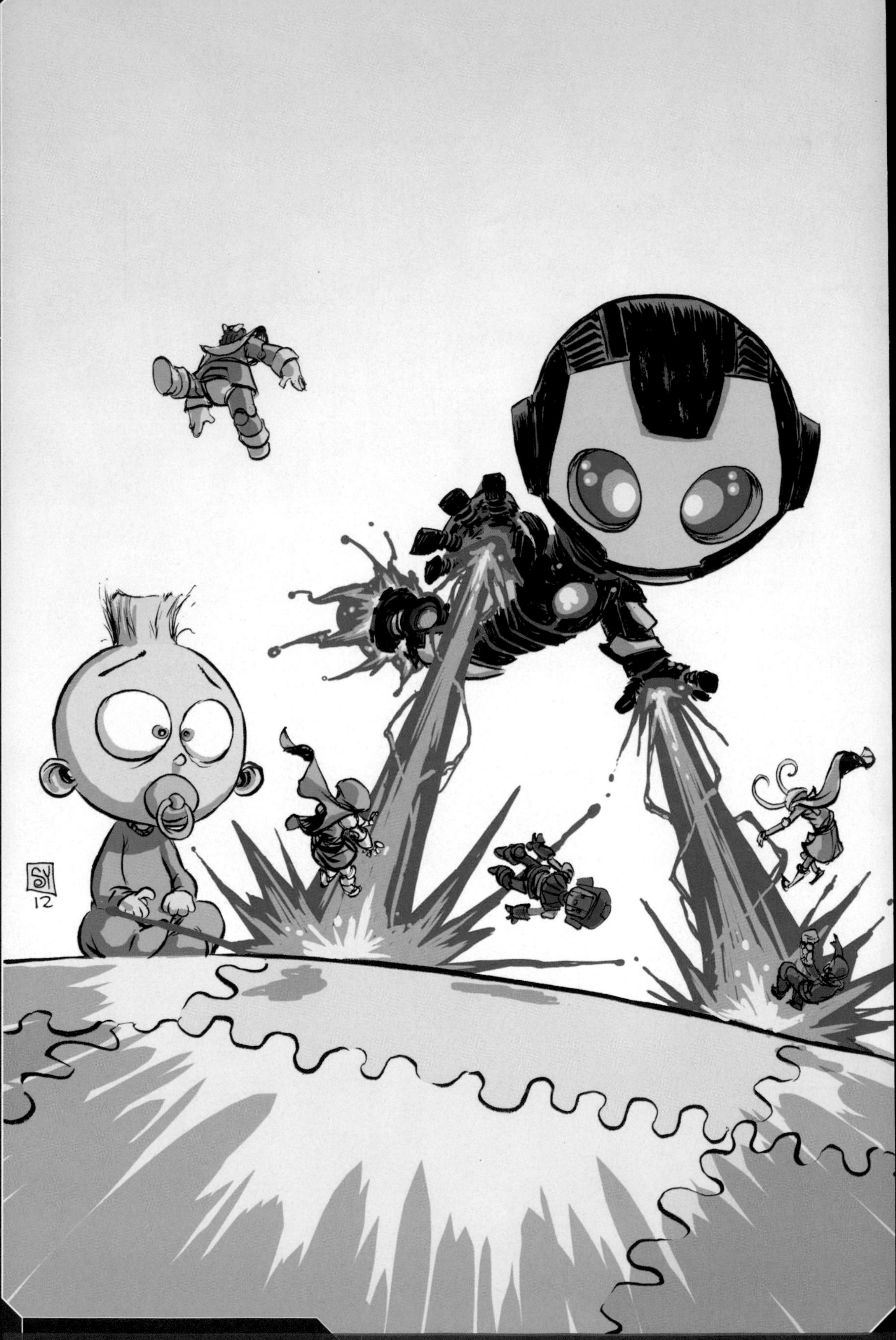
SY
12

#1 YOUNG VARIANT BY SKOTTIE YOUNG

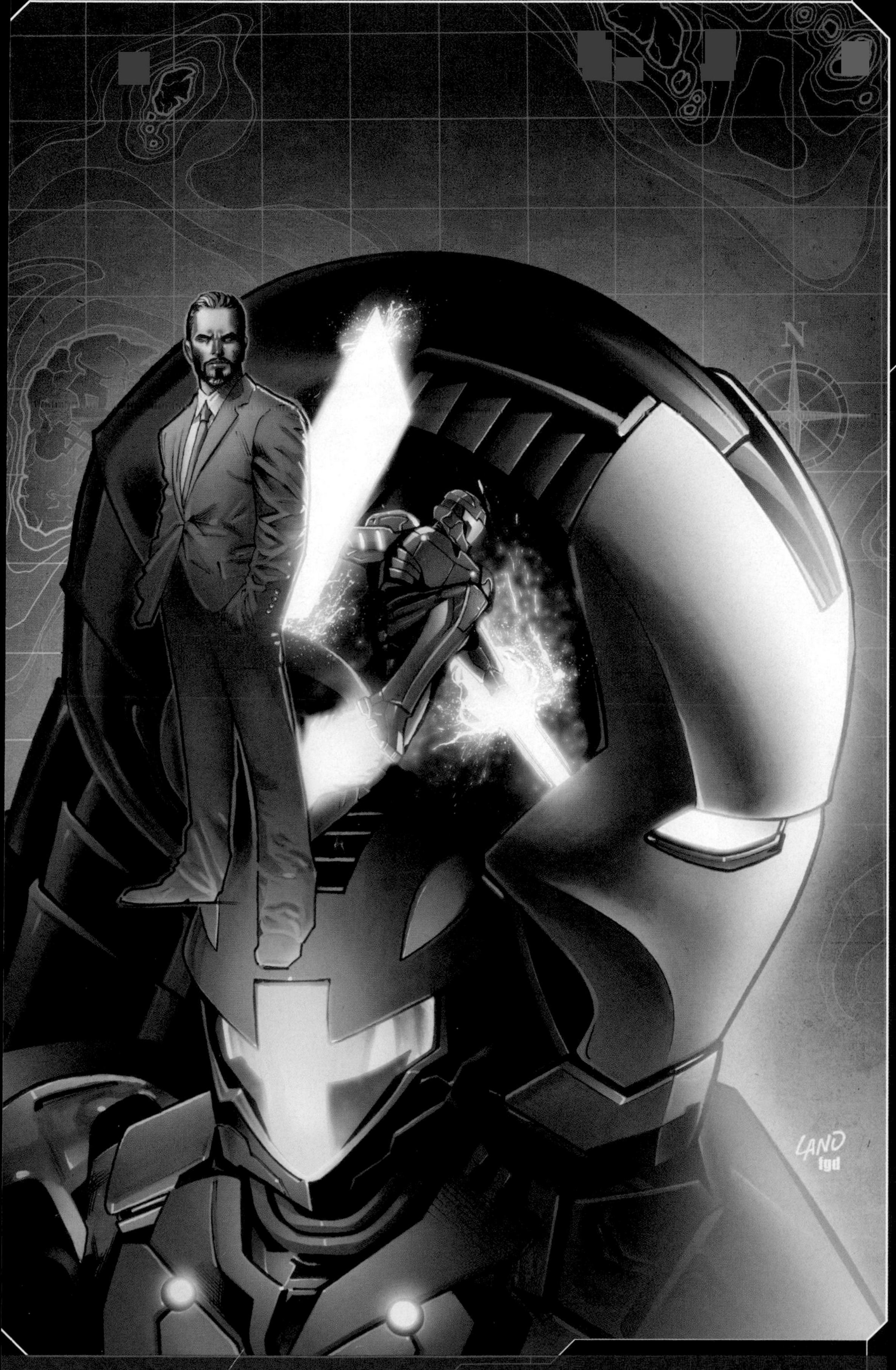
N
LAND
fgd

#2 VARIANT BY GREG LAND & FRANK D'ARMATA

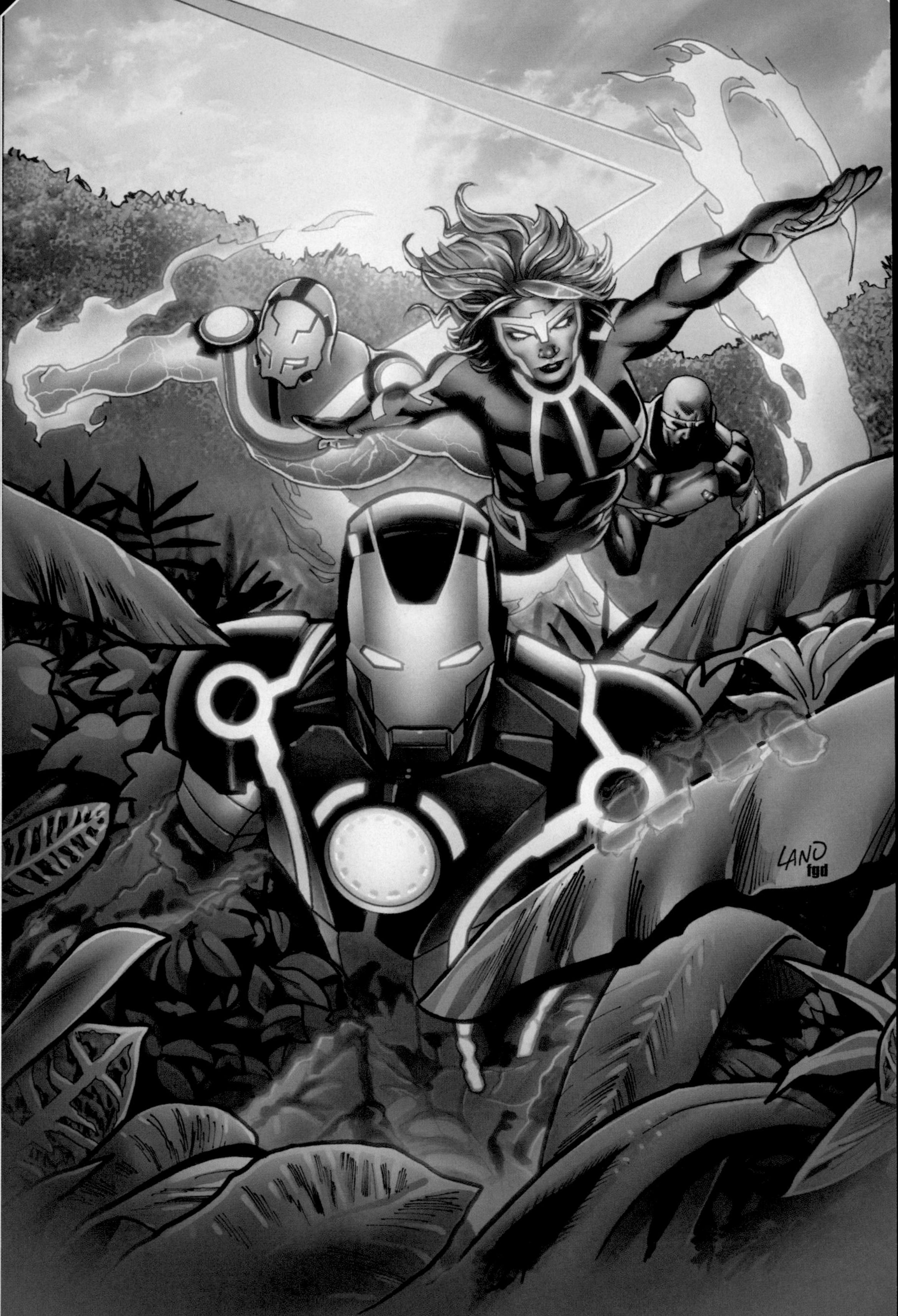
LAND
fgd

#3 VARIANT BY GREG LAND & FRANK D'ARMATA

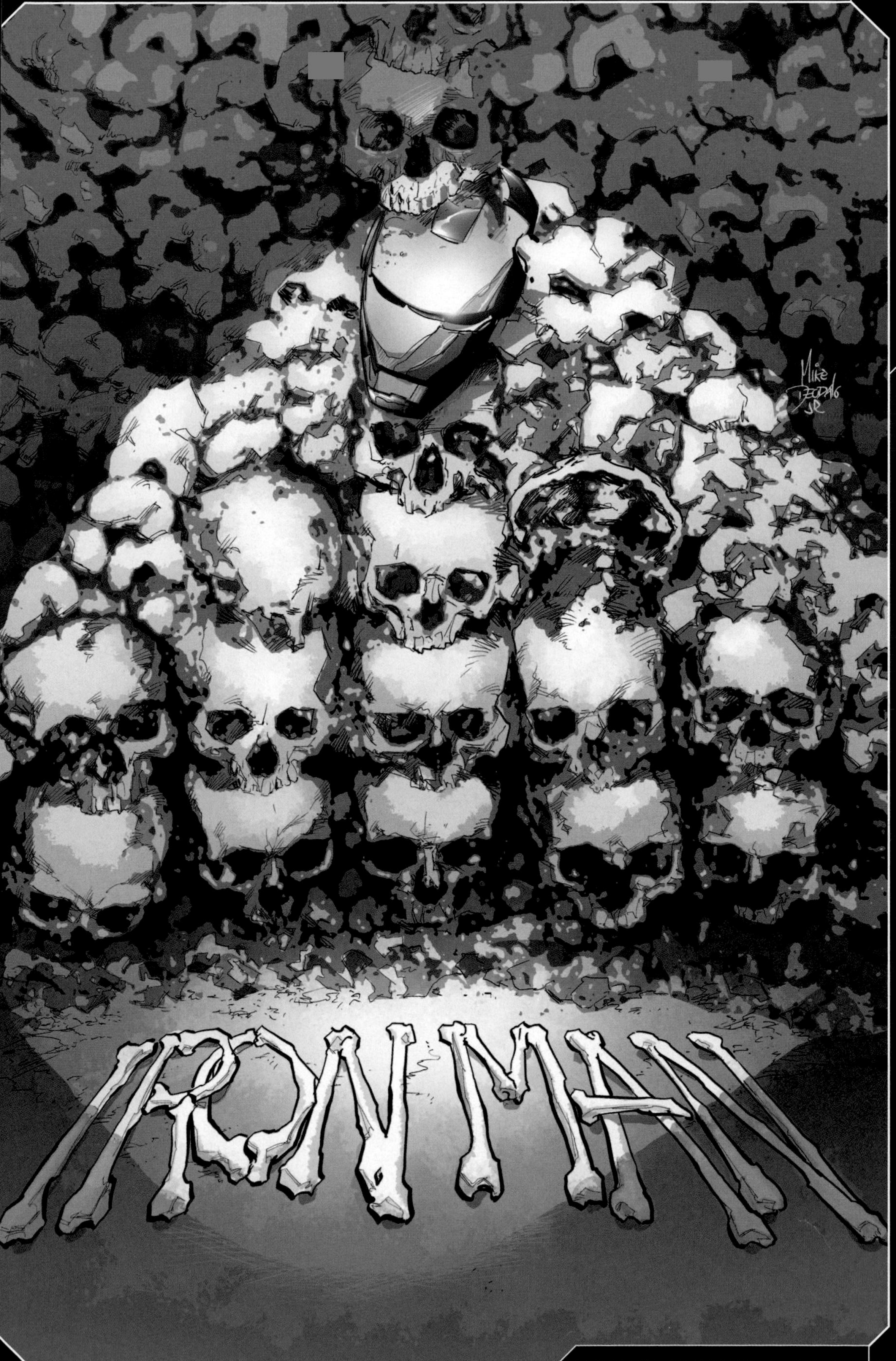
IRON MAN

#4 VARIANT BY MIKE DEODATO & RAIN BEREDO

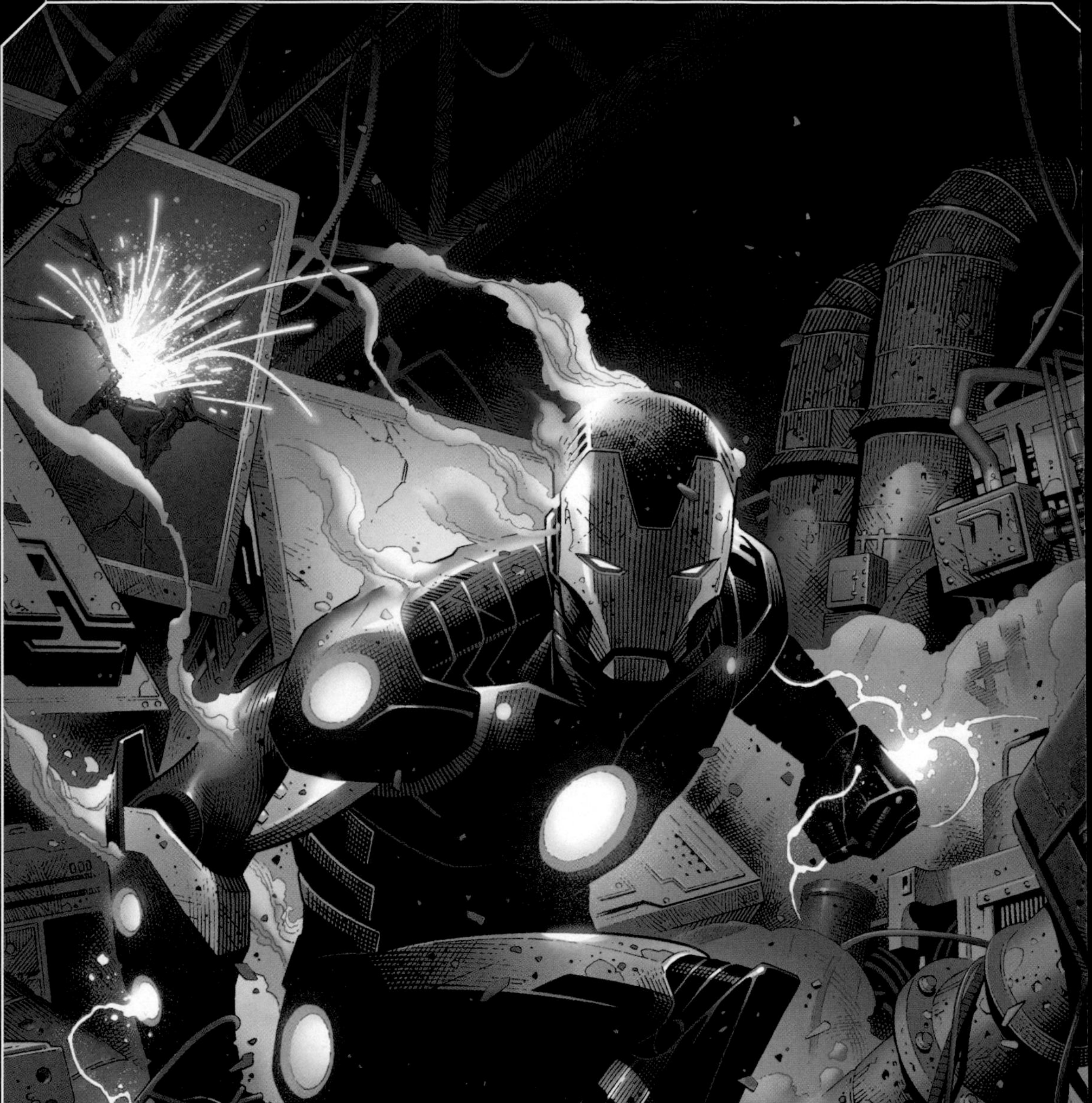

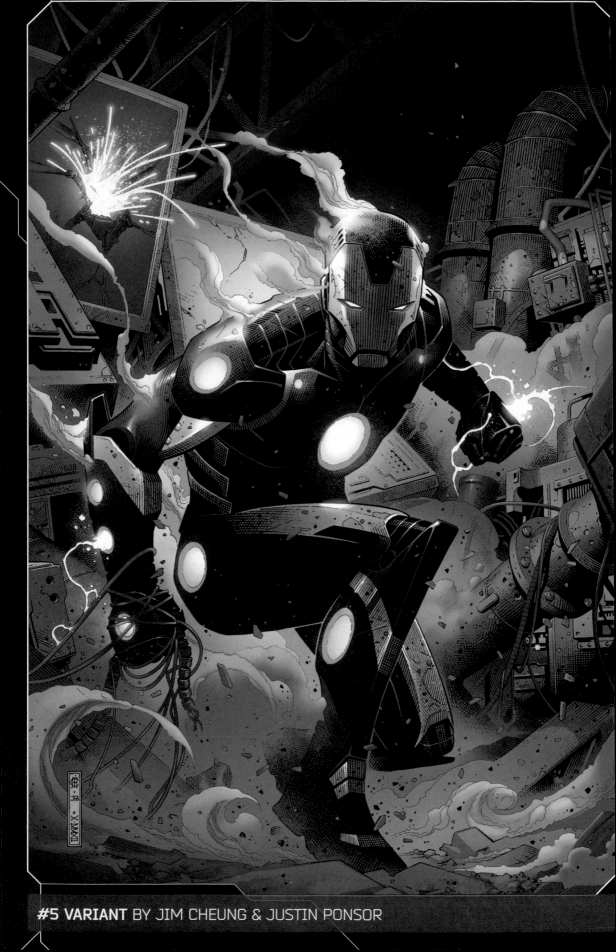

#5 VARIANT BY JIM CHEUNG & JUSTIN PONSOR

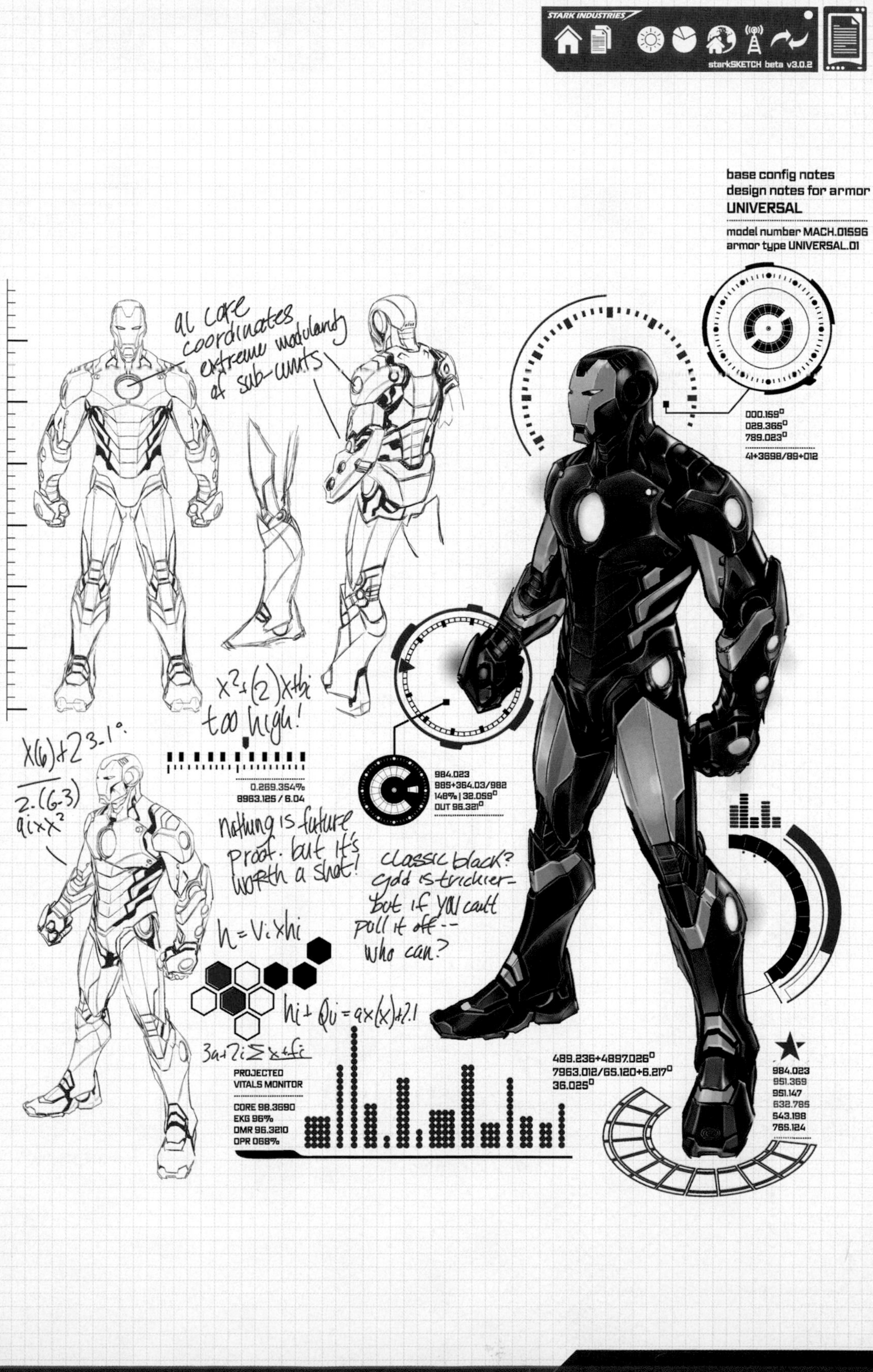
STARK INDUSTRIES
starkSKETCH beta v3.0.2
base config notes
design notes for armor
UNIVERSAL
model number MACH.01596
armor type UNIVERSAL.01
ai core coordinates extreme modularity of sub-units
000.159°
029.365°
789.023°
41+3698/89+012
x²+(2)x+hi
too high!
X(6)+2³-1°
2.(6-3)
9ixx²
0.269.354%
8963.125 / 6.04
984.023
985+364.03/982
148% | 32.059°
OUT 96.321°
nothing is future proof. but it's worth a shot!
classic black? gold is trickier- but if you can't pull it off -- who can?
h=Vixhi
hi+Qi=9x(x)+2.1
3a+2iΣx+fi
PROJECTED
VITALS MONITOR
CORE 96.3690
EKG 96%
DMR 96.3210
DPR 068%
489.236+4897.026°
7963.012/65.120+6.217°
36.025°
984.023
951.369
951.147
632.785
543.198
765.124

#1 ARMOR DESIGN VARIANT BY CARLO PAGULAYAN & JARED FLETCHER

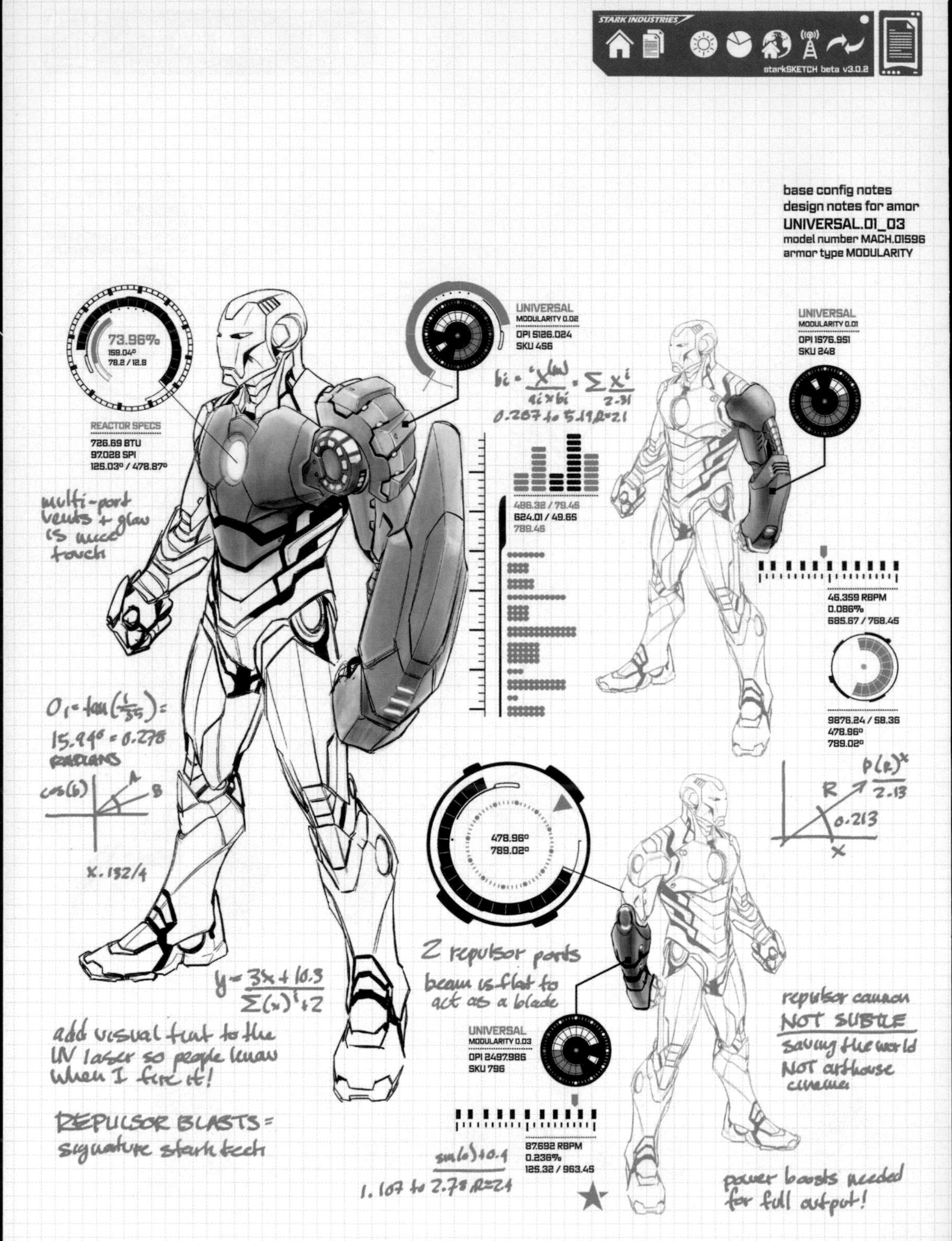
STARK INDUSTRIES
starkSKETCH beta v3.0.2
base config notes
design notes for amor
UNIVERSAL.01_03
model number MACH.01596
armor type MODULARITY
73.96%
159.04°
78.2 / 12.8
REACTOR SPECS
726.69 BTU
97.028 SPI
125.03° / 478.87°
UNIVERSAL
MODULARITY 0.02
OPI 5126.024
SKU 456
UNIVERSAL
MODULARITY 0.01
OPI 1576.951
SKU 248
multi-port vents + glow is nice touch
486.32 / 79.45
624.01 / 49.65
789.46
46.359 RBPM
0.086%
685.67 / 768.45
9876.24 / 58.36
478.96°
789.02°
478.96°
789.02°
x.132/4
2 repulsor ports
beam is flat to act as a blade
UNIVERSAL
MODULARITY 0.03
OPI 2497.986
SKU 796
add visual tint to the UV laser so people know when I fire it!
REPULSOR BLASTS = signature stark tech
87.692 RBPM
0.236%
125.32 / 963.45
repulsor cannon NOT SUBTLE saving the world NOT arthouse cinema
power boosts needed for full output!

#2 ARMOR DESIGN VARIANT BY CARLO PAGULAYAN & JARED FLETCHER

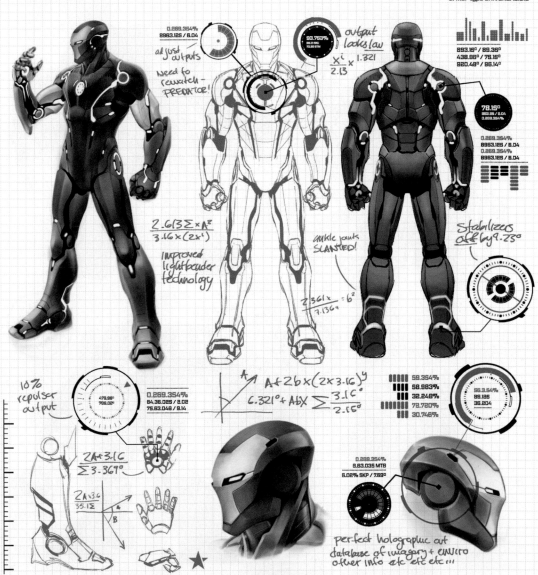

base config notes
design notes for amor
STEALTH
model number MACH.01598
armor type UNIVERSAL.01S

adjust outputs

Need to rewatch PREDATOR!

output looks law

$\dfrac{x^i}{2.13} \times 1.321$

$\dfrac{2.613 \Sigma \times A^2}{3.16 \times (2x^i)}$

Improved lightbender technology

ankle joints SLANTED!

$\dfrac{2.361x}{7.1364} = 6^2$

Stabilizers off by 9.23°

10% repulsor output

$\dfrac{2A \neq 3.16}{\Sigma 3.369°}$

$\dfrac{2A \times 36}{35.1 \Sigma}$

$A \neq 2b \times (2 \times 3.16)^y$

$6.321° + A b \times \Sigma \dfrac{3.16}{2.56°}$

perfect holographic out database of imagery + enviro other info etc etc etc !!!

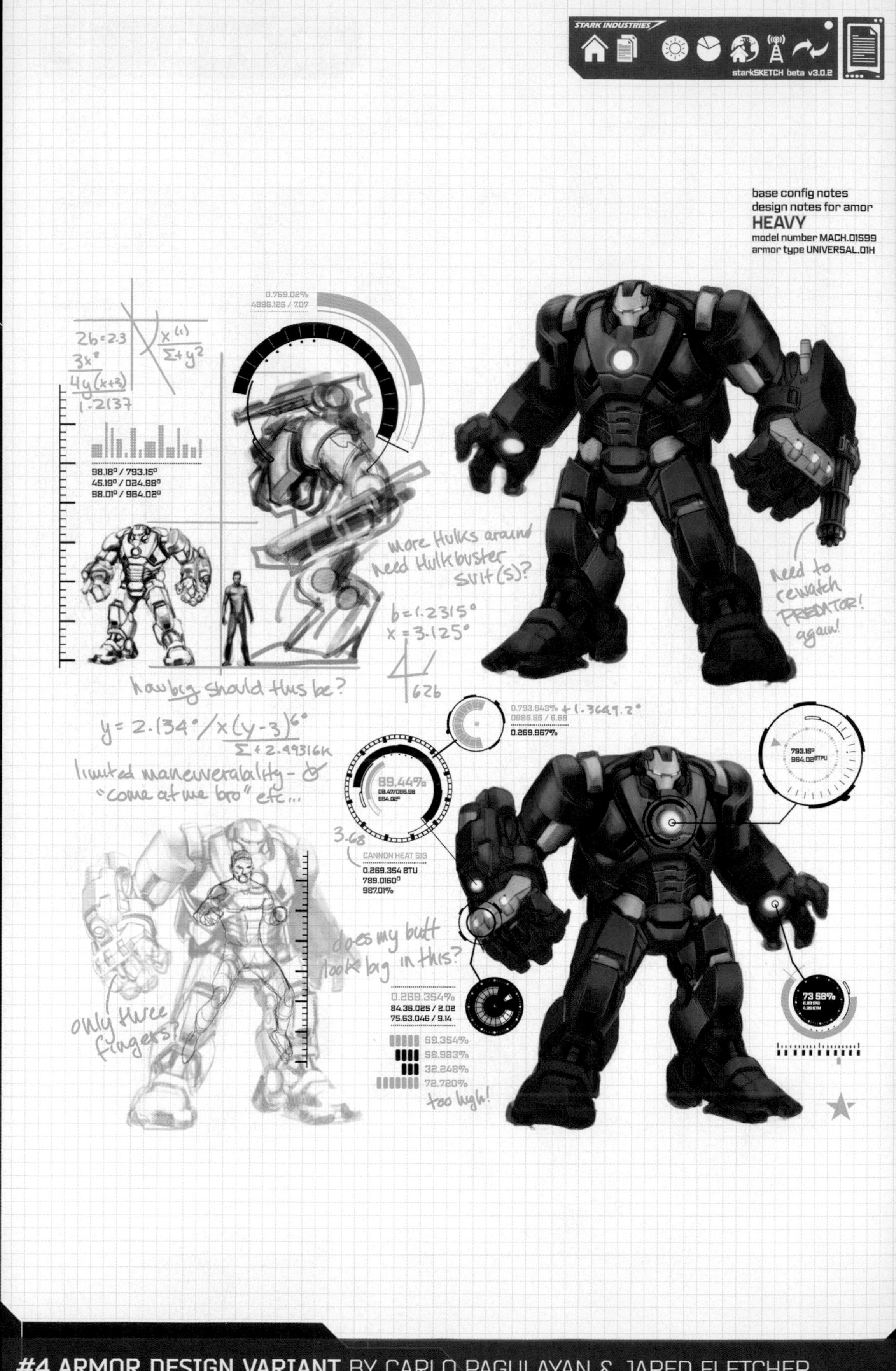
STARK INDUSTRIES
starkSKETCH beta v3.0.2
base config notes
design notes for amor
HEAVY
model number MACH.01599
armor type UNIVERSAL.01H
98.18° / 793.15°
45.19° / 024.98°
98.01° / 964.02°
0.769.02%
4896.126 / 7.07
more Hulks around
need Hulkbuster
suit(s)?
b = 1.2315°
x = 3.125°
626
need to
rewatch
PREDATOR!
again!
how big should this be?
y = 2.134° / x(y-3)6°
limited maneuverability -
"come at me bro" etc...
0.793.843% + 1.3649.2°
0.269.967%
89.44%
3.68
CANNON HEAT SIG
0.269.354 BTU
789.0160°
987.01%
793.15°
964.02°BTPU
does my butt
look big in this?
only three
fingers?
0.269.354%
84.36.025 / 2.02
75.63.046 / 9.14
59.354%
58.983%
32.248%
72.720%
too high!
73.58%

#4 ARMOR DESIGN VARIANT BY CARLO PAGULAYAN & JARED FLETCHER

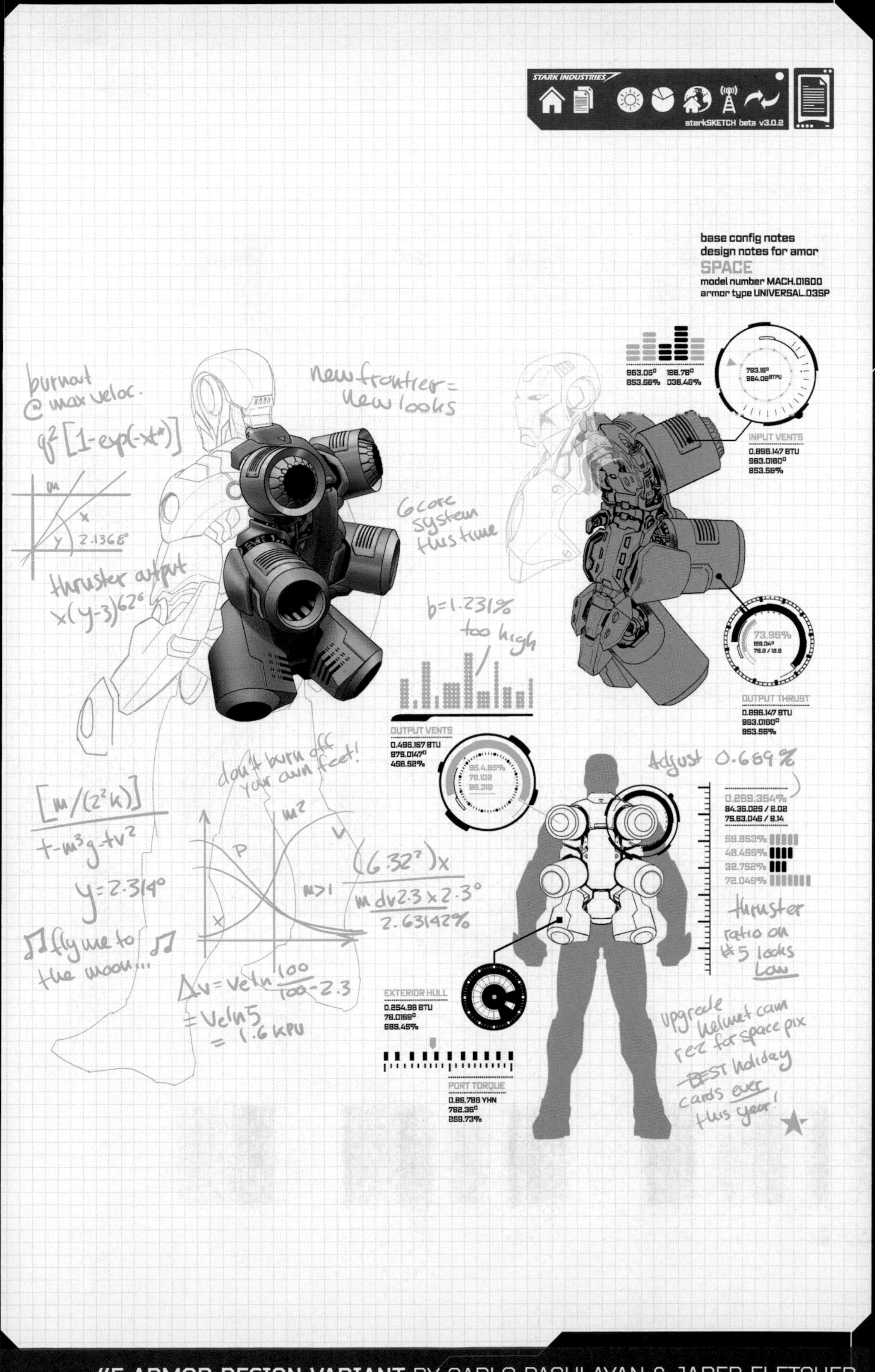
STARK INDUSTRIES
starkSKETCH beta v3.0.2
base config notes
design notes for amor
SPACE
model number MACH.01600
armor type UNIVERSAL.03SP
burnout @ max veloc.
new frontier = new looks
6 core system this time
thruster output
b=1.231% too high
don't burn off your own feet!
fly me to the moon...
INPUT VENTS
0.896.147 BTU
963.0160°
853.56%
OUTPUT THRUST
0.896.147 BTU
963.0160°
853.56%
OUTPUT VENTS
0.496.157 BTU
975.0147°
456.52%
Adjust 0.689%
thruster ratio on #5 looks Low
EXTERIOR HULL
0.254.96 BTU
78.0159°
986.45%
PORT TORQUE
0.86.786 YHN
782.36°
259.73%
upgrade helmet cam rez for space pix
BEST holiday cards ever this year!

#5 ARMOR DESIGN VARIANT BY CARLO PAGULAYAN & JARED FLETCHER

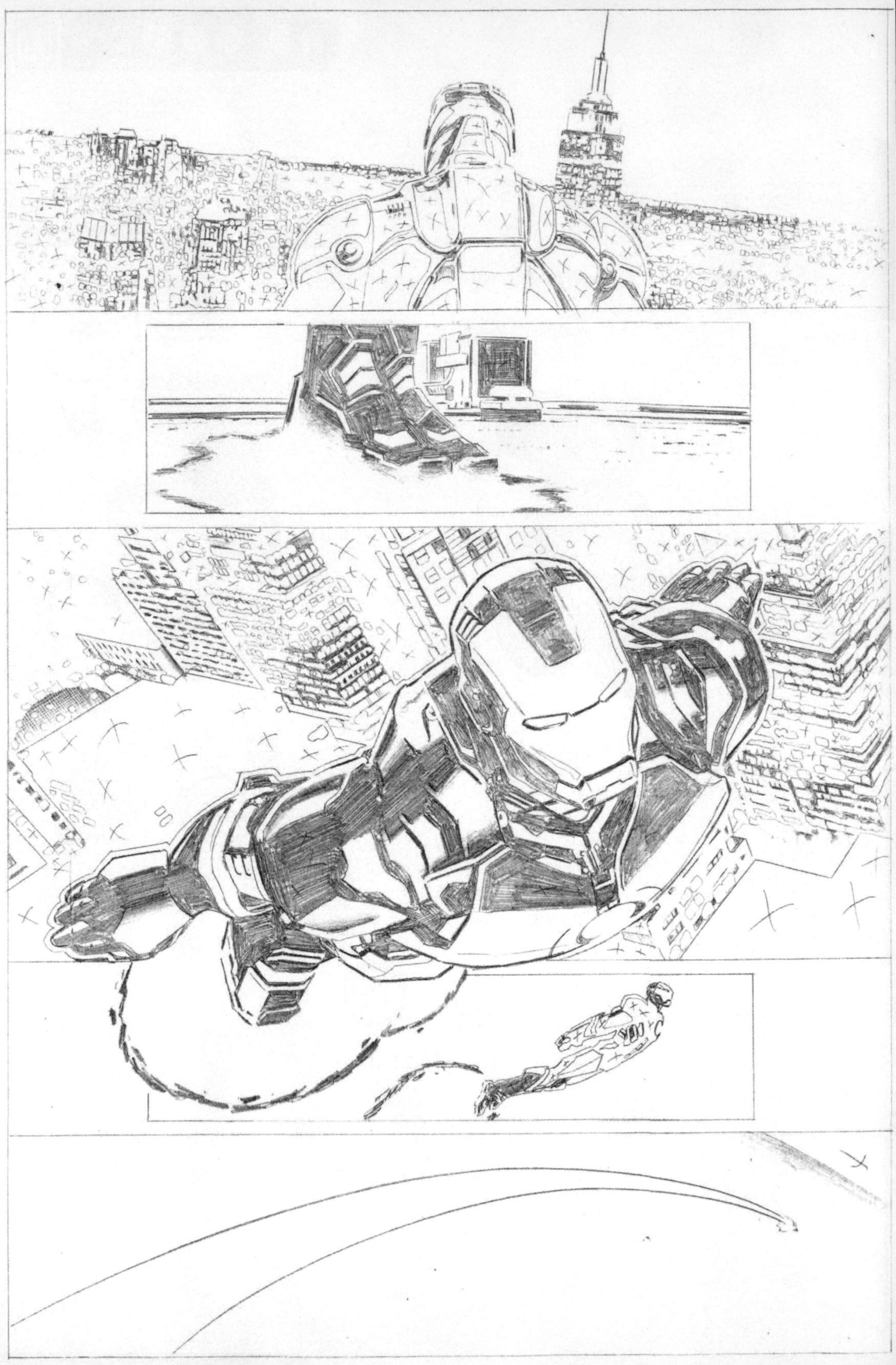

PENCILS BY GREG LAND & INKS BY JAY LEISTEN

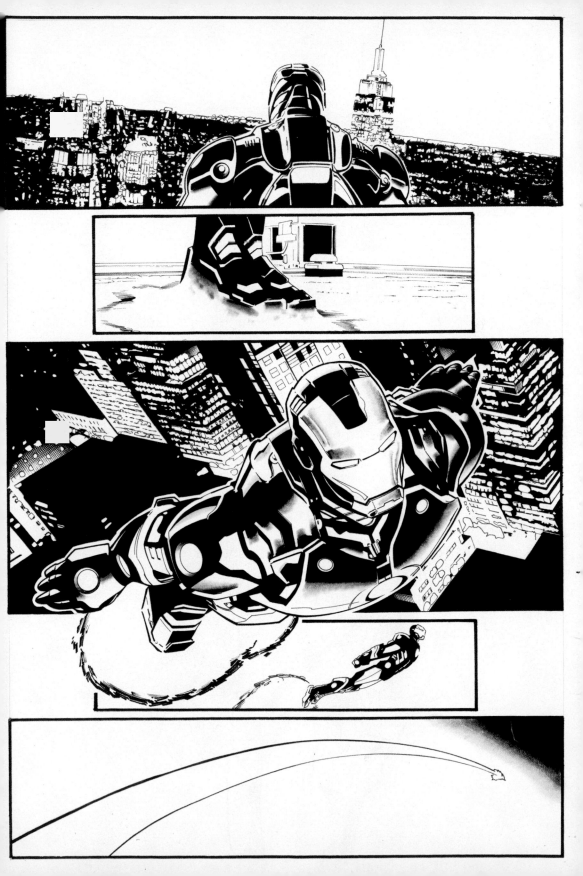

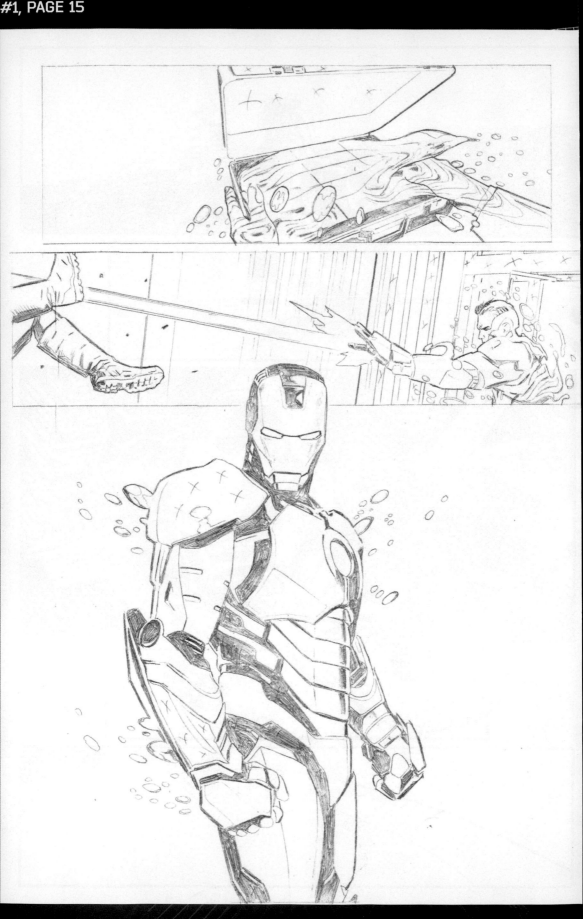

PENCILS BY GREG LAND & INKS BY JAY LEISTEN

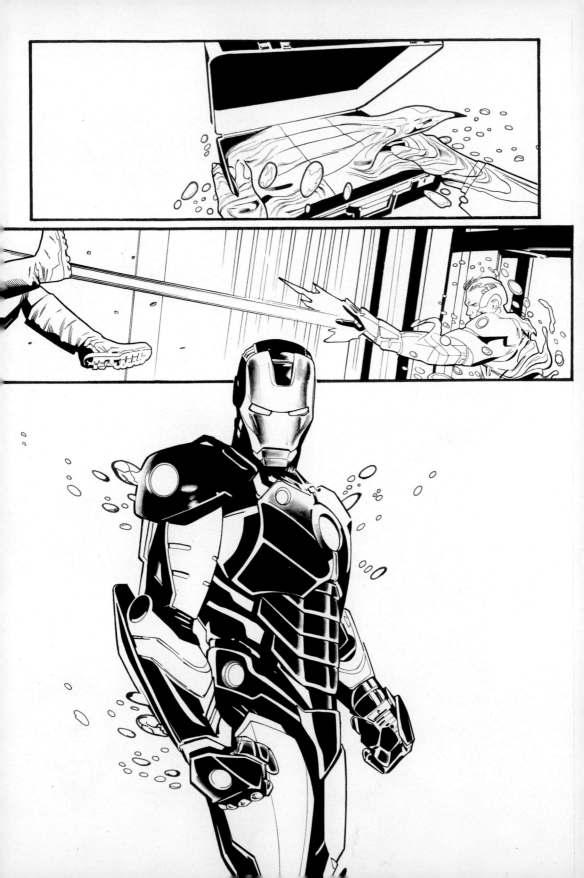

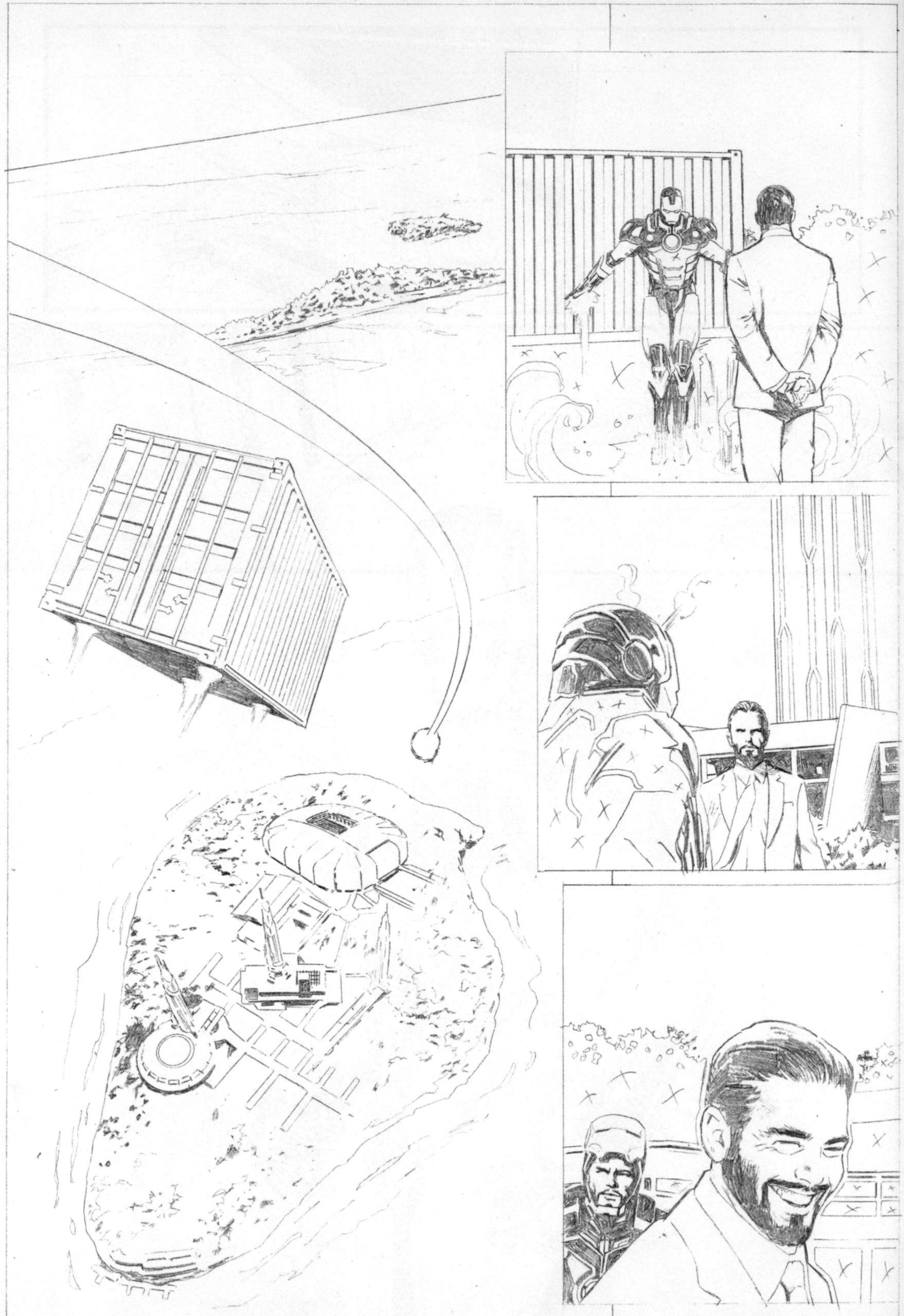

PENCILS BY GREG LAND & INKS BY JAY LEISTEN

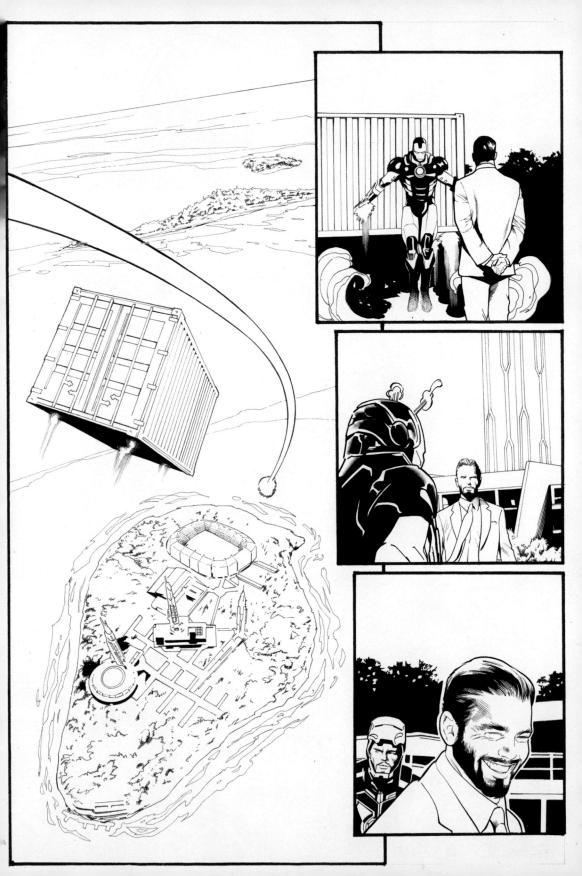

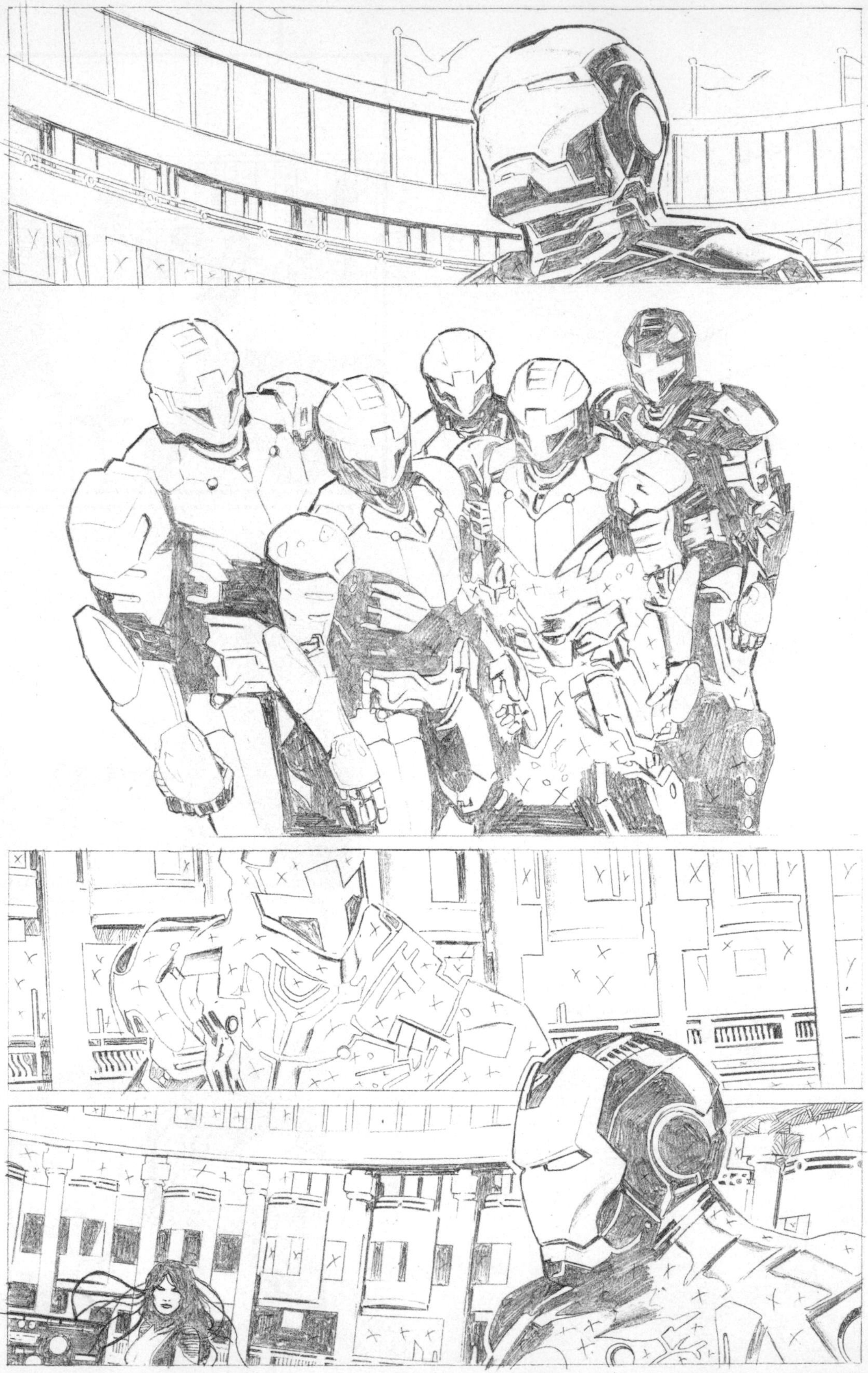

PENCILS BY GREG LAND & INKS BY JAY LEISTEN

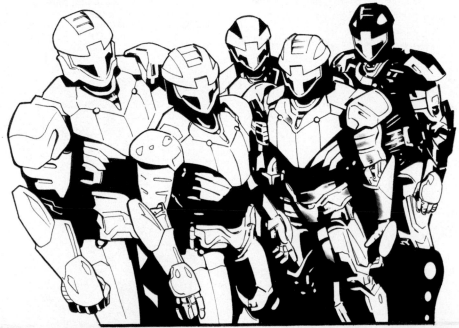

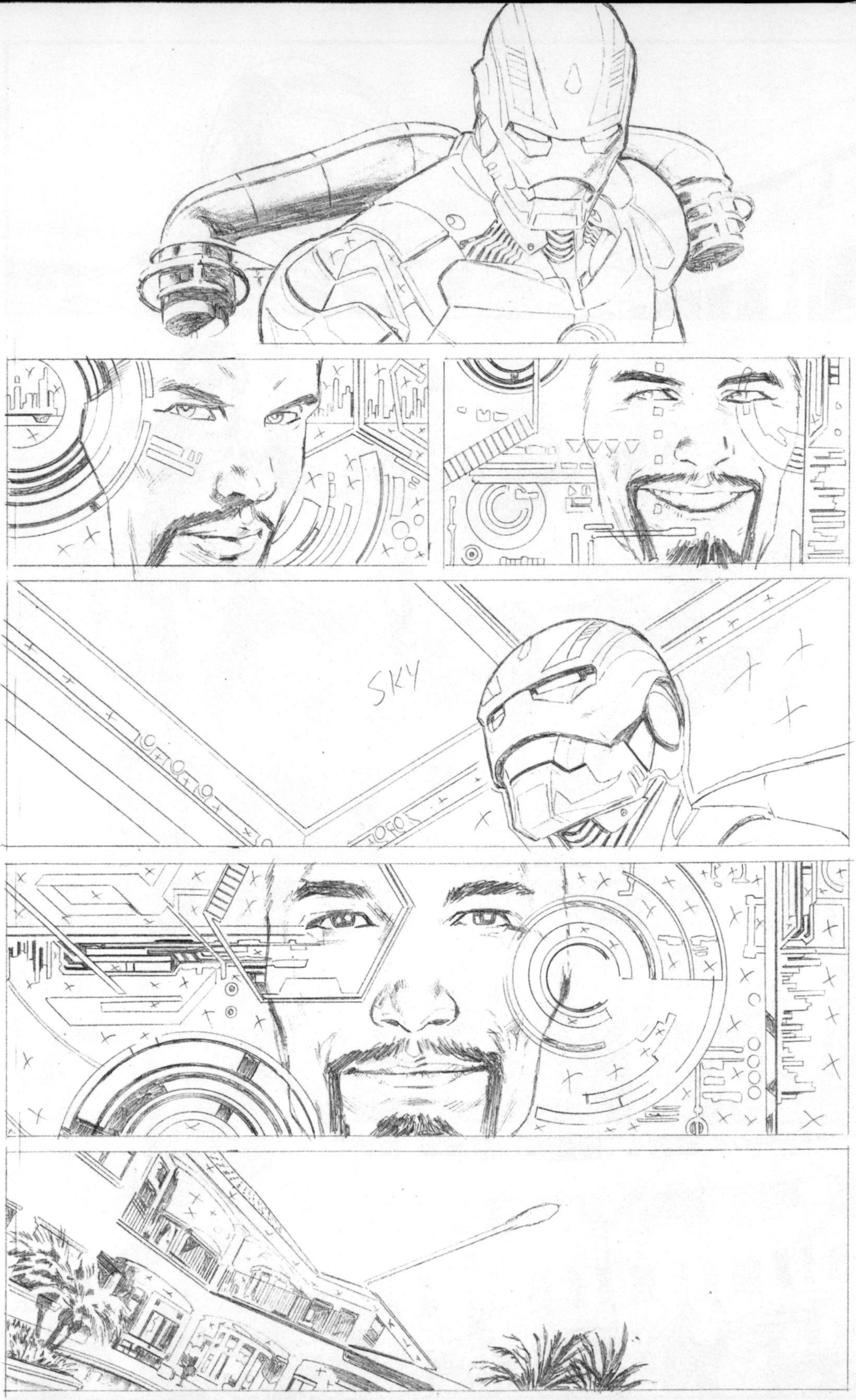
SKY

PENCILS BY GREG LAND & INKS BY JAY LEISTEN

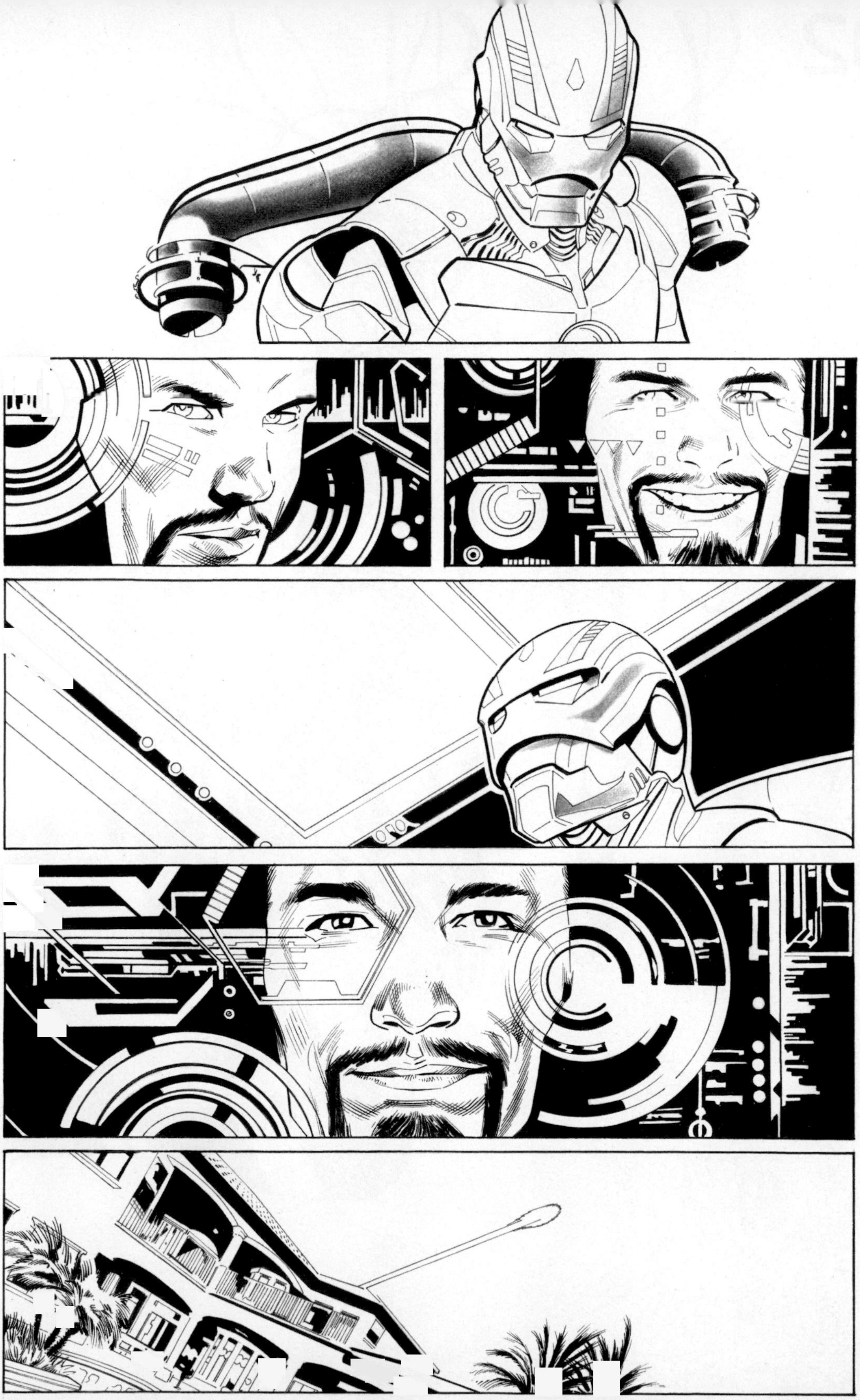

02

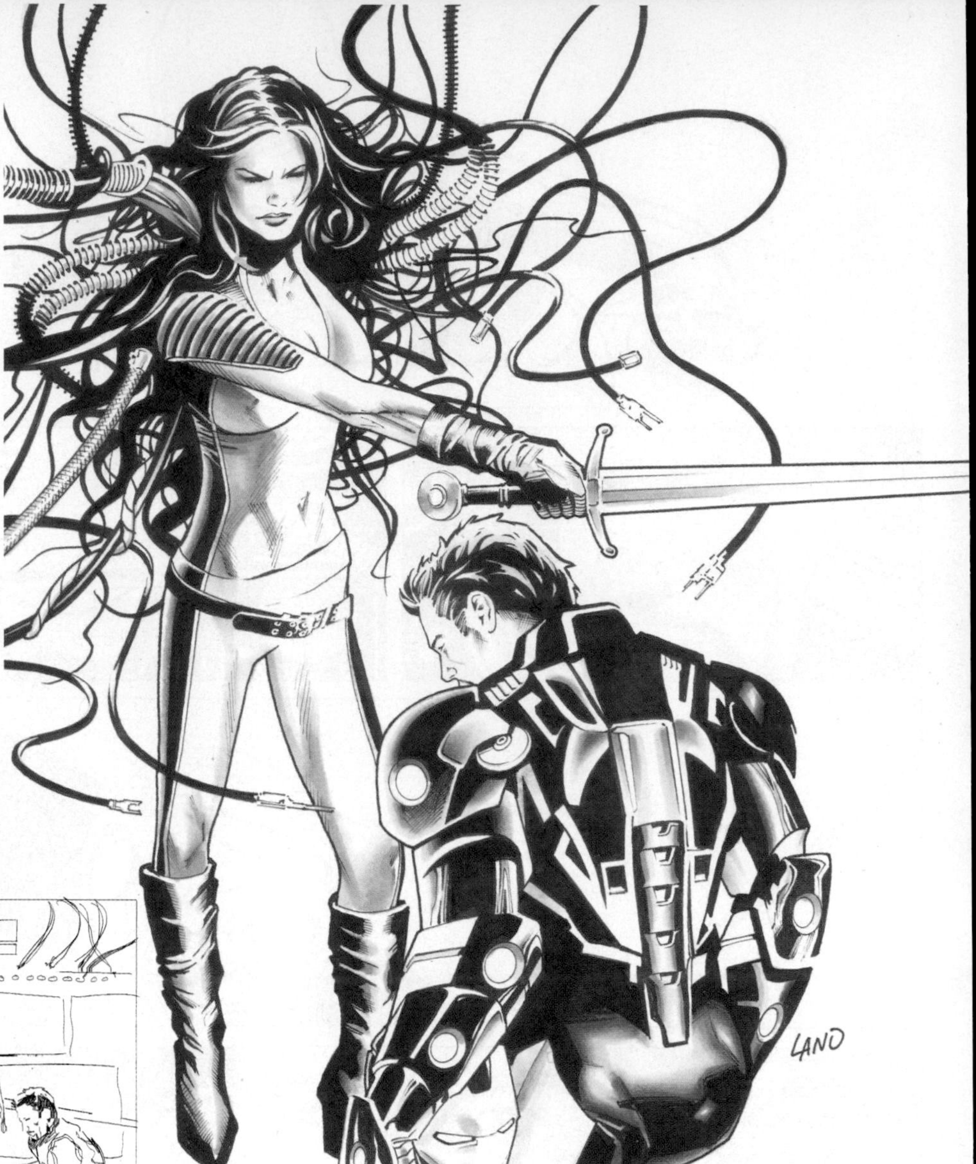
LAND

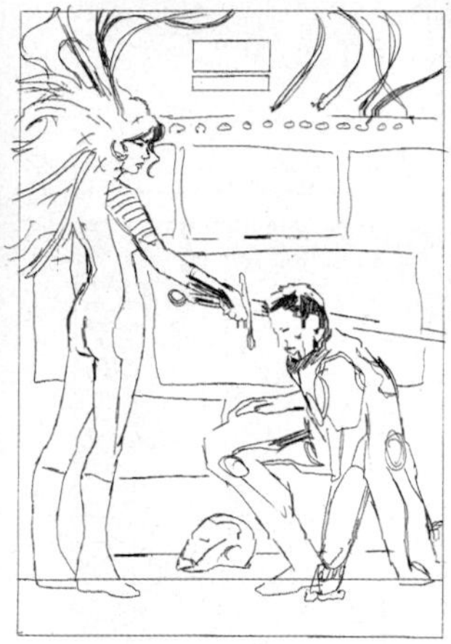

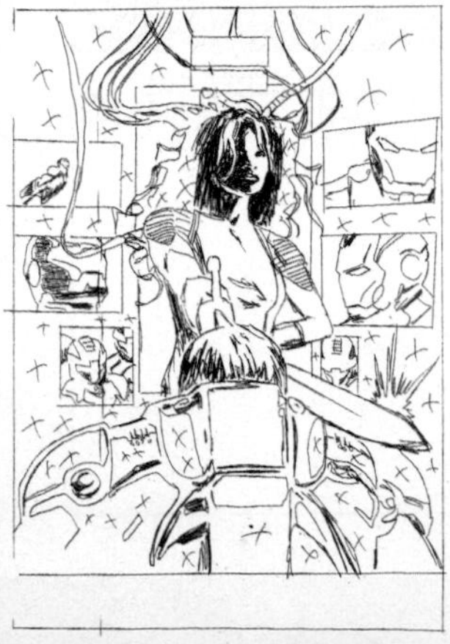

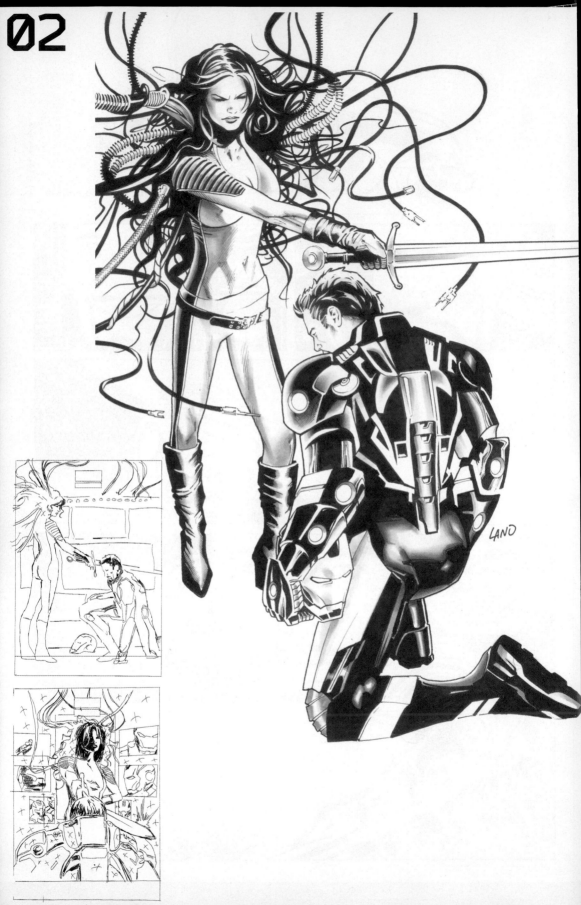

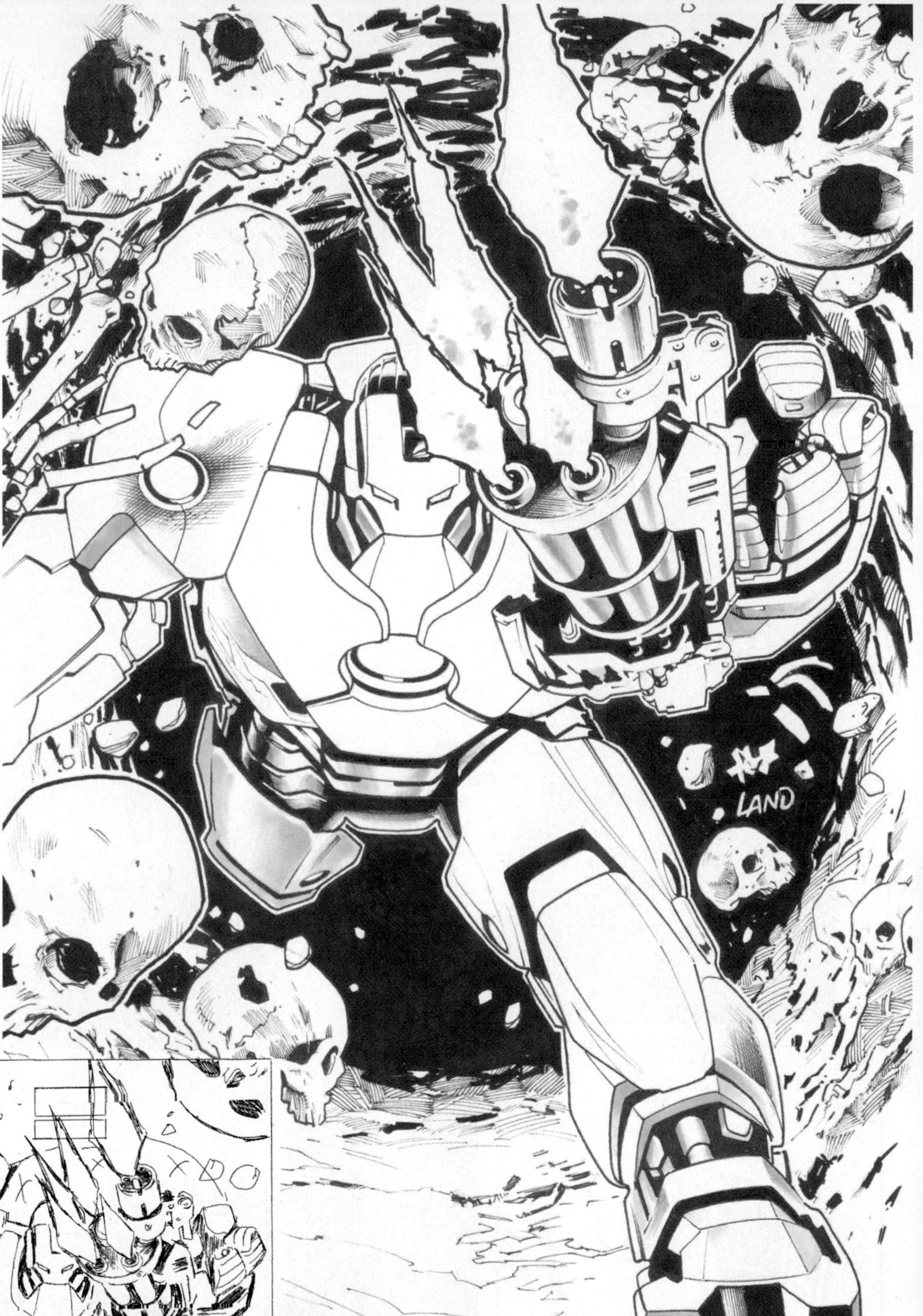
LAND

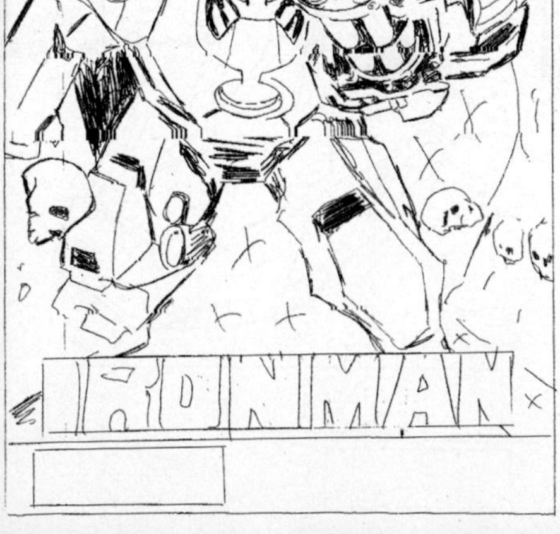
IRONMAN

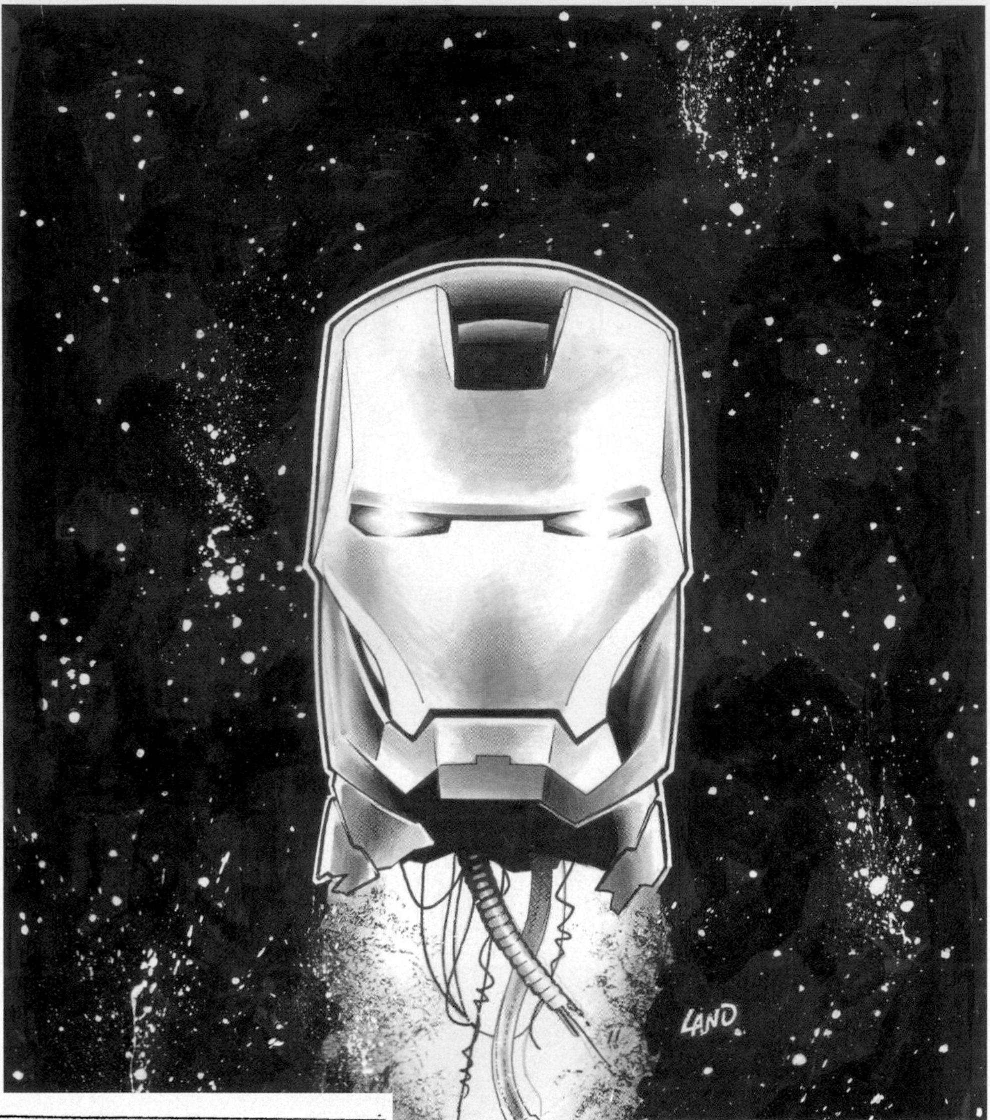
LAND

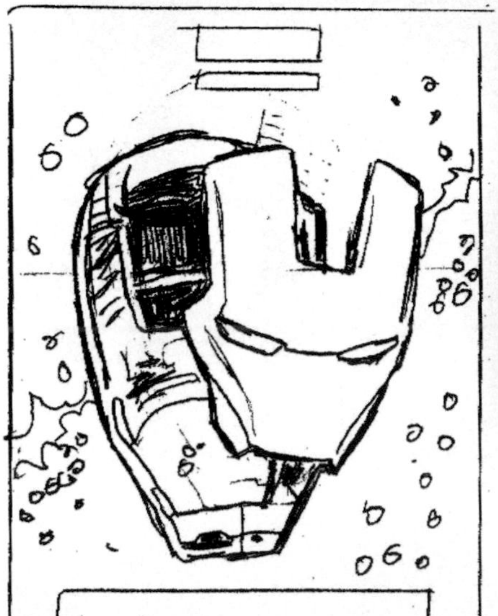

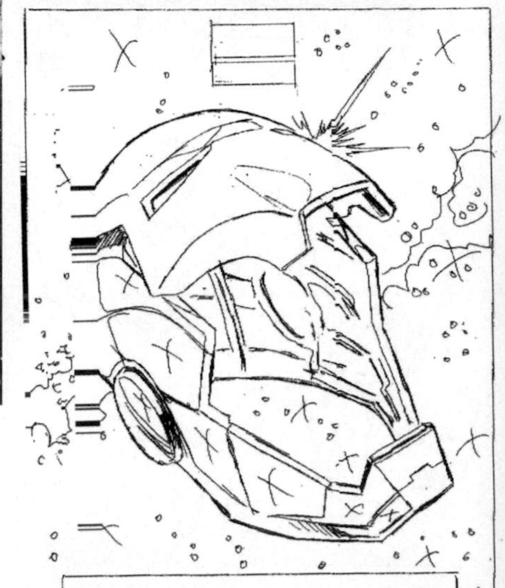

05

THE FREE *MARVEL AUGMENTED REALITY APP*
ENHANCES AND CHANGES THE WAY YOU EXPERIENCE COMICS!

To access the Marvel Augmented Reality App..

- Download the app for free via marvel.com/ARapp
- Launch the app on your camera-enabled Apple iOS® or Android™ device*
- Hold your mobile device's camera over any cover or panel with the **AR** graphic.
- Sit back and see the future of comics in action!

*Available on most camera-enabled Apple iOS® and Android™ devices. Content subject to change and availability.

IRONMAN

AR INDEX